COLLECTIBLE PIN-BACK BUTTONS 1896-1986

An Illustrated Price Guide

By

Ted Hake & Russ King

WALLACE-HOMESTEAD BOOK COMPANY
Radnor, Pennsylvania

This book is dedicated to the memory of Joseph L. Stone of Toledo, Ohio. Mr. Stone began his button collection as a boy in 1921 with a single button found while on an errand for his mother. Fifty years later the collection contained 50,000 different buttons. Mr. Stone's efforts preserved a remarkable record of America's past and many of the photos in this book are of buttons from his wonderful collection.

Library of Congress Catalog Card No. 86-80807
ISBN 0-87069-602-5 *hardcover*
ISBN 0-87069-604-1 *paperback*
Manufactured in the United States of America

1 2 3 4 5 6 7 8 9 0   0 9 8 7 6 5 4 3 2 1

TABLE OF CONTENTS

FOREWORD

Collectible Pin-Back Buttons 1896-1986 is a greatly expanded and re-organized version of *The Button Book,* 1972. This revision, devoted to buttons of an advertising, commemorative or non-political nature, is the only reference book of its kind for collectors, dealers and everyone interested in American history, popular culture, and graphic design.

Over 5,000 buttons are illustrated, dated and priced. This broad selection includes hundreds of the most desirable buttons as determined by collectors over the years. A comprehensive listing of all designs ever produced is an impossibility. Several collectors have amassed collections of 50,000 or more buttons and are still making additions.

Interest in this particular collectible continues to grow. Due to more collectors, choice buttons are not as commonly available at flea markets, antique or hobby shows. Prices on better pieces have consequently risen steadily since 1972 and in *Collectible Pin-Back Buttons* values are increased accordingly. Collectors exist for virtually all early button categories and interest is expanding in 1950's-1960's buttons as new generations of collectors emerge from these eras.

The 1972 *Button Book* noted that button-hunting is a hobby that can bring great satisfaction to the collector who enjoys surprises and new finds. This is still the case and this expanded reference will hopefully be welcomed by collectors old and new, in addition to dealers, historians, librarians, advertising researchers, designers and others who enjoy America's unique past.

The Button Book included a section on presidential campaign buttons which since was revised and expanded into three volumes picturing 12,000 items: *Encyclopedia of Political Buttons 1896-1972, Political Buttons Book II 1920-1976,* and *Political Buttons Book III 1789-1916,* plus price revisions.

Similarly, the original book contained information about non-political buttons in sets and sports buttons. Although samples of these buttons are included in this revision, subsequent specialized reference books *Buttons In Sets 1896-1972* and *Non-Paper Sports Collectibles: An Illustrated Price Guide* contain comprehensive information about these areas.

Your comments or inquiries are welcomed about buttons illustrated in this book or our other reference books. After twenty-five years of dealing in collectibles, buttons are still our favorite subject.

Ted Hake
Hake's Americana & Collectibles
York, Pa.

INTRODUCTION

Ninety-five years have passed since that era's 'miracle' substance—celluloid—was first used to manufacture buttons. Thousands of buttons were produced at the 1896 outset and for the next 30 years, yet it is remarkable that so many early examples remain today. That they do is tribute to the durability of the product and its attractiveness. Although most early buttons were simple product giveaways or handouts, many recipients found them delightful enough to keep—fortunately for the sake of button history, American history and today's collectors.

Buttons are nearing their first century of existence but actually are a 'latter-day' use of celluloid. The mid-1890's began the flourishing button era, but the origin of celluloid in some form started as early as 1839 with the recognition of cellulose as a substance by a French chemist, Anselme Payeu. His discovery led to more research by other scientists and eventually, to the vast plastics industries of today.

The perfection of celluloid, however, is generally attributed to John Wesley Hyatt, a prolific American inventor, in his search for an ivory substitute. His first known creation was an unsuccessful 1863 "collodion" billiard ball which unfortunately detonated in play due to its flammable composition. The composition was subsequently refined and in 1870 Hyatt obtained a patent for "celluloid." The substance was to become the nation's first commercially-profitable synthetic material.

Celluloid use grew rapidly. Although flammable, celluloid had many desirable qualities—warmth to the touch, pliability for easy molding, inexpensive cost—and hundreds of household and personal vanity items were conceived and successfully marketed.

Celluloid was first used in a presidential campaign in 1876, but sparingly. By the campaign of 1888, celluloid lapel studs picturing candidates Harrison, Cleveland and Fisk were introduced by Baldwin & Gleason Co., Ltd., an early New York City novelty firm. At the same time, early celluloid advertising pieces were being produced. The time was at hand for the birth of the button industry and boom years for all types of celluloid advertising. (See supplemental photo pages for "other" types of celluloid pieces.)

Buttons, as made today, were first patented by the Whitehead & Hoag Company of Newark, N.J. in 1896 although related, preparatory patents were acquired as early as 1893 and 1895. (See supplemental article about this company.)

Following these patents, the remainder of 1896 produced an amazing variety and number of Whitehead & Hoag buttons. The flurry was stimulated both by the McKinley-Bryan presidential campaign and introductions of free buttons by manufacturers of candy, chewing gum and tobacco products.

Other major button producers (see separate listing) quickly joined the marketplace and a 25-year era of button magnificence followed. Buttons produced from 1896 into the early 1920's attained a beauty that was to disappear almost as rapidly as it appeared. Lithographed tin buttons were introduced in huge quantities by the J.E. Lynch Company of Chicago for World War I Liberty Loan and War Savings Campaigns. Additional millions of "litho" buttons were used by the American Red Cross and the Salvation Army in their drives for funds. This was a much less expensive mass production process for buttons and reduced the production of celluloid buttons quite drastically. While litho buttons could feature several colors, the colors could not be blended to obtain the immense color range displayed on the best celluloid covered buttons. By the early 1920's production of beautiful multicolor buttons plummeted, although the button concept survived and continued to prosper.

Patriotic red-white-blue colors dominated the countless buttons produced during World War II and continued to dominate political buttons during the post-war years. Advertising buttons, meanwhile, tended to become larger and designed principally for easy legibility. The 1960's produced a revival of sorts with many colorful and nicely-designed 'cause' buttons and the late 1970's brought a flood of colorful 'rock group' buttons.

The number of giveaway buttons has diminished greatly over the years. Today buttons have largely become the province of greeting card manufacturers and retail gift shops. Modern political buttons, although frequently using color, are usually candidate photo or text-only pieces with few references to campaign issues. Nevertheless, button creativity appears in a mild resurgence. Hopefully this trend will continue as buttons head for their '100th birthday.'

NUMBERING SYSTEM

The numbering system adopted for *Collectible Pin-Back Buttons* serves a dual purpose: (1) each button is assigned an individual number for means of communication between collectors or dealers, and (2) parts of each individual number represent the button's age, color and value range.

Buttons in this book have been separated into 13 subject categories; each category is assigned a Roman numeral:

I. ANIMALS, BIRDS, CREATURES	VII. GEOGRAPHIC AREAS
II. CELEBRATIONS, EXPOSITIONS, WORLD'S FAIRS	VIII. MILITARY
	IX. ORGANIZATIONS, ASSOCIATIONS
III. ENTERTAINMENT	X. PRODUCTS, SERVICES
IV. FAMOUS PEOPLE	XI. SOCIAL CAUSES
V. FARM EQUIPMENT	XII. SPORTS
VI. FOOD, BEVERAGE, TOBACCO	XIII. TRANSPORTATION

Within each Roman numeral category, each button is assigned number and letter designations representing:

Individual Button Number-Age-Color-Value

The letter "L" after an individual button number indicates that it is lithographed metal rather than celluloid; an asterisk at the end of some designations indicates a supplemental footnote at the end of that section about that particular button.

As an example, button 58-4-D-C in Category III (Entertainment):

"58" is that button's individual number in Category III; "4" indicates that the button was issued in the 1920's; "D" indicates that the button is multicolor; and "C" indicates that its value is in the range of $10 to $15.

Each button is thus coded with its identification number in the first position followed by coded information in this sequence:

AGE	COLOR	VALUE
(Second position)	(Third position)	(Fourth position)
1 = 1896-1900 A = black/white (bw)	A button which does not fall into a	A = $5-10
2 = 1901-1910 B = sepia	preceding category is coded by its	B = $10-15
3 = 1911-1920 C = 3-5 colors	dominant color:	C = $15-25
4 = 1920's D = multicolor	O = blue	D = $25-50
5 = 1930's E = red/white/blue	P = green	E = $50-75
6 = 1940's F = red/white/blue/bw	Q = red	F = $75-100
7 = 1950's G = blue/white	R = gold or silver or metallic	G = $100-125
8 = 1960's H = blue/white/bw	S = gray	H = $125-150
9 = 1970's or I = red/white	T = tan or buff or brown	I = $150-175
later J = bw/red or red/bw	U = aqua or turquoise	J = $175-200
K = brown/white	V = maroon	K = $200-250
L = green/white	W = pink	L = $250-300
M = orange with black or brown or blue	X = purple	M = $300-350
N = yellow with black or brown or blue	Y = yellow or chartreuse	N = Over $350
	Z = other (including fleshtones, woodtones)	

BUTTON AGE

The age of a button is sometimes self-evident by inclusion of a year in its inscription. Most buttons, however, are undated and those are assigned an approximate age in this book by (1) designs of back (insert) papers known to have occurred within a specified time period; (2) knowledge of the pictured event or person; (3) the button's style of illustration which dates it within certain periods such as art nouveau or art deco. Many buttons have back papers with patent dates, but these years are not necessarily the actual date of issue. Patent dates are very commonly several years older than the actual issue date of the button. A button, for example, with an "1896" patent date on the back paper may well have been issued under that patent but not until a decade later. (See supplemental sections on dating celluloid buttons and button manufacturers.)

BUTTON COLOR

Most buttons fall into a fixed color description code. Still, many color combinations exist that are not specifically listed. A listing of all possible color combinations would be virtually endless, hence a "3-5 colors" designation on several buttons. This designation generally refers to pure color differences, not to "multicolor" buttons which have color overlays to produce rich, life-like tones.

BUTTON VALUE

Each value is the typical retail price for a button in bright condition with no damage. These are nationwide prices, meaning that a majority of collectors in a particular category would probably be willing to buy the item in the price range indicated. All values specified are approximations and the publisher shall not be held responsible for losses that may occur in the purchase or sale of items.

Factors in arriving at prices are (1) the number of collectors looking for that particular category of buttons, (2) the scarcity of the button, (3) the design and/or color quality, (4) whether it is a picture or text-only button, (5) age, (6) size and (7) condition.

A dealer will normally pay about half of the typical retail value since, as in any other business, subsequent added cost is required to successfully re-sell the items.

The buttons pictured in this book are an excellent collective example of the immense variety available, but no conclusion should be drawn about the values of buttons included vs. those excluded. Study of the prices can show what button groups have greater values. A few button groups are largely excluded from this book because they are so common and/or collector interest is minimal. Examples include flags of various countries, fraternal orders, funny sayings, and labor union monthly dues buttons.

BUTTON CONDITION & REPRODUCTIONS

Celluloid buttons are nearly immune to dirt and age, and sometimes may be actually brightened by proper cleaning techniques. The slightest bit of liquid wax on a soft rag will usually remove layers of dust from the celluloid surface. No liquid should get near the back rim or be applied to buttons with celluloid cracks as the liquid can seep through the paper to the metal back with resulting stains. Celluloid covered buttons are quite vulnerable to moisture and severe temperature extremes. In addition, prolonged exposure of a button to either sunlight or artificial light will tend to fade the inks used to produce the button's illustration or wording.

The term 'foxing' applies to the stain which occurs if water or moisture rusts the metal rim (collet) or metal backing under the button paper. A few light spots decrease the button's value about 15%-25%; if the stain is large or dark, the value may decrease to almost nothing. Rusting on lithographed tin buttons has the same effect on value.

Color fade frequently results from too much sun exposure from outdoor display at flea markets. Red is a particularly sensitive color and can fade perceptibly even with only a few hours exposure to direct sunlight.

Other common forms of damage—both to celluloid and lithographed tin buttons—include scratches and dents. Cracks may appear on celluloid pieces, or the celluloid may begin to separate from the paper, usually along the rim.

These defects decrease the button's desirability and may decrease its value by 15%-25% or more, depending on the extent of damage. Many collectors or dealers will not buy buttons with damage that detracts from the button's appearance even if the price is a small fraction of that for the same button in perfect condition.

While condition certainly affects value, some tolerance for minor, non-defacing damage is advisable. Buttons from the early 1930's are now over 50 years old and those from the early years may be 75-90 years old. The rarity and attractiveness of an available button must be weighed against the likelihood of ever finding another example in flawless condition. Often it is best to acquire a less than perfect, but desirable, button when the opportunity arises and then sell or trade that button should a better example come along later.

Modern-day reproductions are more common for presidential campaign buttons than for the non-political types pictured in this book. Non-political reproduction buttons exist, however, particularly in the area of entertainment figures such as Shirley Temple, Elvis Presley, The Beatles and others. Reproduction buttons are sometimes issued with a false date of manufacture intended to mislead the purchaser.

Original character and personality buttons from the 1950's and earlier are popular collectibles and most dealers are not likely to radically underestimate the value. A Shirley Temple button priced at a dollar or two is probably a reproduction or newly created design. Visits to a few flea markets will reveal many of the reproductions or "fantasy" items currently available. Buying from established dealers who do not handle any type of reproductions and who will guarantee in writing the authenticity of the item is the purchaser's best assurance of obtaining a genuine item.

BUTTON SIZE

Buttons are pictured actual size in this book. In a very few cases, a photo from another source was used but even then the size is not off by more than 1/8".

I. ANIMALS, BIRDS, CREATURES

Animals and birds were often depicted on advertising buttons as stereotype characterizations of the quality of the product. Staunch bulldogs, wise owls and sturdy elephants were common motifs. Other animal kingdom members such as tigers and lions were used for eye-catching appeal in addition to the qualities they represented. Farm animals, particularly horses, were commonly portrayed on buttons.

ANIMAL WELFARE

Buttons promoting human care for domestic animals and wildlife have existed since the turn of the century and several early examples are nicely colored and designed. Buttons urging animal welfare have been issued for various beasts, but dogs, cats, and horses are the most frequently pictured.

1-2-D-E   2-3-H-B   3-3-H-B*   4-4-A-B   5-3-E-D   6-3-E-B*

7-2-D-C   8-2-K-B   9-3-F-B   10-2-D-B   11-5-J-A   12-5-N-B

13-3-D-D   14-3-D-C   15-4-G-B   16-5-J-B   17-3-D-C   18-3-L-B

19-4-G-B   20-3-B-B   21-5-J-B*   22-5-A-B   23-2-A-C   24-5-C-C

25-2-K-B   26-3-Q-A   27L-7-O-A   28L-5-C-A   29-5-D-C   30-4-D-D

I.F.A.W.
STOP THE SEAL HUNT

31-9-D-A*

HELP SAVE THE WHALES

RARE ANIMAL RELIEF EFFORT, Inc.
National Audubon Society 950 Third Ave., N.Y., N.Y. 10022

32-9-A-A

BEARS

Early buttons were frequently colorful, nicely-designed, and often depicted bears as Roosevelt-inspired "Teddies."

33-2-D-F

34-2-C-F

35-2-D-F

36-2-D-F

37-2-D-F

38-1-D-E

39-3-D-B*

40-2-D-C

41-3-D-D*

42-7-N-A

BIRDS

A large number of buttons exist picturing birds as advertising symbols. The protective eagle was a common insurance company theme, and other birds were used to promote magazines, chewing gum, gunpowder and a host of other products. Bird buttons were issued in great numbers by the Audubon Society and gum companies.

43-1-D-A   44-2-D-A   45-2-D-A   46L-5-D-A*   47-1-D-A   48-4-D-A

49-3-C-A   50-5-J-A   51-5-L-A   52-5-M-B   53-5-D-B   54-5-D-A

55-2-B-B   56-5-D-B*   57-2-A-B*   58-5-E-D*   59-3-K-C

CATS

Cats have been admired since pre-historic times and manufacturers frequently used this animal as a product symbol, although often in caricature form. Only a few button examples are known which illustrate actual breeds of cats.

60-1-D-B*   61-2-G-C   62-2-C-C   63-2-A-C   64L-6-E-A

65-1-A-A*   66-2-A-A   67L-5-E-A*   68-5-A-B   69-7-M-A*   70-7-P-A*

DOGS: DOG SHOWS, FEED, MEDICINE

Many breeds of dogs were used as advertising symbols with pug bulldogs being the favorite. Various types of hunting dogs appeared on gunpowder and firearm buttons. Unlike cats, several dog breeds appear on buttons which were often related to eastern dog shows.

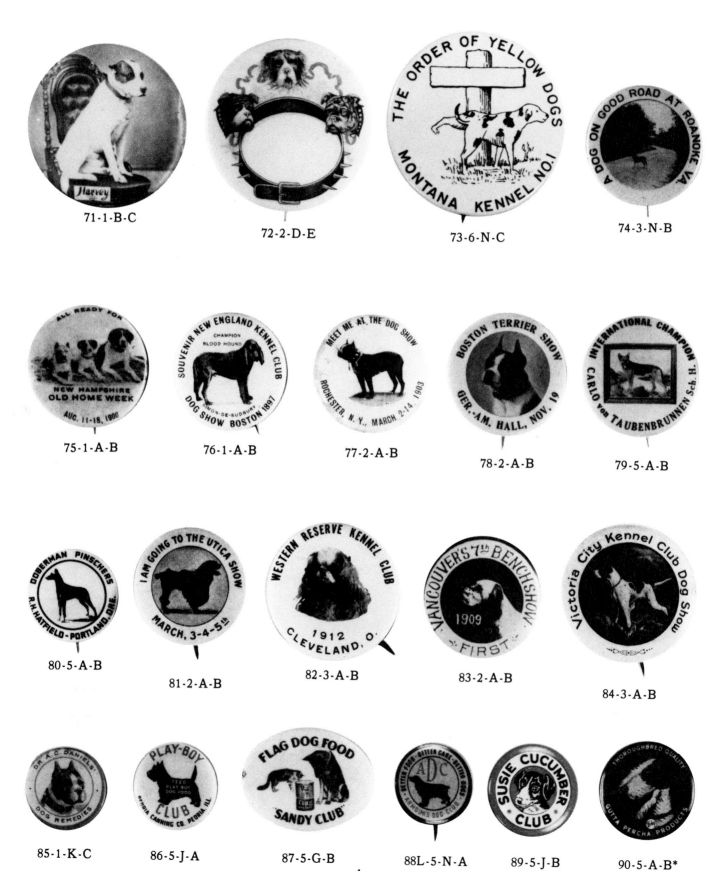

71-1-B-C

72-2-D-E

73-6-N-C

74-3-N-B

75-1-A-B

76-1-A-B

77-2-A-B

78-2-A-B

79-5-A-B

80-5-A-B

81-2-A-B

82-3-A-B

83-2-A-B

84-3-A-B

85-1-K-C

86-5-J-A

87-5-G-B

88L-5-N-A

89-5-J-B

90-5-A-B*

4

CATTLE: FEED, MEDICINE, EQUIPMENT

Milk cows and beef cattle were a standby of the early 20th century American farmer before the days of livestock specialization. A nice assortment of buttons was produced for the different breeds of dairy cattle, although not many in vivid colors. Among the depicted breeds are Holsteins, Jerseys, Guernseys, Brown Swiss and Herefords.

91-2-A-D

92-2-D-E

93-2-J-E*

94-2-A-B

95-2-D-D

96-2-D-D

97-2-J-C

98-1-R-D

99-4-I-B

100-5-K-B

101-4-D-B

102-5-M-B

103-5-V-B

104-3-K-B

105-2-D-B

106-2-A-B

107-4-A-B

108-2-A-B

109-3-A-B

110-3-A-B

111-3-J-B

112-3-M-B

113-1-J-B

114-4-G-C

115-2-M-C

116-2-D-C

HORSES: FEED, MEDICINE, EQUIPMENT

Before the farm tractor took over, horses were the essential animal for breaking, tilling and harvesting the land. Buttons depict a number of workhorse varieties, frequently associated with stock farms or breeders. Buttons were also issued for horse racing events (see Sports miscellaneous section).

117-2-D-E

118-1-A-C

119-1-A-C

120-3-C-C

121-2-D-C

122-2-D-C

123-2-B-B

124-1-B-C

125-2-A-C

126-3-D-D

127-3-A-B

128-2-B-C

129-2-A-B

130-4-A-C

131-5-I-B

132-2-K-B

133-2-N-B

134-3-L-B

135-2-K-D

136-3-D-E

137-2-D-E*

138-2-D-E*

139-2-D-E

140-3-D-E

141-2-J-B

142-3-C-C

143-1-A-B

144-1-K-D

145-2-J-E

146-2-C-D

147-2-K-C

PIGS: FEED, MEDICINE, EQUIPMENT

Hogs were a good cash commodity for early 20th century farmers if they could be kept fat and healthy. Several swine breeds are pictured on buttons, and several cleverly-designed swine tonic buttons exist.

148-3-E-D

149-3-J-E

150-2-I-D

151-2-T-D

152-2-D-D

153-3-G-C

154-4-J-B

155-2-A-C

156-3-I-B

157-3-G-B

158-3-A-B

159-2-G-B

160-4-O-B

161-2-R-B

162-2-M-B

163-2-A-B

164-1-G-C

165-1-D-B

166-2-K-B

167-2-E-B

POULTRY: FEED, MEDICINE, EQUIPMENT

Perhaps due to their relatively short life and production span, egg-layers were the subject of a good number of feed and tonic buttons. Poultry buttons were often quite colorful and several have nice caricature or realistic designs.

168-4-X-A

169-4-Z-A

170-4-C-B

171-3-E-B

172-3-E-A

173-1-J-B

174-4-E-A

175-3-D-B

176-5-M-B

177-2-D-D*

178-2-E-A*

179-3-I-B

180-2-J-A

181L-5-E-B

182-3-E-B

183-3-I-B

184-3-E-A

185-1-J-B

186-3-D-D

187-3-A-C*

188-3-A-C

189-2-D-C

190L-5-Y-A

191L-5-N-A

192L-5-D-B

193-2-B-C

194L-5-N-A

195-3-A-A

196-6-C-B

197-3-A-A

198-1-A-A

199-3-D-A

200-3-A-A

201-1-G-B

202-2-A-B

203-4-D-B

204-5-D-B*

205-2-D-C

206-1-I-A

207-5-C-B

208-2-D-D

209-3-D-C

210-1-E-E*

211-2-J-B

212-2-D-D

SHEEP & GOATS

Sheep and goats did not attain the same button popularity as other types of livestock, although sufficient examples are known to comprise a small collection.

213-6-G-B

214-2-A-B

215-3-G-B

216-2-A-A

217-1-A-C

218-2-Y-B

219-2-F-B

220-4-Q-A*

221-1-A-C

222-3-A-B

223-5-G-A

LIVESTOCK MERCHANTS & ASSOCIATIONS

Moving livestock to market was a major cash decision for early American farmers, and there was no shortage of stockyard dealers soliciting their business. Several midwestern livestock merchants issued nicely-colored and designed buttons to promote their assets and service.

224-2-D-D

225-2-D-D

226-1-J-C

227-2-D-D

228-1-D-D

229-2-B-D

230-2-D-D

231-2-D-D*

232-2-D-D

233-2-D-D

234-2-A-D

235-3-D-D

236-2-D-C*

237-2-G-B

238-2-J-D

239-2-D-B

240-4-C-B

241-1-D-E

242-1-D-D

WILDLIFE, MISCELLANEOUS ANIMALS, ZOOS

A nice assortment of animals appears in isolated instances, either as an advertising symbol or simple illustration. Zoo buttons usually depict tigers, chimpanzees or monkeys.

243-2-A-B

244-1-A-B

245-5-A-B

246L-5-A-B

247-2-D-D

248-1-H-D*

249-2-A-C

250L-5-G-A

251-7-D-A

252-1-I-A

253-1-B-B

254-2-G-A

255-1-B-B

256-5-I-A

257-5-L-A

INSECTS & REPTILES

Although not a large category, several insect buttons were produced for various purposes. A number of "anti" buttons exist for the house fly, and the honeybee was depicted for both its product and its industriousness.

258-4-G-B

259-5-A-B

260-2-N-A

261-2-L-B

262-2-G-A

263-2-J-B

264-3-J-B

265-3-J-B

266-2-Y-A

267-2-D-D*

268-2-D-A

269L-5-D-A

270L-5-D-A

271L-5-D-A

272L-5-D-A

273-5-J-A

274-5-L-A

275-2-H-C

276-2-D-C

277-3-K-B

278-4-A-A

NOTES

I. ANIMALS, BIRDS, CREATURES

ANIMAL WELFARE

    3. BACK PAPER: "AMERICAN HUMANE EDUCATION SOCIETY/OFFICES AT BOSTON"

    6. BACK PAPER: "FUNDS ARE URGENTLY NEEDED BY THE American Red Star Animal Relief ALBANY, N.Y."

    21. ON EDGE: "MADE IN ENGLAND"

    31. ON EDGE: "MADE IN CANADA"

BEARS

    39. BACK PAPER: "MEMBER of the DELI CLUB/THE DELINEATOR BUTTERICK BLDG. N.Y.C."

    41. ATTACHED RIBBON AT TOP: "CALIFORNIA PHARMACEUTICAL ASSOCIATION"

BIRDS

    46. FROM A SET. SEE *BUTTONS IN SETS,* PAGE 5.

    56. FROM A SET. EDGE INSCRIBED: "LONG CHEW GUM"

    57. FRATERNAL ISSUE: ORDER OF OWLS.

    58. FROM AN ANNUAL SERIES. ALSO SEE SECTION XII #112.

CATS

    60. FROM "CAMEO PEPSIN GUM" SET. SEE *BUTTONS IN SETS,* PAGE 64.

    65. ARTIST "HAL HOFFMAN" CARTOON FROM "HASSEN CIGARETTES" SET.

    67. BACK INSCRIBED: "NATHAN ALBERT HEADWEAR/NEW YORK"

    69-70. FROM A SET. BACK INSCRIBED: "ARMOUR STAR FRANKS"

DOGS

    90. ON EDGE: "by STANLEY. TORONTO"

CATTLE

    93. BACK PAPER: "DOUGHERTY BROS., LOGAN, KANS./ESTABLISHED 1886/CATTLE AND HOG RANCH IN CONNECTION "

HORSES

    137. BACK PAPER: "This is a true picture of 'Dr. LeGear,' the largest horse in the world. He is 21 hands tall, takes a 33-inch collar, weighs 2995 lbs. and is valued at $25,000.00. Owned in St. Louis, Mo., by L.D. LeGear Medicine Co./Mfrs. of Dr. LeGear's Stock and Poultry Remedies."

    138. BACK PAPER: "This button shows a true picture of 'Dr. LeGear,' the largest horse in the world. He is 21 hands tall, 16 feet from tip to tip, takes a 32-inch collar, is 8 years old. Owned by DR. L.D. LeGEAR CO./Mfrs. of Dr. LeGear's Stock Remedies/St. Louis, Mo."

POULTRY

    177. BACK PAPER: "GLOBE POULTRY FEEDS MANUFACTURED BY THE ALBERT DICKINSON CO./CHICAGO, ILL." W/BRANCH LOCATIONS.

    178. BACK PAPER: SAME AS NO. 177.

    187. BACK PAPER: INCLUDES "RADIO LE GEAR/THE $500.00 WHITE ROCK ROOSTER YOU HAVE HEARD CROW BY RADIO"

    204. PERMANENT WHITE METAL RIM.

    210. ON EDGE: "WJ WOODBURN & SON, MONTREAL"

SHEEP

    220. BACK PAPER: "EFFICIENT DISENFECTANT FOR FARM AND HOUSEHOLD. BEST FOR DIPPING ALL STOCK "

LIVESTOCK MERCHANTS & ASSOCIATIONS

    231. BACK PAPER: "THIS IS OUR HUMP. INCREASE OVER LAST TEN YEARS' AVERAGE." W/LIVESTOCK STATISTICS.

    236. BACK PAPER: "WE SOLICIT YOUR CONSIGNMENTS, GUARANTEEING FULL PRICES, QUICK SALES AND PROMPT RETURNS "

WILDLIFE, MISC. ANIMALS, ZOOS

    248. BACK PAPER: "SOUVENIR OF THE CHUTES/SAN FRANCISCO "

INSECTS & REPTILES

    267. RIM INSCRIPTION: "THE BEST THING YOU EVER STRUCK/FRISBEE'S ALFALFA CLOVER HONEY/THE FRISBEE HONEY CO./PHONE 50-298, DENVER, COLO."

II. CELEBRATIONS, EXPOSITIONS, WORLD FAIRS

HOLIDAYS & SEASONS

No major holiday escaped the creative talents of early button designers. July 4th buttons with Uncle Sam or firecracker designs were the most-frequently issued holiday commemoratives since the day often was associated with a local celebration. Buttons exist for approximately 14 secular holidays in addition to numerous religious days. Of the secular holidays, Labor Day and Mother's Day closely follow Independence Day in frequency of issue and nice design and colors. The birthday anniversaries of Presidents Washington and Lincoln prompted a number of well-done variations. Nice examples, but fewer of them, were issued for Christmas, Memorial Day, Thanksgiving. Early buttons exist but are scarcer for Valentine's Day, Halloween and Father's Day. The church-related holiday buttons offer an excellent opportunity for the color-oriented collector.

1-3-B-B	2-3-B-B	3-2-R-A	4-6-E-A	5-3-D-D

		8-4-I-A	9-3-R-A	10-1-A-A	11-5-L-A
6-5-E-B	7L-2-D-C				

12-5-D-A	13-4-N-A	14-4-D-A	15-4-N-B	16-4-I-A	17-4-D-A	18-4-D-A

19-2-D-A	20-5-N-A	21-5-Y-A	22-1-J-A	23-5-E-A

24-3-D-B

25-3-D-B

26-2-D-B

27-2-F-B

28-2-D-C

29-3-D-B

30-1-D-D

31-1-E-B

32-1-J-B

33-2-D-B

34-2-D-C*

35-3-D-A

36-4-D-A

37-3-M-A

38-5-M-A

39-3-J-A

40-3-D-A

41-2-D-A

42-3-I-A

43-2-D-A

44-2-D-A

45-5-D-A

46-3-D-A

SANTA CLAUS

Both children and adults love Santa Claus, a fact not lost on retailers who used his presence on buttons as pre-Christmas rewards for shoppers. Santa buttons from 1900 into the late 1920s are usually superbly multi-colored. An early Santa depiction in black and white is indeed a rarity. His imagined appearance varies from jolly to stern, and visualizations of his attire range from jaunty to patriotic. Not only is Santa pictured with his sleigh and bag of toys; he is also an auto driver, an aircraft pilot and a telephone user. He often is pictured entering a chimney (in one example, he enters headfirst and only his legs are visible) or at a fireplace mantle. Some depictions were repeated with only the name of the retailer changed. Early Santa buttons are charming, graphically delightful and the favorite theme of many collectors.

47-3-C-D

48-2-D-E

49-3-D-D

50-2-D-D*

51-2-D-E

52-4-D-D

53-3-D-D

54-3-D-C

55-2-C-C

56-3-D-E

57-3-D-E

58-3-D-D

59-3-D-D

60-3-D-D

61-3-D-D

62-3-D-D

63-3-D-D

64-3-D-D

65-3-D-D

66-3-D-D

67-3-D-D

68-3-D-D

69-3-D-E

70-3-D-D

71-3-D-D

72-3-D-D*

73-3-D-D

74-3-D-D

75-3-D-D

76-3-D-E

77-3-D-D

78-3-D-D

79-3-D-D

80-3-D-D

81-3-D-D

82-3-D-D

83-3-D-D

84-3-D-D

85-3-D-D

86-3-D-D

87-3-D-D

88-3-D-D*

89-3-D-D

90-3-D-D

91-3-D-D

92-3-D-E

93-3-D-D

94-4-D-B

95-5-D-B

96-5-A-C

18

LOCAL EVENTS: FAIRS, PICNICS, CARNIVALS, RODEOS

Many colorful and cleverly-designed buttons announced community carnivals, street fairs, town anniversaries, agricultural exhibits and similar local events. Clowns, dancing ladies and cartoon animals are a frequent motif. Buttons in this category were issued for events in towns from New England to the West Coast and are an increasingly popular collectible due to their wide range of unique designs and frequent superb color.

97-2-D-K

98-1-D-E

99-1-D-D

100-2-D-D

101-2-E-C

102-2-D-C

103-1-D-C

104-1-C-C

105-3-D-D

106-1-D-B

107-1-D-B*

108-2-C-B

109-2-C-B

110-1-D-B

111-2-D-C

112-1-D-C*

113-1-D-C

114-1-D-C

115-1-D-C

116-1-D-C

117-1-D-C

118-1-D-C

119-1-D-C

120-1-D-C

121-1-C-C

122-1-D-C

123-1-D-C

124-1-C-B

125-1-C-B

126-1-C-B

127-1-B-B

128-1-D-B

129-3-E-B

130-2-B-B

131-1-C-B

132-3-I-A

133-2-D-I

134-2-D-F

135-2-A-D

136-1-B-C

137-1-D-C

138-2-D-C

139-1-D-C

140-2-D-C

141-1-D-C

142-1-D-C

143-1-D-C

144-2-D-C

145-1-D-C

146-2-C-C

147-3-C-B

148-2-C-C

149-2-G-B

150-2-D-B

151-3-D-A*

152-3-D-B

153-3-D-B

154-2-C-C   155-2-D-A   156-3-D-B   157-5-E-A   158-5-E-A

159-2-D-B   160-3-A-B   161-3-J-B   162-3-E-B

163-3-L-B   164-5-M-A   165-5-A-A   166-5-C-A

1898-1899 TRANS-MISSISSIPPI/GREATER AMERICAN EXPOSITION, OMAHA, NEB.

As the new century neared, most of the vast western segment of the United States had been explored, settled and developed. Omaha, a bustling trade center of the ''West,'' was a logical site to parade the products, resources and industries of states and territories west of the Mississippi River. Although not a great number of buttons are known to exist from this fair, several examples are nicely designed and quite colorful.

167-1-D-D   168-1-H-C   169-1-B-C   170-1-D-C

173-1-L-B*

171-1-D-C   172-1-D-B   174-1-D-B   175-1-D-B

1901 PAN-AMERICAN EXPOSITION, BUFFALO, N.Y.

The United States was asserting itself as a leading nation in the international community and Buffalo, N.Y. was selected as the site of an exposition to "demonstrate the cultural, commercial and technical progress of the Western Hemisphere" during the preceding century. The fair featured a 375-foot Electric Tower powered by the waters of Niagara Falls and the introduction of Edison's wireless telegraph. The fair ran May 1 through November 1 and was the site of President William McKinley's September 6th assassination. The fair produced a nice assortment of well-designed and extremely colorful buttons.

176-2-B-D

177-2-D-C   178-2-D-C   179-2-D-C   180-2-D-C   181-2-D-C

23

182-2-J-C

183-2-C-C

184-2-D-D

185-2-B-D

186-2-D-C

187-2-D-C*

188-2-D-D

189-2-D-C

190-2-D-C

191-2-D-D

192L-2-C-D*

193-2-A-D

194-2-E-D

195-2-E-C

196-2-D-C*

197-2-D-C*

198-2-D-C*

199-2-D-C*

200-2-D-C*

201-2-D-C*

202-2-D-C*

203-2-D-C*

204-2-G-C

205-2-D-D

24

1904 LOUISIANA PURCHASE WORLD'S FAIR, ST. LOUIS, MO.

"Meet Me At St. Louis" was the theme song of the Louisiana Purchase Exposition that commemorated the 100th anniversary of the 1803 purchase of the Louisiana Territory from France and opening of the west. The fair, scheduled to open in 1903, did not open until 1904 due to the need for more preparation time upon the six years already spent. Nevertheless, it was one of the nation's most colossal fairs and was held concurrently with the first Olympic games on U.S. soil. Among the attractions were some 1500 buildings including one from nearly each state, international exhibits, and the 750-foot Ferris Wheel which had been re-constructed from the 1893 Columbian Exposition. The fair, opened April 30 by telegraph from President Roosevelt in Washington, ran through December 1 and produced a large number of buttons depicting the "Education" theme, buildings and exhibits, and Louisiana Purchase President Thomas Jefferson.

206-2-D-D 207-2-D-D 208-2-A-C 209-2-A-C

210-2-D-D 211-2-D-C 212-2-D-C 213-2-D-D 214-2-D-C

215-2-B-D 216-2-D-D 217-2-D-D 218-2-D-D* 219-2-D-D

220-2-D-C* 221-2-N-C 222-2-E-C 223-2-C-C 224-2-D-C*

225-2-L-C

226-2-C-C

227-2-D-C

228-2-D-C

229-2-D-C

230-2-D-C

231-2-C-C

232-2-D-C*

233-2-D-C*

234-2-D-C*

235-2-D-C*

236-2-D-C*

237-2-D-C*

238-2-D-C*

239-2-D-C*

240-2-D-C*

241-2-D-C*

242-2-D-C*

243-2-D-C*

244-2-D-C*

1905 LEWIS & CLARK EXPOSITION, PORTLAND, ORE.

The Lewis & Clark Exposition commemorated the 100th anniversary of the explorers' famed geographical and scientific exploration in 1804-1806 of the vast, uncharted territory resulting from the Louisiana Purchase. A beautiful button from the exposition pictures Lewis & Clark and a symbolic Miss Liberty first sighting the Pacific Ocean on November 7, 1805.

245-2-D-D

246-2-D-F

247-2-D-D*

248-2-C-C

1907 JAMESTOWN EXPOSITION, HAMPTON ROADS, VA.

The Jamestown Exposition, held at Hampton Roads, Va., commemorated the 300th anniversary of the first U.S. English settlement May 13, 1607 at Jamestown. A few buttons depict the colonists' early meeting with the Indians, and one unusual button issued during the fair depicts the battle between the ironclad war vessels *Merrimac* and *Monitor* which occured at Hampton Roads in 1862 during the Civil War.

249-2-D-G

250-2-D-D

251-2-B-C

252-2-C-C

253-2-C-C

254-2-B-C

1909 ALASKA-YUKON-PACIFIC EXPOSITION, SEATTLE, WASH.

Seattle, the nearest northwest major city to late 1890s gold discoveries in Alaska and the Yukon territories, used this advantage to promote itself as the gateway to the northern goldfields. The AYP Exposition in 1909-1910 was developed for this purpose and attracted an estimated 3.75 million visitors. Although a large number of buttons did not result from the fair, a select few are exquisite in color and design and appropriately reflected the "richness" of Seattle's prosperity and access to Northwest gold areas.

255-2-D-E*

256-2-D-D

257-2-D-C

258-2-Y-C

1909 HUDSON-FULTON CELEBRATION, HUDSON, N.Y.

This regional "centennial" celebration was of brief duration, but it inspired some of the most beautifully-designed and colored buttons of any fair. The fair was a dual tribute to explorer Hendrick Hudson's 1609 discovery of the Hudson River in his *Half Moon* sailing ship and inventor Robert Fulton's 1807 introduction of steam navigation on the river in the steamboat *Clermont*.

259-2-D-C

260-2-D-C

261-2-D-C

262-2-D-C

263-2-D-C

267-2-A-B

264-2-D-E

265-2-D-D

266-2-D-D

1915 PANAMA-CALIFORNIA EXPOSITION, SAN DIEGO; PANAMA-PACIFIC EXPOSITION, SAN FRANCISCO

Both fairs were tributes to the 1914 opening of the Panama Canal which linked the Atlantic and Pacific Oceans for maritime trade. The San Francisco Exposition closed at the end of 1915 and a number of exhibits were moved to the concurrent San Diego Exposition which continued into 1916. Few buttons are known from the San Francisco fair although most examples are very well-designed and quite colorful. Fewer yet buttons emerged from the San Diego fair, despite its intent as a more 'international' event.

269-3-D-D*

270-3-D-C

271-3-C-C

272-3-D-D*

268-3-F-C*

273-3-D-C   274-3-C-C   275-3-O-C*   276-3-D-D   277-3-J-C

1926 SESQUICENTENNIAL, PHILADELPHIA, PA.

It was 1926 and the United States of America was 150 years old. Philadelphia, the site of the signing of the Declaration of Independence, was the fair site of the nation's birthday party. Among the outstanding buildings were the Palace of Liberal Arts and Manufactures and the Palace of Agriculture. Guests included President and Mrs. Coolidge, Queen Marie of Rumania, and Prince Gustav Adolf of Sweden. The exposition, running from June 1 to November 30, was judged a patriotic, but not financial, success despite an attendance of about six million visitors. A number of buttons were issued for the fair, many with the Liberty Bell as a centerpiece, and a few are noted for exceptionally nice design and color.

278-4-D-D   279-4-E-C   280-4-C-C   281-4-D-C

282-4-A-C   283-4-O-C   284-4-E-C   285-4-C-C*

1933 CENTURY OF PROGRESS WORLD'S FAIR, CHICAGO

Despite the effects of the Great Depression, the 1933-1934 "Century of Progress" Chicago World's Fair opened May 17, 1933 and continued a successful 17-month run before ending on Halloween night, 1934. The 8-acre Hall of Science, later to become the Museum of Science and Industry, was the fair's focal point. The fair's theme was based on 100 years of progress since the 1833 incorporation of the city of Chicago. The opening night fair lights were activated by starlight from the heavens. Over its span, The Century of Progress attracted approximately 140 million visitors. A good variety of buttons was issued by the fair and many of its exhibitors.

286-5-N-C   287L-5-G-B   288L-5-G-B   289L-5-G-B   290L-5-E-B   291L-5-R-C*   292-5-G-B

293-5-D-D

294-5-A-D

295-5-G-C

296L-5-E-C

297-5-A-C

298-5-I-C*

299-5-G-C

300-5-A-C

301-5-G-C

302L-5-Y-B

303-5-P-B

304-5-T-B

305L-5-M-C

306L-5-G-B

307-5-A-B*

308-5-G-B*

309-5-A-B*

310L-5-C-B

311L-5-C-B

1939 GOLDEN GATE EXPOSITION, SAN FRANCISCO

The Golden Gate International Exposition ran from February 1939 through September 1940 to celebrate the new Golden Gate and Oakland Bay bridges, plus the "progress of art and beauty in the Western Hemisphere." Site of the fair was man-made "Treasure Island" which was reached by bay ferry. A 400-foot Tower of Sun was the fair's symbol. Only a few button examples are known from this fair.

312-5-E-C

313-5-G-B

1939 NEW YORK WORLD'S FAIR, NEW YORK, N.Y.

World War II loomed as the 1939-1940 "World of Tomorrow" New York World's Fair opened. Centerpieces of the fair were the Trylon, a 728-foot tapering column, and the Perisphere, a huge globe. The fair, held in Flushing Meadow Park in Queens, boasted more than two million flowers and 10,000 trees on the site of an original dump. Among the "World of Tomorrow" previews were air conditioning, television, nylon, and General Motor's "Futurama," a prediction of auto freeway systems which reportedly drew 28,000 visitors daily. Almost 45 million visitors attended the 1½ year fair, which also commemorated the 150th anniversary of George Washington's presidency. Many button variations in orange, blue and white depicted the Trylon and Perisphere. "I Have Seen The Future" buttons by the thousands were given to each visitor at the end of the "Futurama" ride. Less common buttons were issued by Ford, I.B.M., and for special single day events.

314-5-G-B*

315-5-O-B

316-5-J-D*

317-5-M-C

318L-5-G-B

319L-5-E-B

320-5-G-A

321-5-K-C

322-5-R-B

323-5-M-D*

324-5-N-B

325-5-M-C

326-5-E-B

327-5-N-B

329-5-A-C

330-5-A-D*

328-5-M-B

331-5-G-C

332-5-M-C

333-5-I-B*

334-5-M-B

335-5-M-B

336-5-M-B

337-5-M-B

338-5-M-C   339-5-C-C   340-5-M-A   341-5-M-A   342-5-M-A   343-5-M-A

344-5-M-A   345-5-M-A   346-5-M-A   347-5-M-B   348-5-M-A

1962 SEATTLE WORLD'S FAIR; 1964 NEW YORK WORLD'S FAIR

The Seattle "Century 21 Exposition" was themed "Man in the Space Age" and featured a 607-foot steel and glass Space Needle. The 1964-1965 New York Fair, on the same site as its predecessor in 1939-1940, was themed "Peace Through Understanding" along with a concurrent celebration of the city's 300th year. The fair's symbol was the Unisphere, a stainless steel globe 135 feet tall.

349-8-R-B   350-8-M-A   351-8-E-A   352-8-G-A

1976 U.S. BICENTENNIAL CELEBRATION

America's 200th year was celebrated at countless locations, cities to villages, across the land. Numerous buttons from these sites and other buttons by greeting card manufacturers were issued for the nation's year-long birthday party.

353-9-R-A   354-9-G-A   355L-9-L-A   356-9-E-A

NOTES

II. CELEBRATIONS, EXPOSITIONS, WORLD'S FAIRS

HOLIDAY & SEASONS
    34. BRASS 'POCKET WATCH' RIM DESIGN.
SANTA CLAUS
    50. BACK PAPER: ''The Big Christmas Store contains Everything in gifts dear to the heart of childhood''
    72. GREEN RIM.
    88. BACK PAPER: ''A MERRY CHRISTMAS/The Big Daylight Store/A.H. Meyer & Co.''
LOCAL EVENTS
    107. BACK PAPER: ''To Find/XENODACHY/VISIT MECHANICS FAIR''
    112. BACK PAPER: ''W. F. MILLER & CO./134 PARK ROW, NEW YORK''
    151. BACK PAPER: ''SHRYOCK-TODD NOTION CO., Importers and Jobbers of Streetmen's Goods of all kinds''
1898 TRANS-MISSISSIPPI
    173. BACK PAPER INCLUDES: ''GERMAN VILLAGE/The Gaiety Resort of the Exposition/CONTINUOUS VAUDEVILLE''
1901 PAN-AMERICAN
    187. ON EDGE: ''OFFICIAL BUTTON''
    192. CRIMPED METAL EDGE AND BACK PIN ATTACHED AT TOP.
  196.-203. PART OF A SET.
1904 LOUISIANA PURCHASE
    218. BACK PAPER: ''WORLD'S FAIR/ST. LOUIS/1904''
    220. BACK PAPER: ''ST. LOUIS SEED CO'S. EXHIBIT/SIZE 120 FEET DIAMETER/20,000 PLANTS''
    224. DIECUT CELLULOID MOUNTED ON DIECUT METAL BACK W/INSERT PIN.
  232.-244. PART OF A SET.
1905 LEWIS & CLARK
    247. BACK PAPER INCLUDES: ''ALAMEDA COUNTY/COUNTY SEAT/THE ATHENS of the PACIFIC/The great commercial and educational centre of the Pacific Coast/Nature's Garden Spot''
1909 ALASKA-YUKON-PACIFIC
    255. ALSO SEEN IN 1¼" SIZE. THIS SIZE, VALUE D.
1915 PANAMA-CALIFORNIA & PANAMA-PACIFIC EXPOSITIONS
    268. W/RED/ORANGE/BLUE RIBBON AND BRASS HANGER BAR.
    269. BACK PAPER: ''Official Souvenir/Panama-Pacific International Exposition/PAN-PACIFIC SOUVENIR CO./SAN FRANCISCO, CAL./Distributors ''
    272. W/SILVER RIBBON AND BRASS HANGER BAR.
    275. BACK PAPER: ''CALL YOUR 1915 MEETINGS FOR SAN FRANCISCO ''
1926 SESQUICENTENNIAL
    285. CLOTH BUTTON W/PAPER HAT & SILK RIBBON.
1933 CHICAGO WORLD'S FAIR
    291. BACK INSCRIPTION: ''This SHIRT MANUFACTURED BY RELIANCE MFG. CO. at their exhibit during A CENTURY OF PROGRESS'' SILVER/BLUE.
    298. BELOW CENTER DESIGN: ''CHICAGO'S NEW CENTURY CELEBRATION''
  307.-309. PAPER BUTTON ON METAL COLLET.
1939 NEW YORK WORLD'S FAIR
    314. BACK PAPER: ''GENERAL MOTORS EXHIBIT/WORLD'S FAIR 1940 IN NEW YORK''
    316. 'FUTURAMA' GM HOST BUTTON W/RED & WHITE RIBBON.
    323. SOLID BACK INSCRIPTION: ''THE ICE INDUSTRY EXHIBIT/FOOD B'L'D'G./WORLD'S FAIR, NEW YORK CITY, 1940''
    330. FACE AND COLLAR ARE TINTED.
    333. BUTTON ATTACHED TO BLUE/WHITE DIECUT CELLULOID.

III. ENTERTAINMENT

AMUSEMENT PARKS, BEACHES

Brooklyn's Coney Island is generally considered the country's first major amusement park with its origin in the mid-1840s. Between 1897 and 1905, three additional amusement sites—Steeplechase Park, Luna Park and Dreamland Park—were opened in the greater New York area and enjoyed immense popularity along with the venerable Atlantic City, N.J. boardwalk and beach. Colorful buttons depicting rides, attractions, buildings and beach scenes were issued by these major parks in addition to numerous local and smaller amusement sites across the nation.

1-2-D-H

2-2-D-C

3-3-D-D

4-2-D-D

5-3-D-D

6-2-D-C

7-2-D-C

8-1-D-D

9-3-E-C

10-3-D-C

11-1-D-C

12-3-D-C

13-3-A-B

14-2-D-E

15-5-J-A

16-2-D-C*

17-3-D-E

18-3-I-B

19-2-E-C

20-2-D-D*

21-2-G-A

22-2-I-A

23-2-E-A

24-3-G-A

25-5-E-A

26-2-J-B

27-2-G-C   28-2-J-C   29-4-N-A

30-2-D-C

31-3-E-D   32-3-K-B   33-2-B-C*   34-3-D-C   35-3-H-B

ARTISTS, PAINTERS, CARTOONISTS

Prior to the 1960's few buttons were devoted to the visual arts other than an ''Art Scene'' series depicting classic paintings. These buttons were a turn-of-the-century premium from Cameo Pepsin Gum. In the 1960's the work of several well-known artists appeared on buttons.

36-1-D-B*   37-1-D-B*   38-1-D-B*   39-5-D-B*   40-5-D-B*

41-8-W-B   42-8-A-C*   43-8-A-C*   44-8-I-C*

CIRCUSES, CLOWNS, FREAKS

Although a circus in America first appeared in 1792, the 1890s-1930s are usually considered to be the finest—and certainly most famed—era of circus entertainment. Barnum & Bailey's "Greatest Show On Earth" was purchased in 1907 by the equally successful Ringling Bros. The two circuses performed separately until 1919 when, combined under a single name, the first joint performance opened in New York City. Other famed names among the nearly 100 circus touring companies by 1909 included Forepaugh, Hagenbeck-Wallace, Sells-Floto, Al G. Barnes, Sparks and John Robinson. "Wild West Shows" also enjoyed great popularity, particularly "Buffalo Bill" Cody's. Numerous circus buttons with standard clown designs were issued for performances in various communities across the nation.

45-1-B-D

46-2-K-D

47-2-A-C

48-2-A-E

49-2-G-D

50-1-A-B

51-1-B-E*

52-3-A-E

53-5-C-C

54-5-G-B

55-2-J-D

56-4-D-C

57-4-C-C

58-4-D-C

59-5-J-B

60-5-J-B

61-5-C-C

62-7-C-B

63-5-C-B

64-5-C-B

65-5-G-A

66-2-C-B

67-2-B-E

68-1-A-C

69-6-E-B

MARATONA

70-2-A-E*

BOB YOKUM'S BUFFALO
PIERRE. S.D.

71-2-B-D

SAM LOCKHARTS ELEPHANT
HADDIE

72-2-B-D

SAM LOCKHARTS BABY ELEPHANT
TOM-TOM

73-2-A-D

HAGENBACK'S NEW MEMBER
CLOVER CLUB'S IRRESISTIBLY YOURS.
HAM, JR.

74-2-A-C

CONSUL AT BOSTOCKS

75-2-B-C

BOSTOCK THE ANIMAL KING.

76-2-B-C

J.W. GORMAN'S KING & QUEEN
FAMOUS HIGH DIVING HORSES

77-2-C-C

ADGIE
LION TAMER

78-1-B-D

79-2-B-C

SOUVENIR
TERRELL JACOBS

80-5-A-C

CLYDE BEATTY

81-5-A-C

82-5-A-C

COLE BROS. CIRCUS

83-5-A-C

CLYDE BEATTY CIRCUS

84-6-H-C

SALLY STARR

85-7-D-D

38

86-2-D-E*

87-1-D-E*

88-1-B-D*

89-2-A-D*

90-2-B-C*

91-2-B-C*

92-2-B-C*

93-2-B-C*

94-2-B-C*

95-2-J-C

96-2-B-D*

97-2-R-D*

98-5-A-D

CHILDREN'S CLUBS

Clubs for youth flourished in the 1930s. Radio stations, newspapers and movie theaters as well as food producers were the primary club sponsors.

99-2-B-B

100-2-A-A

101-5-C-B

102-5-C-B

103-5-C-B

104-5-J-B

105-5-E-B

106-5-E-B

107-5-R-B

108-5-C-B*

109L-5-M-A

110-5-G-A

COMIC CHARACTERS

No child and few adults or retailers could resist the button popularity of characters from early comic strips and later radio shows, film cartoons, and movies. The popularity of such themes remains to the present although not to the same extent as yesteryear. Comic character buttons are generally considered to have begun with Outcault's "Yellow Kid" series in 1896 and hundreds of different character buttons followed. Comic buttons were frequently given as premiums by newspapers, retailers and food manufacturers. The variety and continued popularity of comic characters makes this category one of the most-frequently sought by today's button collectors.

111-5-J-C*

112-2-D-D

113-2-D-D

114-4-M-B

115-6-E-D

116-5-F-C

117-5-A-B

118-5-A-B*

119-5-A-B*

120-5-A-B*

121-5-D-C

122L-5-D-C

123-5-J-A

124-7-E-B

125-9-M-A

126-6-C-E

127-5-W-D*

128-5-J-C

129-5-D-C

130-5-J-C*

131L-8-F-B

132L-8-C-A*

133L-8-F-A*

134L-8-C-A*

135L-8-F-A*

136-5-J-C*

137-5-A-E

138-5-A-D

139-5-A-D

140L-5-J-D*

141-9-D-A

142-2-D-E

143-2-D-E

144-2-D-E

145-5-C-C*

146-5-D-C*

147-5-D-E

148L-5-D-E*

149L-5-M-G

150-5-E-H*

151-6-I-E

152L-7-J-C

153L-9-E-A*

154-6-E-D

155L-6-E-D

156L-6-J-D

157L-6-D-D*

158L-6-D-D*

159L-6-D-D*

160L-6-D-D*

161L-6-D-D*

162L-6-D-D*

163L-6-D-D*

164L-6-D-D*

165-8-C-B

166-5-C-D*

167-5-D-D*

41

168-5-E-F

169L-5-R-C

170-5-D-D*

171-5-D-D*

172-5-R-D

173L-5-R-D

174-5-R-D

175-8-J-B

176-5-J-D

177-5-N-C

Not Too Close

178-5-A-E*

179-5-J-E

180-5-J-D*

181L-5-N-C*

182L-5-J-G

183L-5-D-D*

184-2-D-C*

185-2-D-C*

186-2-D-C*

187-2-D-D

188-9-J-A*

189L-7-I-C

190-2-E-C

191-2-K-C

192L-5-N-B*

193-5-A-C*

194-2-D-C

195-5-C-D*

196-5-A-D

197L-5-J-B*

42

198-5-J-C*

199L-5-N-B*

200-5-A-B*

201-5-I-B

202-5-F-B

203-5-F-B

204-6-J-C*

205-5-D-C*

206-5-D-B*

207-5-D-B*

208-5-D-B*

209-5-D-B*

210-5-D-B*

211-5-D-B*

212-5-D-B*

213-5-D-B*

214L-5-N-B*

215L-7-C-B*

216L-7-C-B*

217L-5-F-C

218-5-E-C

219-9-J-A*

220L-5-P-B*

221-3-D-B*

222-5-J-C*

223-2-D-C

224-6-H-C*

225-7-I-C

226-6-E-D

227-6-P-D

228L-5-F-B*

229-1-D-B*

230-1-D-B*

231-1-D-B*

232L-5-N-B*

233L-7-C-B*

234L-5-J-B*

235L-5-G-B

236-9-N-A*

237-9-Y-A*

238-5-J-B*

239-3-A-D

240-3-N-D

241-6-P-C*

242-5-J-B*

243-5-C-L

244-5-D-E*

245-5-D-E*

246-5-D-E

247-5-D-E

252-9-D-C

248-5-D-E

249-5-A-C

250-5-J-C*

251-8-M-A*

44

253-6-D-F*

254L-6-C-C*

255-2-D-E*

256L-7-M-E

257L-7-M-B

258-8-C-B*

259-5-G-D

260-6-E-C

261L-5-P-B*

262L-5-J-C*

263-5-E-C

264-5-D-C

265-5-J-C

266-5-M-C

267-5-D-D*

268-5-C-D*

269-5-I-C

270L-5-G-C

271-5-C-E*

272-5-C-D*

273-6-M-C*

274L-7-F-C

275L-7-H-C

276-5-J-C*

277L-5-J-B

278-5-C-C

279-5-M-C

280-5-H-A

281-6-F-D

282-5-D-C

283-5-D-C*

284-5-D-C

285-5-D-D

286-5-R-D

287-5-D-C*

288-5-D-B*

289-5-A-C

290-5-N-C

291L-5-A-C

292L-5-R-D*

293-5-P-D

294-5-S-D

295-5-D-B*

296-5-D-B*

297-5-D-B*

298-5-D-B*

299-5-D-C*

300-5-C-D*

301-5-C-D*

302-5-R-C*

303L-7-J-B*

304L-7-C-B*

305L-5-J-B*

306L-7-J-D

307L-9-F-A*

308L-7-N-B

309L-6-E-C

310L-6-C-D*

311L-6-F-B*

312L-6-E-D*

313L-6-E-D*

314L-6-M-E*

315L-7-C-D*

316-6-J-I

317-6-D-D*

318-7-D-D*

319-8-D-C*

320-6-D-G*

321L-8-F-B*

322L-8-F-B*

323L-8-F-B*

324L-8-F-B*

325L-8-F-B*

326L-8-F-B*

327-5-F-D

328-5-J-C*

329-5-P-F

330-5-J-E*

331L-5-J-C*

332L-5-J-C*

333L-9-M-A*

334-5-G-A

335-5-R-B

336L-7-J-C

337-7-N-B

338-1-D-C*

339-1-D-F*

340-1-N-G*

341-1-N-D

342-1-N-F

343-3-N-D

47

COWBOYS, WESTERN HEROES

The American West and its cowboy heroes were a combination of gunsmoke, rearing horses, fistfights and justice-done in the imagination of early book and magazine readers, radio listeners and film-goers. Tom Mix was among the most-famed early cowboys to gain increased popularity through buttons. The cowboy fascination continued longer than most button topics with heroes such as Gene Autry, Roy Rogers and Hopalong Cassidy carrying the popularity into the 1940s through 1950s. Among the fictitious heroes, The Lone Ranger still ranks high among cowboy collectors. Although cowboy buttons are not generally noted for beautiful colors or inspired design, they are a widely-sought category by today's collectors.

344-6-N-C

345-6-M-D*

346-6-M-D

347-6-A-D

348L-6-E-D

349-6-A-D

350-6-M-G

351-6-A-D

352-6-C-C*

353-6-A-C

354-6-A-C

355-6-A-B

356-6-E-C

357-7-H-C*

358-7-C-B*

359-7-R-D

360-5-A-D

361-5-M-E

362-5-J-E

364-5-M-C

363-5-A-D

365-7-A-C

366-7-Q-F

367-7-M-C*

368-7-J-C*

369-7-A-C

370L-7-J-C

371L-7-A-D

372-7-P-B*

373L-7-C-C

374L-7-N-C

375-7-J-C

376-7-P-D

377L-7-E-C

378L-7-N-C

379-7-J-C

380-7-J-C

381L-7-P-C

383L-7-N-B*

384L-7-M-B*

385L-7-J-B*

382L-7-J-E*

386L-7-H-B*

387L-7-Y-B*

388-7-R-D*

389-7-R-D*

390L-7-R-E*

391L-7-R-E*

392-7-J-A

393-7-C-D

394L-7-I-C

395-7-M-B

396-7-M-B

397L-7-J-D

398-7-G-B

399L-7-C-B

400L-7-C-B

401-7-P-B

PFEIFERS DAVY CROCKETT FAN CLUB

402-7-K-C

DAVY CROCKETT

403-7-M-B

JERRI-JANE Tots to Teens
DAVY CROCKETT
INDIAN SCOUT
NORRISTOWN, PA

404-7-G-B

DAVY CROCKETT

405-7-N-B

PIONEER OF THE MONTH
KING OF THE Frontier
1786-1836

406-7-T-B

MEMBER
DAVY CROCKETT CLUB
S.S. KRESGE CO.

407L-7-N-B

S. S. KRESGE CO.
DAVY CROCKETT
INDIAN SCOUT

408L-7-K-B

DAVY CROCKETT
INDIAN SCOUT

409L-7-C-B

MATT DILLON'S FAVORITE
ALL STAR DAIRIES

410L-7-E-C

RUSSELL BROS. CIRCUS
Hoot Gibson

411-5-A-E

MONTE HALE

412-7-N-B

MONTE HALE

413-7-N-B

Wild Bill Hickok and Jingles
WE'RE PARDNERS

414L-7-N-D

Buck Jones Rangers' Club of America

415-5-A-D

FOR U. S. MARSHAL
BUCK JONES

416-5-A-E

BUCK JONES
PHANTOM RIDER CLUB

417-5-F-F

BUCK JONES CLUB
291

418-5-J-E

BUCK JONES
RED RIDER

419-5-J-E

Club Member
BUCK JONES
"Roaring West"
Every Sat. - Sun. Mat.
RKO CAPITOL
Union City

420-5-I-D

BUCK JONES
A UNIVERSAL STAR

421-5-A-E*

ALLAN "Rocky" LANE

422-7-M-C

THE LONE RANGER
SUNDAY HERALD and EXAMINER

423L-5-M-C*

HI-YO, SILVER
THE LONE RANGER

424-5-J-E

LEE POWELL
ORIGINAL MOTION PICTURE
LONE RANGER

425-5-A-E

MEMBER
LONE RANGER SAFETY CLUB

426-5-N-D

LONE Reading TIMES RANGER

427-5-E-D

LONE RANGER CLUB
DR. WEST'S TOOTH PASTE

428-5-J-D

LONE RANGER

429-6-E-D*

HI-HO STERLING SILVER

430L-5-G-B*

"LONE RANGER"
Buchan's
ENRICHED BREAD

431-6-S-B*

"HI-YO SILVER"
Buchan's
"PLAY SAFE"

432-6-I-B*

51

438L-7-W-C*

433-5-J-E   434-5-J-E*   435-5-E-C*   436-5-E-D*   437-7-D-C

439-5-A-D   440-5-G-E

443L-5-G-D

441-6-N-D   442-5-C-E

444-5-F-E   445-5-A-G   446-5-G-G   447-5-C-F   448-5-C-F

452L-5-C-D*

449-5-M-H

450-5-A-E   451-5-A-E

453L-5-J-C*   454L-5-J-C*   455L-5-J-C*   456L-5-J-C*   457L-5-J-C*

458-5-N-E

459-5-M-E

460-9-I-A*

461-9-I-A*

462L-6-N-B

463-6-J-C

464-6-N-C

465-5-A-C

466-5-A-C

467-5-K-D

468-5-A-C

469-5-C-C

470-5-G-C

471L-5-K-A

472-5-N-B

473-5-C-C

474L-7-D-B*

475-5-J-D

476-6-A-D

477-6-A-D

478-7-N-C

479-7-N-C

53

480-7-J-E*

481-6-N-F

482-7-C-D

483-7-J-D

484-7-N-C*

485-7-N-D

486-6-A-F*

487-6-A-F

488-6-A-D

489-7-A-B

490-6-A-C

491-7-P-C

492-7-N-B

493-7-H-B

494-7-P-B

495L-7-D-C*

496L-7-D-C*

497L-7-D-B*

498L-7-D-B*

499L-7-D-B*

500L-7-D-B*

501L-7-D-B*

502L-7-D-B*

503L-7-D-B*

504L-7-D-B*

505L-7-D-B*

506L-7-D-B*

507L-7-D-B*

508L-7-D-B*

509-9-A-A*

510-5-A-B

511-7-X-B

512-5-A-D

513-5-C-E

514-7-H-C

515-7-W-B

516-5-J-E

517-5-N-E

518-5-E-E

519-5-C-E

520-5-M-E

521-5-A-E

522-5-J-E

523-5-N-E

524L-7-N-A

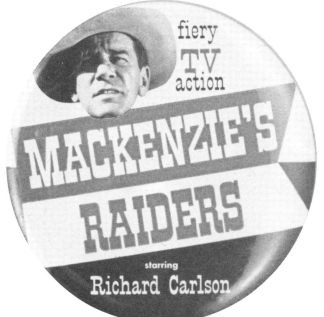
525-8-F-C

DISNEY, DISNEYANA

A mouse named Mickey was born in 1928 and, along with other Disney characters to follow, helped the nation's morale through the Depression years. Mickey Mouse products, including buttons, were produced in great numbers. The buttons frequently were associated with bread, children's clothing, or clubs sponsored by movie theaters. Early Disney buttons, often designated "Walt Disney Enterprises" rather than the later "Walt Disney Productions," are sought widely by collectors. There also is a growing interest in post-World War II Disney buttons, particularly "studio issues" from the Disney parks in California and Florida.

526-5-J-F

529-5-C-H*

527-5-M-F

528-5-C-H*

530-5-C-H*

531-5-C-E

532-5-C-L*

533-5-M-E

534-5-C-H*

535-5-J-F

536-5-C-H*

537-5-A-F   538-5-A-E   539-5-A-E   540-5-H-E   541-5-C-F   542-6-A-E

543L-5-C-F   544-5-J-F   545-5-J-F   546-5-J-E

547-5-M-J

548-5-H-E*   549-5-J-F   550-5-M-F   551-5-M-E

552-5-D-H   553-5-J-E   554-5-J-F   555-5-J-F   556-5-J-F

557-5-M-H   558-5-J-F   559-5-J-D*   560-5-C-F*   561-5-C-F*

562-5-F-G*   563L-5-R-G*   564L-5-C-D   565L-7-J-B   566L-7-J-C*

57

567-7-C-D

568L-9-J-B

569L-9-J-A

570-9-W-B

571-9-C-D*

572-9-C-C*

573-9-D-B

574-9-D-D

575-5-M-H

578L-7-C-D

579L-9-C-A*

576-8-P-H

577-5-M-F

580L-7-J-C* 581L-7-J-C* 582L-7-J-C* 583L-7-J-C* 584L-7-J-C* 585L-7-J-C* 586L-7-J-C*

587L-7-J-C*

588-5-J-E

589-5-E-D

592-5-E-H

590-5-X-D

591-5-E-D

593-6-J-D

594-6-D-E

595-6-J-E

596-7-J-C

597L-7-C-C

598-6-J-D

599L-6-C-E

600-6-D-D

601L-7-C-C

602L-7-D-C

603-7-K-C

604L-7-M-B

605-9-D-B

606-9-D-A

607-9-J-B

608-9-C-B

609-9-D-B

610-9-C-B

611-9-C-E*

ICE SHOWS, ROLLER SKATING, DANCING, MISC. ENTERTAINMENT EVENTS

Professional ice show tours originated in the 1930's with Sonja Henie the first of a succession of skating idols. Various entertainment events have also captured the nation's imagination, with the Evel Knievel feats among the latter-day attractions.

612-2-A-C

613-5-W-C

614-6-C-B

615-6-A-C

616-7-A-B

617-4-I-A

618-1-A-A

619-4-A-A

620-6-E-A

621-6-E-A

622-6-N-A

623-7-A-B

624-7-N-A

625-6-I-A

626-9-D-B

627-9-D-B

MUSICIANS, SINGERS, COMPOSERS

Among the early musicians, the two known versions of "Roney's Boys" are quite colorful and choice items of entertainment button collectors. In recent years, many nicely-designed buttons have emerged with the popularity of musical groups and their records or videos. Singers, like musicians, did not appear on a large number of buttons until the 1950s. More buttons in this category have been issued since the emergence of Elvis Presley and the Beatles than were produced in the preceding 60 years.

628-2-D-D

629-2-D-D

630-1-B-B

631-2-B-C*

632-5-A-B

633-5-A-B

634L-5-J-B

635L-5-G-B

636-6-A-C

637-5-A-C

638-6-A-D

639-7-A-D

640L-7-A-B

641-7-J-B

642-7-A-B

643L-7-A-B

644L-7-A-B

645-7-A-B

646-7-J-B

647L-7-A-B

648L-7-J-B

649-7-G-B

62

650-7-N-D

651L-7-W-E

652-7-I-C

653-7-E-C

654-7-A-D

655L-7-R-B*

656L-7-R-B*

657-7-A-D

658L-7-R-B*

659L-7-R-B*

660-7-D-D

661L-7-E-B*

662L-7-E-B*

663-7-D-C

664L-7-E-B*

665-7-H-B

63

666L-8-L-B*

667-7-G-C

668L-8-L-A*

669L-7-A-C

670-7-J-C

671-8-A-C

672L-7-A-C

673-7-A-C

674L-7-Y-B

675-7-W-D

676-7-M-D

64

678-8-X-A

677-8-A-D

679L-9-N-A

680L-9-M-B

681-9-T-B

682-9-A-B

683-9-A-B

684L-9-M-B

685L-8-J-A*

686L-8-J-A*

687L-8-J-A*

688L-8-J-A*

689-8-A-D*

690-8-A-D*

691L-8-J-A*

692L-8-E-A*

693L-8-J-A*

694-8-A-B

65

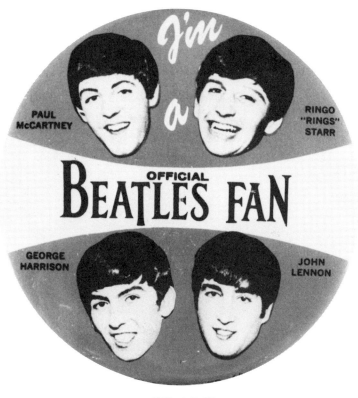

695L-8-J-C*

696-8-C-C*

697-8-D-C*

698-8-D-C*

699-8-D-C*

700-8-D-C*

701-9-D-A

702-9-D-A

703-9-D-A

MOVIES

The appeal of early "silver screen" stars prompted buttons as an inducement to youngsters to enter the movie house (or return to it), as if further inducement was needed. Many series of buttons depicting movie stars appeared between the 1920s and the advent of the television age. Button issues for movies which remain classics today—e.g. *Gone With The Wind* and *Wizard of Oz*—are rare and fervently sought by collectors. Also extremely popular are buttons showing major stars such as Valentino, Harold Lloyd, Mickey Rooney, Judy Garland, Our Gang, Clark Gable, and Charlie Chaplin.

704-6-C-D

705-6-G-B

706-4-A-C*

707-5-F-C

708-5-W-D

709-4-C-D

710-6-A-C

711-6-A-C

712-7-K-D

713-5-J-C

714-6-A-C

715-5-S-C

716L-5-A-C*

717L-5-A-C*

718L-5-A-C*

719L-5-A-C*

720L-5-A-C*

721L-5-A-C*

722L-5-A-C*

723L-5-A-C*

724L-5-A-C

725L-5-A-C*

726L-5-A-C*

727-6-A-C

728L-6-G-C

729-5-A-C

730-4-A-G*

731-4-A-E

732-5-A-D

733-5-G-E

734-5-M-D

735-6-G-C

736-6-G-C

737-5-C-D

738-4-J-E

739-4-A-D

740-4-M-D

741-4-G-D

742-4-A-D

743-4-M-D

744-5-H-B

745-5-A-C

746-5-F-D

747-5-E-D

748-5-H-D

749-7-A-D

750-6-G-C

751-5-A-C

752-5-A-D

753-7-D-D

"Sampeck"
TRIPLE-SERVICE SUIT

754-4-A-D*

DOUGLAS FAIRBANKS in the BLACK PIRATE
STRAND THEATRE

755-4-A-E

DON Q.
SON OF ZORRO

756-4-C-F

SUPERVISOR

757-6-A-E

JUDY GARLAND IN "THE HARVEY GIRLS"

758-6-C-E

293 WIZARD OF OZ
JUDY GARLAND M-G-M's

759-5-M-F*

2419 WIZARD OF OZ
JACK HALEY M-G-M's

760-5-M-E*

EL MAGO DE OZ

761-5-M-D*

DON'T MISS THE WIZARD OF OZ AT LOEW'S PALACE

762-5-C-G

GRACIE FIELDS
QUEEN OF HEARTS

763-5-J-D

VOTE FOR JOHNNY HINES
"THE SPEED SPOOK"

764-3-A-C

JACKIE HOORAY
GANG'S CLUB

765-5-B-C

CHARLES HUTCHISON

766-4-J-C

AL JOLSON in "MAMMY"
A Warner Bros. Production

767-5-A-H

TOMMY KELLY
TOM SAWYER CLUB

768-5-P-C

DEMAND THAT UNIVERSAL PROGRAM
FLORENCE LAWRENCE

769-4-A-E

JANET DID IT

770-7-A-B

DAVEY LEE
SONNY BOY CLUB

771-5-D-B

"THE SHOW IS ON"
BEATRICE LILLIE

772-5-A-C

HAROLD LLOYD Talks
RIALTO NOW
in "WELCOME DANGER"

773-5-F-E

LONESOME LUKE

774-3-A-D

775-4-A-C

69

776-5-A-D*

777-5-A-D*

778-5-A-D*

779-5-A-F*

780-5-A-D*

781-5-A-D*

782-5-A-F*

783-5-A-D*

784-5-A-D*

785-4-J-E

786-5-G-C

787-5-J-D

788-3-J-D

789-5-A-C

790-3-A-C

791-6-C-C

792L-4-G-C*

793L-4-G-C*

794L-4-G-C*

795L-4-G-C*

796L-4-G-C*

797L-4-I-C*

798L-4-G-C*

799-5-A-D

800-5-G-C

801-5-D-D

802-5-A-D

803-5-A-D

804-5-A-C

805-5-A-C

806-5-N-D

807-5-A-D

808-5-J-C

809-4-J-D

810-6-N-C

811-5-N-E

812-5-N-E

813-6-N-E

814L-5-G-B

815L-6-A-C

816-4-A-B

817-4-A-B

818-4-A-B

819L-5-G-E

820-5-A-E

821-5-W-D

822-5-J-D

823L-9-D-A

824-4-J-D

825-5-M-E

826-3-M-B

827-5-C-E

828-3-A-C

829-5-Y-D

830-5-Y-D

831-5-N-D

832-3-F-C

833-5-E-D

834L-7-Y-C

835-5-C-G

836-3-E-C

837-3-Y-C

838L-6-I-B

839-6-G-E

840-5-D-C*

841-6-C-G

842-6-P-G

843-6-P-G

844-5-N-C

845-9-J-A

846-5-E-C

847-3-D-C

848-5-E-E

849-3-R-C*

850-3-C-C

851-5-G-B

852-5-N-E

853-3-X-C

854-6-O-E

855-5-J-E

856-5-P-F

857-5-F-D

858-6-J-E

859-4-G-C

860-4-G-C

861-5-G-E

862-5-J-E

863-5-M-F

864-4-A-F*

865-4-T-C*

866-4-T-C*

867-4-T-C*

868-4-T-C*

869-4-T-C*

870-5-M-E

871-5-J-E

872-3-A-C

72

873-3-G-B

874-5-G-B

875-3-D-C

876-5-J-C

877-5-N-C

878-5-D-C

879-4-A-B

880-5-E-B

881-5-M-B

882-5-J-C

883L-5-J-B

884L-5-G-B

885-6-I-B

886-4-G-B

887-5-G-B

888-5-J-B

889-5-F-B

890-3-G-C

891-7-J-D

894-9-D-A

892-5-R-D

893L-8-W-B

895-8-F-B

RADIO

The miracle of wireless radio opened an enormous new medium of communication between advertiser and customer. Youngsters and their buying moms or dads were a prime target for radio advertisers. Buttons by the thousands were issued as premiums for buying products and joining clubs which would ensure the continued use of the product. In addition, buttons were issued to promote the popularity of radio program personalities with the intent of continued listenership. Although radio buttons are not generally as beautiful as some other categories, the variety available has great appeal to both the beginning and advanced collector.

896L-5-I-A

897-8-F-B

898-5-N-B*

899-5-N-B*

900L-7-G-A

901L-5-E-A

902-5-A-A

903-5-A-B

904-5-A-B

905-5-I-A

909L-5-C-C

906-5-I-A

907-5-G-A

908-5-E-A*

910-5-M-A

911-6-F-B

912L-6-M-B

913-5-A-A

914-6-K-C

915-5-E-A

916-7-A-B

917-5-C-B

918-5-A-C

919-5-P-A

920-5-N-A

921-7-J-A

922-5-A-B

923-5-A-A

924-5-R-A

925-5-C-A

926L-7-G-B

927-5-J-C

928-5-A-A

929L-5-G-A

930-5-N-A

931-6-E-B

932-5-N-B

933-5-N-B*

934-5-A-B

935L-5-M-A

936L-5-H-A

937-5-A-A*

938-6-J-B

939-6-J-B

940-5-I-A

941-5-A-B

RENFREW
OF THE
MOUNTED

942-5-J-B

WILL ROGERS
He Chews To Run

943-5-J-C*

AUNT SALLY'S DUTCH OVEN KIDDIES CLUB
W.G.S.T.

944-5-G-A

I AM A LULLABY LISTENER
Sears Roebuck Station

945-5-E-A

THE SHADOW

946-5-A-H*

UNCLE SID'S ABC CLUB
ALWAYS BE CAREFUL
AB WCLO

947-5-J-A

MEMBER
SINBAC
RADIO CLUB

948-5-C-A

SINBAC
Radio Club

949L-5-E-A

THE SKY CLIMBERS

950-5-D-B

Kate Smith's Philadelphia A & P Party

Nov. 4   1935

Hello Everybody

951-5-J-C

JUNIOR SMITH'S
WMCA
RED CROSS
SMILE CLUB

952-5-K-A

Steffen's
SAFE MILK   ICE CREAM
SPARKIE CLUB

953-7-A-A

MEMBER
I·S·P
Speed Gibson
BUTTERFLY BREAD

954-5-J-B

SPEED GIBSON
SECRET POLICE
I.S.P.

955L-5-L-B

TREAT CRISPS CLUB
W·L·T·H
SAT. NOON
SPEED MEMBER
00000

956-5-E-A

PAUL SPORS RIVIERA
WHOOPEE CLUB

957-5-A-A

FRED STRITT
MONDAY CLUB

958-5-A-A

SUNSET·CLUB
WSB
The Atlanta Journal

959-5-I-A

SIGNAL
TARZAN CLUB

960-5-L-D*

THUNDER FIRE'S SAFETY TRIBE
WSPD

961L-5-M-A

TIM TYLER
IVORY PATROL CLUB
Viva

962-5-C-C

UNCLE BOB FOR SAFETY
HYDROX
FOR HEALTH

963-5-O-A

MEMBER OF
"UNCLE BOB'S"
Curb is the Limit Club
K.Y.W.
Chicago Evening American

964-5-G-A

UNCLE DON'S KIDDIE CLUB DENVER
KFEL
CHARTER MEMBER

965-5-F-A

UNCLE DON'S
RADIO CLUB

966-5-H-B

UNCLE DON'S
FT. UNDERWEAR RADIO CLUB

967-5-H-B

UNCLE DON'S
FISCHER BAKING CO. CLUB

968-5-H-B

UNCLE DON CLUB
Happylad Shirts
Peter Pan

969-5-J-B

UNCLE DON'S
MODEL SOUP CLUB

970-5-L-B

UNCLE DON'S MTF CLUB
MY-T-FINE

971-5-L-B

MEMBER
UNCLE DON'S WESSON VEG OIL CLUB

972-5-L-B

973-5-M-C

974-5-L-C

975-5-J-B

976-5-H-B

977-5-E-C

978-5-D-B

979-5-C-B

980-5-N-A

981-5-M-A

982-5-A-A

983-5-N-A

984-5-A-A

985-5-H-A

986-5-R-A

987-5-G-A

988-6-J-A

989L-5-N-B

990-5-G-A

991-5-G-A

992-5-G-B

993-5-I-B

994L-5-Q-A*

995L-5-J-A*

996-5-H-A*

997-5-E-B

998-5-A-A

999-5-W-A

1000-5-Q-A

STAGE, THEATER, VAUDEVILLE, MAGICIANS & OCCULT

Vaudeville was an era of popular entertainment with attractions ranging from the bizarre and risque to near-legitimate theatre and musicals. Many vaudeville stars were depicted on buttons. Of note is the "strong woman" Charmion pictured in various poses on a series of approximately 30 buttons. Vaudeville buttons are commonly black/white or sepia and rich colors are rare. Magician buttons, although scarce, were usually nicely-done. Theater never developed the mass appeal of other entertainment media, a fact demonstrated by the comparative small quantity of buttons for this art form. There are series buttons depicting feminine early stage stars but theater productions were seldom advertised by buttons.

1001-2-D-C

1002-2-A-B

1003-2-A-B

1004-2-A-B

1005-2-A-B

1006-4-A-C

1007-2-B-B

1008-2-B-B

1009-2-B-B

1010-2-B-B

1011-2-B-B*

1012-1-A-B*

1013-2-B-B*

1014-1-A-B

1015-2-I-B

1016-1-I-B

1017-7-F-C

1018L-5-A-C

1019L-5-A-C

1020-2-B-D

1021-2-D-E

1022-2-B-C

1023-5-A-A

1024-2-B-C*

1025-2-B-C*

1026-2-B-C*

1027-2-B-C*

1028-2-B-C*

1029-2-B-C

1030-2-B-D*

1031-2-B-D*

1032-2-C-C

1033-5-B-C*

1034-8-A-D

1035-1-Y-D

1036-1-A-D

1037-4-B-D

1038-5-J-D

1039-3-D-D

1040-5-G-B

1041-5-G-B

1042-5-M-C*

1043-9-C-D*

1044-9-C-D*

TELEVISION

Beginning in the early 1950s, the television set became the nation's most popular household appliance. Promotion buttons for various stars or program series have been issued from the outset to the present. This category of buttons can be expected to appreciate in future years as nostalgia-minded early TV viewers join the ranks of collectors.

1045L-7-D-B

1046-7-A-B

1047L-9-E-A*

1048L-9-E-A*

1049-7-L-C

1050L-9-J-B

1051-8-A-B

1052-9-D-A

1053L-9-C-A*

1054L-9-C-A*

1055L-9-C-A*

1056L-9-C-A*

1057L-9-C-A*

1058L-9-C-A*

1059L-9-C-A*

1060L-8-F-B*

1061-6-C-E*

1062-9-D-A*

1063-9-A-B

1064-8-N-B*

1065-7-A-B

1066-8-F-B

1067L-7-L-D

1068L-8-M-A*

1069L-8-M-A*

1070L-8-M-A*

1071-7-A-B

1072L-8-A-B

1073L-8-A-B

1074-7-N-B

1075-9-C-A

1076-9-D-A

1077-8-H-B

1078-7-M-C

1079-7-A-B

1080-7-D-C

81

1081-7-C-C

1082-7-J-C*

1083-8-A-B

1084L-7-D-B

1085-8-A-B

1086-8-A-B

1087-7-N-B

1088L-7-C-B

1089-9-A-A

1090-7-A-B

1091-7-J-B

1092L-7-M-A

1093L-7-A-C

NOTES

III. ENTERTAINMENT

AMUSEMENT PARKS, BEACHES

     16. PICTURES ALFONSE AND GASTON.

     20. BACK PAPER INSCRIBED: "Free Excursions Every Day to LENA PARK, IND., the New Manufacturing City . . . "

     33. FRONT INSCRIBED: "Shooting the Shoots/Wonderland Park/Revere. Mass."

ARTISTS, PAINTERS, CARTOONISTS

     36.-38. FROM "CAMEO PEPSIN GUM" SET. SEE *BUTTONS IN SETS,* PAGE 64.

     39.-40. DESIGN BY "HANS FLATO"

     42.-44. THREE BUTTONS BY ARTIST ERNEST TROVA INCLUDED IN THE *INDEX,* A MULTIPLE-OBJECT WORK PUBLISHED IN 1969.

CIRCUSES, CLOWNS, FREAKS

     51. BACK PAPER: "SANDOW'S SCHOOL OF PHYSICAL CULTURE/ST. JAMES ST., LONDON"

     70. LADY SNAKE HANDLER WITH PYTHON AROUND HER NECK.

     86.-94. ALL PICTURE "CHIQUITA," A MIDGET KNOWN AS THE "CUBAN ATOM."

     96. BACK PAPER: "32 YEARS OLD/27 INCHES HIGH/WEIGHT, 16½ LBS."

     97. SAME PHOTO APPEARS ON ANOTHER BUTTON INSCRIBED "BABY MYRTLE."

CHILDREN'S CLUBS

     108. BACK PAPER: "TWINKIES/SHOES THAT MAKE HEALTHY-HAPPY FEET/MADE BY HAMILTON-BROWN SHOE CO."

COMIC CHARACTERS

     111. PART OF A SET. SEE *BUTTONS IN SETS,* PAGE 17.

     118. BACK PAPER: "SEE THE GUMPS IN THE COURIER"

     119.-120. BACK PAPER: "FOLLOW ANDY IN THE EXPRESS"

     127. PART OF A SET. SEE *BUTTONS IN SETS,* PAGE 15.

     130. PART OF A SET. SEE *BUTTONS IN SETS,* PAGE 17.

     132.-135. PART OF A SET. SEE *BUTTONS IN SETS,* PAGE 59.

     136. PART OF A SET. SEE *BUTTONS IN SETS,* PAGE 16.

     140. PART OF A SET. SEE *BUTTONS IN SETS,* PAGE 29.

     145. PART OF A SET. SEE *BUTTONS IN SETS,* PAGE 15.

     146. PART OF A SET. SEE *BUTTONS IN SETS,* PAGE 8.

     148. PART OF A SET. SEE *BUTTONS IN SETS,* PAGE 15.

     150. PART OF A SET.

     153. FROM 1976, MARVEL COMICS GROUP.

     157.-164. FAWCETT PUBLICATIONS, 1948. ISSUED AS A SET THAT ALSO INCLUDES "IBIS" AND "NYOKA."

     166.-167. PART OF A SET. SEE *BUTTONS IN SETS,* PAGE 15.

     170. BACK PAPER: "READ DICK TRACY EVERY DAY IN THE NEWS/NEW YORK'S PICTURE NEWSPAPER"

     171. BACK PAPER: "Read DICK TRACY Every Day in THE CHICAGO TRIBUNE". ON THE ORIGINAL, TRACY'S FACE AND HANDS ARE BEIGE. ON THE REPRODUCTION, THEY ARE PINK. ALSO THE ILLUSTRATION AND LETTERING IS LARGER ON THE ORIGINAL.

     178. BUTTON IS FABRIC COVERED WITH DIECUT BLACK CARDBOARD EARS AND A BLACK ON PINK RIBBON. CARDBOARD HAS A "PAT SULLIVAN" COPYRIGHT NOTICE PRINTED ON IT.

     180. PART OF A SET. SEE *BUTTONS IN SETS,* PAGE 15.

     181. PART OF A SET.

     183. PART OF A SET. SEE *BUTTONS IN SETS,* PAGE 11.

     184. BACK PAPER: "FOXY GRANDPA PRIZE BADGE. See him and the boys every Sunday in the NEW YORK JOURNAL."

     185. BACK PAPER: "GRANDPA YOU'RE A WONDER! WM. A. BRADY PRESENTS THE MUSICAL SNAPSHOT 'FOXY GRANDPA.' Made famous by The New York Herald with Joseph Hart and Carrie DeMar."

     186. BACK PAPER: "GRANDPA YOU'RE A WONDER! 2ND YEAR/THE MUSICAL SNAPSHOT 'FOXY GRANDPA' BOOK BY R.M. BAKER/MUSIC BY JOS. HART"

     188. EDGE INSCRIBED: "©1971 R CRUMB" (FRITZ THE CAT)

     192. PART OF A SET.

193. PART OF A SET.

195. PART OF A SET. SEE *BUTTONS IN SETS*, PAGE 15.

197. PART OF A SET. SEE *BUTTONS IN SETS*, PAGE 29.

198. PART OF A SET. SEE *BUTTONS IN SETS*, PAGE 17.

199. PART OF A SET.

200. PART OF A SET.

204. PART OF A SET.

205. PART OF A SET. SEE *BUTTONS IN SETS*, PAGE 8.

206.-213. PART OF A SET. SEE *BUTTONS IN SETS*, PAGE 9.

214. PART OF A SET.

215.-216. PART OF A SET.

219. A 1980's COMIC STRIP BY ROBERT LAUGHLIN.

220. PART OF A SET.

221. PART OF A SET. SEE *BUTTONS IN SETS*, PAGE 7.

222. INSCRIBED "KRAZY KAT" BUT PICTURES FELIX.

224. PART OF A SET.

228. PART OF A SET.

229.-231. PART OF A SET. SEE *BUTTONS IN SETS*, PAGE 11.

232. PART OF A SET.

233. PART OF A SET.

234. PART OF A SET. SEE *BUTTONS IN SETS*, PAGE 29 .

236. EDGE INSCRIBED: "©1971 R CRUMB"

237. EDGE INSCRIBED: "©1971 KALEIDOSCOPE ENT-(?)"

238. PART OF A SET. SEE *BUTTONS IN SETS*, PAGE 17.

241. PART OF A SET.

242. PART OF A SET. SEE *BUTTONS IN SETS*, PAGE 17.

244.-245. PART OF A SET. SEE *BUTTONS IN SETS*, PAGE 8.

250. PART OF A SET. SEE *BUTTONS IN SETS*, PAGE 17.

251. PART OF A SET. SEE *BUTTONS IN SETS*, PAGE 12.

253. AUSTRALIAN ISSUE.

254. PART OF "KELLOGG'S PEP" SET OF 86. SEE *BUTTONS IN SETS,* PAGE 10.

255. INSCRIBED: "yores trulie Pickle Neary". COPYRIGHT 1903.

258. PART OF A SET. SEE *BUTTONS IN SETS*, PAGE 13.

261. PART OF A SET.

262. PART OF A SET.

267.-268. PART OF A SET. SEE *BUTTONS IN SETS*, PAGE 15.

271.-272. PART OF A SET. SEE *BUTTONS IN SETS*, PAGE 15.

273. PART OF A SET.

276. PART OF A SET. SEE *BUTTONS IN SETS*, PAGE 17.

283. PART OF A SET. SEE *BUTTONS IN SETS*, PAGE 8.

287.-288. "S•S•S•S" STANDS FOR: SKIPPY SKINNER'S SECRET SOCIETY. THE CLUB WAS SPONSORED BY WHEATIES. TEN NEW MEMBERS AND TEN BOX TOPS WERE NEEDED TO EARN THE "CAPTAIN" BUTTON.

292. PART OF A SET.

295.-298. PART OF A SET.

299. PART OF A SET. SEE *BUTTONS IN SETS*, PAGE 8.

300.-301. PART OF A SET. SEE *BUTTONS IN SETS*, PAGE 15.

302. GRADUATING CLASS BUTTON FROM WEST PHILADELPHIA HIGH SCHOOL (WPHS).

303. PART OF A SET.

304. PART OF A SET.

305. PART OF A SET. SEE *BUTTONS IN SETS*, PAGE 13.

307. EDGE INSCRIBED: "Copyright ©1975 by Marvel Comic Group."

310. PART OF A SET. REVERSE INSCRIBED: "COMIC TOGS" SEE *BUTTONS IN SETS*, PAGE 8.

311. PART OF "KELLOGG'S PEP" SET. SEE *BUTTONS IN SETS*, PAGE 10.

312. REVERSE INSCRIBED: "MEMBER IN GOOD STANDING"

313. REVERSE INSCRIBED WITH MESSAGE CODED IN SYMBOLS.

314. REVERSE INSCRIBED: "READ SUPERMAN ACTION COMICS MAGAZINE"

315. CAME IN STORE BOUGHT EXERCISE SET.

317. FIRST CLUB MEMBER'S BUTTON, CIRCA 1940.

318. CIRCA 1950'S RE-ISSUE OF #317, WITH SOME DESIGN CHANGES.

319. THE SAME AS #318, BUT INSCRIBED ON THE LOWER RIGHT EDGE: "©1961 NATIONAL PERIODICAL PUBLICATIONS INC."

320. SIMILAR TO #317 AND CIRCA 1940 BUT RARE IN THIS SIZE.

321.-326. FROM A 1966 SET.

328. PART OF A SET. SEE *BUTTONS IN SETS,* PAGE 17.

330. AUSTRALIAN. ADVERTISES A GLUE PRODUCT.

331.-332. PART OF A SET.

333. EDGE INSCRIBED: "COPYRIGHT ©1979 MARVEL COMICS GROUP"

338.-339. PART OF A SET. SEE *BUTTONS IN SETS,* PAGE 14. NUMBERS 1-40 ARE FAIRLY COMMON. NUMBERS 41-89 AND NUMBERS 101-160 PICTURING FLAGS ARE LESS COMMON. NUMBERS 90-95 ARE SCARCE AND NUMBERS 96-100 ARE UNKNOWN.

340. BICYCLE ADVERTISING. NIGHTSHIRT INSCRIBED: "SAY! WE WONT DO A TING BUT GO TO CHATHAM/SEE!!"

COWBOYS, WESTERN HEROES

345. ORIGINAL HAS ORANGE RIM AND "ECONOMY NOVELTY & PRINTING CO., N.Y.C." ON EDGE. REPRODUCTION HAS RED RIM AND NO EDGE INSCRIPTION.

352. BACKGROUND IS YELLOW, BLUE, OR PURPLE.

357. ORIGINAL HAS EDGE INSCRIBED: "©GENE AUTRY", REPRODUCTION DOES NOT. REPRODUCTION HAS OBVIOUS PRINTING SCREEN ON THE PORTRAIT. THERE IS ALSO AN ORIGINAL 1⅜" LITHO.

358. BACKGROUND IS BLUE, YELLOW, OR PURPLE. ALSO COMES WITH AND WITHOUT THE © SYMBOL ON THE BACKGROUND.

367. ORIGINAL IS 2". REPRODUCTION IS 1¾" AND HAS EDGE INSCRIBED: "Copyright 1950 William Boyd"

368. THE ORIGINAL 1¾" WITH RED BACKGROUND PICTURES "TOPPER" ON THE RIGHT. A SIMILAR BUTTON SHOWING "TOPPER" ON THE LEFT IS A FANTASY ITEM, PRODUCED CIRCA 1982.

372. ALSO COMES WITH A RED BACKGROUND.

382.-391. BUTTONS OF VARIOUS RANK TO PROMOTE CHILDREN'S SAVINGS ACCOUNTS IN BANKS. #382 WAS WORN BY TELLERS. ORIGINALS OF #383-387 ARE LITHO. TIN, BUT THERE IS A CELLULOID REPRODUCTION OF #385 (BRONC BUSTER). THE HIGHEST RANKS—"STRAW BOSS" AND "FOREMAN" EXIST AS 1½" CELLULOIDS OR 2¼" LITHO. TIN.

421. AUSTRALIAN BUTTON.

423. ORIGINAL IS A BW/ORANGE 1" LITHO. THE REPRODUCTION IS A BW/RED 1" CELLULOID.

429. CLUB MEMBER'S BUTTON FOR LONE RANGER VICTORY CORPS, 1942.

430. ADVERTISING BUTTON FOR STERLING SALT.

431.-432. PART OF A SET. SEE *BUTTONS IN SETS,* PAGE 65.

434.-436. ISSUED BY PHILADELPHIA, PA. RADIO STATION-WFIL.

438. PART OF A SET. SEE *BUTTONS IN SETS,* PAGE 66.

452. PART OF SET. SEE *BUTTONS IN SETS,* PAGE 31.

453.-457. COMPLETE SET OF RALSTON CEREAL PREMIUM BUTTONS. SEE *BUTTONS IN SETS,* PAGE 66.

460.-461. ISSUED TO PUBLICIZE THE SHOWING OF "THE MIRACLE RIDER" ON A MICHIGAN PUBLIC TELEVISION STATION. #460 IS DATED "1971" ON THE BOTTOM EDGE. #461 IS DATED "1971" ON THE FRONT.

474. NABISCO PREMIUM, 1956.

480. ISSUED WITH A ROY ROGERS DOLL BY "IDEAL NOVELTY & TOY CO."

484. ON THE ORIGINAL, THE PHOTO COVERS THE RIM EDGE. ON THE REPRODUCTION, THE RIM EDGE IS WHITE.

486. THERE IS A MATCHING HOPALONG CASSIDY.

495.-508. FROM A "POST'S GRAPE-NUTS FLAKES" SET, 1953. SEE *BUTTONS IN SETS,* PAGE 65.

509. SOUVENIR FROM ROY ROGERS MUSEUM, APPLE VALLEY, CALIFORNIA, 1985.

DISNEY, DISNEYANA

528.-530. OFFICER BUTTONS FROM THE FIRST MICKEY MOUSE CLUB.

532. BUTTON SUPPLIED BY KAY KAMEN, INC. AS PART OF MERCHANDISE PROMOTION TO BE WORN BY STORE SALES PEOPLE. CIRCA, 1934. MICKEY IS BW/RED WITH YELLOW GLOVES ON WHITE BACKGROUND.

534.&536. SEE #528.-530.

548. BRASS RIM AROUND ILLUSTRATION PRINTED IN BW ON FABRIC. BACKGROUND COLOR IS BLUE, GOLD, OR RED.

559. ISSUED BY VARIOUS BREAD COMPANIES. SEE *BUTTONS IN SETS*, PAGE 11.

560.-561. PART OF A SET. SEE *BUTTONS IN SETS*, PAGE 15.

562. PART OF A SET.

563. PART OF A SET.

566. PART OF A SET. SEE #580-587.

571. FIFTIETH BIRTHDAY BUTTON. BW/RED ON YELLOW. 1978.

572. ISSUED FOR BI-CENTENNIAL, RWB/YELLOW. 1976.

579. FIFTIETH BIRTHDAY BUTTON. RWB/ORANGE. 1984.

580.-587. FROM A SET OF 10 ISSUED BY DONALD DUCK PEANUT BUTTER. SET INCLUDES MINNIE MOUSE (SEE #566) AND MICKEY MOUSE.

611. IN 1985, A GM CAR WAS AWARDED TO EVERY 30,000TH ADMISSION.

MUSICIANS, SINGERS, COMPOSERS

631. PICTURES CLOCKWISE: PRYOR, SOUSA, HERBERT, DAMROSCH.

655.-656. PART OF A SET. SEE *BUTTONS IN SETS*. PAGE 34.

658.-659. SAME AS #655-656.

661.-662. PART OF A SET. SEE *BUTTONS IN SETS*, PAGE 33.

664. SAME AS #661-662.

666.&668. ISSUED AS A PAIR.

685.-688. PART OF A SET.

689.-690. PART OF A SET.

691.-693. PART OF A SET. SEE *BUTTONS IN SETS*, PAGE 33.

695. A 4" LITHO. THE CELLULOID SMALLER SIZES ARE REPRODUCTIONS.

696.-700. EDGE INSCRIBED: "A.&M. LEATHERLINES, INC., NEW YORK 10012"

MOVIES

706. INSCRIBED: "BEN ALEXANDER SAYS: BE A GOOD SCOUT/SCOTTY OF THE SCOUTS, A MASCOT SERIAL PLAY"

716.-726. BUTTON SET SPELLING OUT: "JAMES CAGNEY"

730. A POCKET MIRROR, RATHER THAN A BUTTON, BUT ONE OF THE EARLIEST CELLULOID CHAPLIN ITEMS.

754. PART OF A SET. SEE *BUTTONS IN SETS*, PAGE 27.

759.-761. PART OF A SET. SEE *BUTTONS IN SETS*, PAGE 25.

776.-784. MOVIE THEATER DRAWING PRIZE BUTTONS. NUMERALS ARE IN RED.

792.-798. PART OF A SET. EITHER BLUE ON WHITE OR RED ON WHITE AND WITH VARIOUS THEATER NAMES.

840. OFTEN FOUND WITHOUT THE ATTACHED FIREMAN'S BODY MADE OF RED/BLUE/YELLOW DIECUT PAPER ON FABRIC.

849. BLUE FLAG WITH REFLECTIVE (FOIL) GOLD STARS. WHITEHEAD & HOAG CALLED THE PROCESS OF USING COLORED METALLIC FOILS UNDER THE CELLULOID "CRYS-TOGLAS."

864. FIRST TARZAN SERIAL, 1920. THE BUTTON PICTURES KAMUELA SEARLE WHO WAS FATALLY INJURED DURING FILMING.

865.-869. PART OF A SET.

898.-899. BOBBY BENSON CLUB MEMBER'S BUTTONS. ISSUED BY HECKER CEREALS.

908. CANADIAN STATION.

933. PART OF A SET IN VARIOUS COLORS AND SPECIFYING VARIOUS BAKERY PRODUCTS.

937. PART OF A SET.

943. BACK PAPER: "READ WILL ROGERS IN *LIFE*"

946. THE WHITE BACKGROUND GLOWS-IN-THE-DARK.

960. ISSUED BY SIGNAL OIL CO.

994.-996. SUNDAY SCHOOL "TEAM" BUTTONS FROM "DAVID C COOK PUBLISHING CO./ELGIN ILLINOIS"

STAGE, THEATER, VAUDEVILLE, MAGICIANS & OCCULT

1011. "BABY LIL"

1012. BACK PAPER: "COMPLIMENTS OF INNOCENT KIDD."

1013. "MAUD JEFFRIES." PART OF A LARGE SET OF ACTRESSES ISSUED BY SWEET CAPORAL CIGARETTES, CIRCA 1900. SEE *BUTTONS IN SETS*, PAGE 57.

1024.-1028. VAUDEVILLE TRAPEZE ARTIST.

1030.-1031. BOTH BUTTONS PICTURE THE SAME WOMAN. #1030 HAS A PENCIL NOTATION ON THE BACK PAPER: "LITTLE EGYPT 1904." NUMEROUS PERFORMERS USED THE "LITTLE EGYPT" NAME AND THIS IS NOT THE SAME WOMAN OF THE 1893 CHICAGO WORLD'S FAIR FAME.

1033. "RUDITH WILLIAMS"
1042. WITH BLUE FABRIC RIBBON INSCRIBED: 6TH ANNUAL CONVEN-
TION/I.B.M./COLUMBUS, OHIO JUNE 3-4-5, 1931."
1043.-1044. STAGE PRODUCTIONS OF WORKS BY MAURICE SENDAK. #1044 IS FROM OPENING
NIGHT IN LONDON.

TELEVISION
1047.-1048. PART OF A SET FROM 1972.
1053.-1059. PART OF A SET FROM 1973.
1060. INSCRIBED ON CURL: "©Hank Ketcham 1968"
1061. DEPICTS THE ORIGINAL DESIGN BY FRANK PARIS, CIRCA 1947.
1062. FROM 1980.
1064. PART OF A SET. SEE *BUTTONS IN SETS,* PAGE 61.
1068.-1070. PART OF A SET. SEE *BUTTONS IN SETS,* PAGE 63.
1082. PART OF A SET. SEE *BUTTONS IN SETS,* PAGE 62.

IV. FAMOUS PEOPLE

Famous people—those that distinguished themselves in non-entertainment professions or careers—offer good collecting possibility. Such buttons number into the thousands, depending on the collector's personal definition of "famous." Such buttons are normally photo depictions of individuals whose contributions ranged from science to the humanities to business, although a complete listing would be endless. Although famous people buttons are rarely very colorful, they do present a cross-section of individuals who shaped America in their own way.

EXPLORERS

Daring excursions to the far points of the globe in the early part of the 20th century prompted national excitement as would excursions in the late 1960s to the moon. Commander Byrd's first polar flight over the North Pole in 1926, his South Pole flight in 1929, and subsequent settlements in the two extreme regions prompted a number of commemorative buttons. Earlier explorers such as Christopher Columbus and historic Pacific Coast voyagers are button subjects, as are the U.S. Northwest's Lewis & Clark (See page 26 for other Lewis & Clark buttons).

1-3-D-C

2L-5-E-B

3-3-B-A

4-2-D-C

5-2-D-A

6-2-A-C*

7-5-A-A   8-5-D-A   9-5-G-A*   10-5-G-A*   11-2-A-A

12-2-A-D

13-2-A-D

14-2-D-D

15-2-D-D

17-5-D-C*

18-5-A-C

19-5-F-C

20-5-A-C

16-2-E-D*

INDIANS

Possibly because the typical American in the early 20th century had not seen an actual American Indian, this subject resulted in a wide assortment of buttons with many in excellent designs and colors. The Indian was obviously an excellent theme for community homecomings and manufactured products, because the feathered head-dress or regalia offered multicolor opportunities befitting the event or product. The Indian theme was also used on a vast number of lodge pins or ribbons.

21-1-D-C

22-2-D-C

23-2-D-C

24-2-D-C

25-1-A-C

26-1-A-B

27-2-D-C

28-2-D-B

29-2-D-C*

30-2-D-C

31-1-D-B

32-2-C-B

33-2-D-B

34-2-D-B

35-1-B-C

36-3-D-C

37-2-D-B

38-2-C-B*

39-2-D-B

40-3-D-B

41-4-D-B

42-5-D-B

43-2-D-B

44-3-D-B

45-1-A-A

46-2-D-B

47-2-G-A

48-3-D-B

49-2-C-A

50-4-A-A

51-5-E-A

52-5-D-A

53-2-C-B

54-4-C-A

55-4-J-A

56-4-R-A

57-2-D-C

58-2-D-B   59-1-C-A   60-2-D-A   61-2-D-B   62-4-C-A

63-1-D-A*   64-1-D-A*   65-2-D-A   66-2-C-A   67-2-C-A   68-2-J-A

NATIONALITY HEROES & PRESIDENTS

Virtually every major nation in the 20th century has had a leader or people's hero who is pictured or commemorated on a button for use by American followers. Although the hero is often a political or military figure, revolutionary figures are pictured in fair share. In addition, nationality persons since the earliest day of recorded history have also been recognized on latter-day buttons. U.S. presidential campaigns are not included in this category (Refer to Hake's *Encyclopedia of Political Buttons*, Books I, II, III,) as they represent a major collecting field by themselves.

69-1-B-B

70-2-D-B   71-5-D-B   72-2-D-A

73-2-D-A   74-5-D-A   75-5-G-A

76-2-B-D   77-2-B-B   78-2-D-A   79-2-A-A*

80-2-D-A

81L-5-D-A*

82L-5-D-A*

83-3-D-B

84-2-B-A

85-2-B-A*

86-2-A-B

87-2-A-B

88-1-D-A*

89-1-A-A

90-2-E-A

91-3-B-A

92-3-A-A

93-2-A-A

94-2-B-A

95-1-A-A

96-3-A-B

97-1-B-A

98-1-B-A

99L-4-F-B

100-3-A-C

101-1-A-B*

102-1-A-A*

103-1-A-A*

104-1-A-A*

105-1-A-A*

106-4-A-B

107-4-G-A

108-5-G-A*

109-5-G-A*

110-5-G-A*

111-5-G-A*

112-5-G-A*

113-5-G-A*

114-5-G-A*

115-2-A-A

116-2-B-A

117-1-D-A*

118-1-D-A*

119-1-D-A*

120-1-D-A*

121-1-D-A*

122-1-D-A*

123-1-D-A*

124-1-D-A*

125-1-D-A*

126-1-D-A*

127-1-D-A*

128-2-B-A

129-1-A-A*

130-5-A-A

131-2-B-A

132-3-A-A

133-8-G-A

134-1-D-A

135-4-A-A

136-5-C-A

137-5-A-A

138-5-A-A

139-5-A-A

140-1-D-A*

141-1-D-A*

142L-5-G-C

143-5-A-C

144-5-E-C

145-5-A-B

146-5-F-A

147-6-A-A

148-6-A-B

149-7-A-A

93

ROYAL FAMILIES

A surprisingly large assortment of buttons portraying the changes in Royal Families has developed since the turn of the century. The British Empire's royal family is the subject of most buttons, although examples exist of ruling families or royalty from the Low Countries and Scandanavian countries. Non-European countries are also represented by royal family buttons, although these are comparatively isolated and scarce.

150-4-D-A

151-1-D-A*

152-1-D-B

153-1-D-B

154-1-A-C

155-1-A-B

156-2-A-B

157-2-D-C

158-2-D-C

159-2-D-B

160-2-D-B

161-2-D-B

162-5-A-B

163-5-A-B

164-5-A-B

165-5-A-B

166-3-D-B

167-3-A-B

168-3-F-B

169-5-E-B

170L-5-F-C

171L-5-F-C

172L-5-F-C

173L-5-F-C

174-5-G-C

175-5-A-B

176-5-D-C

177-5-E-C

178-5-A-B

179-5-C-A

180-7-A-B

181-9-D-A

182-9-D-A

183-9-D-A

184-1-B-C

185-1-D-A

186-1-D-C

187-2-B-B

188-5-A-B

189-5-B-B

190-5-A-A

191-5-A-B

192-2-A-B

193-5-E-B

194-5-A-B

195-3-A-B

196-5-A-B

IV. FAMOUS PEOPLE

EXPLORERS

6. BUTTON HAS BRASS RIM, MAROON FELT OUTER RIM W/RED SILK RIBBON W/GOLD LETTERING.
9.-10. FROM A SET. SEE *BUTTONS IN SETS*, PAGE 68. INKS USED TO PRINT THIS SERIES ARE WATER-SOLUBLE. BUTTONS CANNOT BE CLEANED WITHOUT RISK OF LOSING PICTURE.
16. SMALL WOOD STAKE ATTACHED TO REPRESENT THE NORTH POLE. COOK & PEARY PICTURED.
17. BACK PAPER: "BORN DECEMBER 19, 1933 ON THE BYRD ANTARCTIC EXPEDITION II THE FARTHEREST SOUTH OF ANY DAIRY ANIMAL."

INDIANS

29. BACK PAPER: "PRINCESS Stands for Quality. GREEN & DE LAITTRE COMPANY/ IMPORTERS AND WHOLESALE GROCERS/MINNEAPOLIS."
38. BACK PAPER HAS BLACK/WHITE ILLUSTRATION OF ABRAHAM LINCOLN W/ "CENTENARY CELEBRATION FEB. 12/1809-ABRAHAM LINCOLN-1909 "
63. FROM A SET. SEE *BUTTONS IN SETS*, PAGE 67.
64. FROM A SET. SEE *BUTTONS IN SETS*, PAGE 35.

NATIONALITY HEROES & PRESIDENTS

79. BACK PAPER: "Henry Koch Cafe "
81.-82. FROM "YANK JUNIOR HERO SERIES/RELIANCE MFG. CO." SEE *BUTTONS IN SETS*, PAGE 40.
85. BOTTOM RIM INSCRIPTION: "COMMODORE JOHN BARRY "
88. FROM A SET. SEE *BUTTONS IN SETS*, PAGE 39.
101.-105. FROM A SET. SEE *BUTTONS IN SETS*, PAGE 38.
108.-114. FROM A SET. SEE *BUTTONS IN SETS*, PAGES 67-68.
117.-127. FROM A SET. SEE *BUTTONS IN SETS*, PAGE 39.
129. FROM A SET. SEE *BUTTONS IN SETS*, PAGE 38.
140.-141. FROM A SET. SEE *BUTTONS IN SETS*, PAGE 39.

ROYAL FAMILIES

151. FROM A SET. SEE *BUTTONS IN SETS*, PAGE 39.

V. FARM EQUIPMENT

Even with mushrooming industrial growth, the United States was principally an agricultural nation during the 1890's and early 20th century. Buttons advertised many horse-drawn farm machinery pieces but horse farming began to wane with the introduction of the massive coal-fired steam engine tractors and stationary gasoline engines. The plow and the reaper continued to be improved and although not all farmers could afford it, mechanized farming grew. Early farm equipment buttons are often quite colorful, nicely designed, represent a vivid history of America's agricultural progress, and are a favorite topic among many collectors.

PLOWS

1-2-D-D*   2-2-D-D*   3-2-L-D*   4-2-D-D*   5-2-D-D

6-1-D-C   7-2-D-C   8-2-D-C   9-1-D-C   11-2-D-C

10-1-D-D

12-1-D-D   13-1-R-C   14-1-C-E   15-1-H-C   16-3-G-C

17-2-D-C   18-1-D-D   19-1-D-C   20-1-D-C   21-2-D-D

22-2-C-C   23-2-F-C*   24-2-D-C*   25-1-D-E

SEEDERS, PLANTERS, DRILLS, CULTIVATORS, MANURE SPREADERS

26-1-C-B

27-2-J-D*

28-2-D-C

29-2-K-D

30-4-D-E

31-2-D-D

32-2-D-C

33-2-D-F

34-2-D-C

35-1-J-C

36-1-D-F

37-2-D-C*

38-2-A-C

39-2-A-C

40-2-D-C

41-2-J-D

42-2-D-D

43-1-C-D

44-2-C-D

MOWERS, HARVESTERS, REAPERS

45-2-D-F*

46-2-D-D

47-2-D-D

48-2-D-D

49-2-D-D

50-1-D-D

51-2-D-E

52-1-D-D*

53-2-D-C*

98

54-1-D-D   55-1-D-D   56-1-D-E*   57-1-D-D   58-1-J-D

59-2-J-C   60-2-H-C   61-1-D-D   62-1-Y-D   63-2-D-E*   64-3-C-D

65-1-C-C   66-1-B-C*   67-1-J-C   68-1-C-C*   69-1-D-D   70-2-O-C

WAGONS

71-2-D-D   72-2-I-D   73-1-D-F   74-1-C-C   75-1-I-D

76-2-D-D   77-2-E-D   78-1-F-C   79-1-O-D   80-1-C-D

81-1-G-E   82-1-D-D

FEEDERS, SHELLERS, STACKERS

83-2-J-C

84-1-L-C

85-2-D-D

86-1-C-D

87-2-C-C

88-1-P-E

89-2-D-F

90-1-D-G

91-1-A-C

92-2-D-D

STEAM & GASOLINE TRACTORS

93-2-A-E

94-2-D-D

95-2-D-E

96-2-J-F

97-4-O-C

98-1-C-C*

99-2-D-D

100-3-C-E

101-3-C-E

102-2-A-C

103-3-E-E

104-4-A-D

105-7-C-B

106-1-A-C

107-4-L-C

108-4-L-C

109-2-J-F*

110-1-C-E

111-1-D-E

112-1-D-E

113-1-D-E

114-1-D-E

115-2-E-C

116-2-D-E

117-3-H-E

118-1-D-E

119-1-D-E

120-1-H-E

121-3-Z-C

122-2-C-E

123-2-D-G

124-2-D-F

125-2-J-D

126-2-C-E

127-2-D-D

128-2-C-E

129-2-C-E*

130-5-E-C

131-4-J-D

132-2-D-F

133-2-E-D

134-4-C-B

STATIONARY ENGINES

135-2-C-D

136-2-F-D

137-2-J-D

138-2-J-D

139-2-A-C

140-2-A-D

141-2-C-D

142-2-D-E

143-2-A-D

144-2-A-D

145-2-D-E

146-2-A-C

147-2-J-E

148-4-J-B

149-3-J-C

150-1-D-D

151-1-I-B

152-1-A-E

153-2-E-B

154-2-G-B

155-6-M-A

156-2-Q-B

157-3-P-B

158-3-D-C*

159-2-C-B

160-1-D-C

161-2-E-B

162-2-I-C

163-2-N-B

164-2-J-B

165-2-A-B*

166-1-A-C

167-2-F-B*

168-2-E-B

169-2-B-D

170-2-J-C

171-2-N-D

172-2-E-D

173-2-D-D*

174-1-P-D

175-1-D-E

176-2-D-E

177-2-E-B

178-2-D-C

179-1-J-C

180-2-A-C

181-2-E-C

182-2-C-C

183-1-J-C*

184-2-A-C

185-2-A-B

186-2-A-B

187-2-R-C

188-2-J-B

189-1-J-B

190-4-G-C

191-4-A-B

192-4-J-B

FENCES

193-2-J-C

194-2-C-B

195-2-C-B

196-1-A-C

197-2-C-D

198-2-I-A

199-2-J-C

200-2-J-C

201-2-D-B

CREAM SEPARATORS

202-1-D-E

203-1-C-E

204-2-H-C

205-2-J-C

206-2-E-D

207-2-D-B

208-2-D-B

209-2-D-B

210-2-D-B

211-2-D-B

212-2-D-B

213-2-D-D*

214-2-D-C

215-2-C-A

MISCELLANEOUS AGRICULTURE

216-1-A-E*

217-2-F-B

218-1-D-C

219-1-D-C

220-3-D-B

221-2-D-C

222-2-R-B

223-4-M-B

224-3-D-B

225-2-E-A

226-2-D-C*

227-2-D-C

228-2-D-C

229-3-D-B

230-3-D-B

231-1-D-C

232-1-D-A*

233-1-D-A

234-1-D-A

235-4-E-A

236-2-D-D

237-2-D-B

238-3-D-B

239-3-D-B

NOTES

V. FARM EQUIPMENT

1. BACK PAPER INCLUDES: "E. BEMENT'S SONS, MANUFACTURERS OF BALL-BEARING DISK PLOWS "

2.-3.-4. BACK PAPER INCLUDES: "E. BEMENT'S SONS, MANUFACTURERS OF HIGH GRADE FARM IMPLEMENTS "

23. HAS MOVABLE METAL DIAL HAND.

24. BACK PAPER: "ROCK ISLAND PLOW CO./ROCK ISLAND, ILLS.,/MANUFACTURE THE BEST FARM IMPLEMENTS"

27. SEE NOTE FOR ITEMS #2-3.

37. BACK PAPER: "WRITE FOR PRICES AND TERMS on The Litchfield Manure Spreader."

45. BACK PAPER: "ANY HARVEST HAND CAN WIN IF HE WILL USE ACME BINDERS, MOWERS, HEADERS OR HAY TOOLS."

52. CIRCA 1898-1900 VERSION BY WHITEHEAD & HOAG WHICH DEPICTS THE CASE EAGLE W/ROUNDED SHOULDERS. (SEE # 53).

53. CIRCA 1906-1907 VERSION BY BASTIAN BROTHERS WHICH DEPICTS THE CASE EAGLE W/SQUARED SHOULDERS. (SEE #52).

56. BACK PAPER: "DEERING BINDERS, REAPERS, MOWERS, HAY RAKES. GRAND PRIX, PARIS, 1900"

63. TINY INSCRIPTION AROUND DEPICTION OF LION: "AS TO THE ANIMAL KINGDOM, SO IS 'LEADER' THRESHING MACHINERY IN COMPARISON WITH OTHERS." BACK PAPER HAS COMPANY NAME AND LOCATIONS.

66. TINY INSCRIPTION ON ILLUSTRATION: "QUAIL BRAND"

68. BACK PAPER LISTS "Jones Lever Binders, Jones Chain Mowers, Jones Steel Headers, Jones Adjustable Hay Rakes"

98. HOLE IN RIM FOR METAL CLICKER ATTACHMENT.

109. BACK PAPER: "REMEMBER HART-PARR TRACTORS BURN KEROSENE/A Postal Card Brings Full Information."

129. BACK PAPER: "ADVANCE -RUMELY THRESHER CO., Inc./LA PORTE/INDIANA"

158. BACK PAPER INCLUDES TEXT FOR POULTRY AND PET STOCK SUPPLIES, PORTABLE HOUSES AND FENCES, INCUBATORS AND BROODERS, BIRD SEEDS AND SUPPLIES, DOG FOOD AND MEDICINES.

165. BACK PAPER EXPLANATION OF ACRONYM S.M.T.B: "SATTLEY MAKES THE BEST IMPLEMENTS "

167. TINY INSCRIPTION IN CENTER INCLUDES: "THE BROWN WAGON AND IMPLE-MENTS/ALL GENUINE GOODS BEAR THIS LABEL"

173. TINY "DEMPSTER" IN CENTER OF DESIGN.

183. SMALL INSCRIPTION IN CENTER: "THE ONLY PERFECTION WATER ELEVATOR AND PURIFIER"

213. BACK PAPER: "BEST CREAM SEPARATORS ON EARTH. Tubular, Russian, Belt, Little Giant Safety Hand/P.M. SHARPLES, WEST CHESTER, PA."

216. BACK PAPER HAS SUBSCRIPTION INFORMATION (KANSAS CITY).

226. BACK PAPER: "This is the only box in which you can shove letters, papers and ordinary packages with ONE HAND/locked or unlocked/SIGNAL MAIL BOX CO./JOLIET, ILLINOIS."

232. PART OF A SET. SEE *BUTTONS IN SETS*, PAGE 64.

VI. FOOD, BEVERAGES, TOBACCO

Producers, processors, and packagers of food and drink products embraced the button for advertising purposes immediately upon its introduction in 1896. Trade card advertising was long established but faded fast once button collecting swept the country. Many companies stimulated interest by issuing "sets" of buttons and thousands of others ordered and gave away single-issue buttons to keep up with the competition.

ALCOHOLIC DRINKS

Brewery buttons issued between 1900-1920 were often nicely designed and beautifully colored. They were not to regain this excellence after the 13 years of Prohibition ending in 1933. Although most of the choice early buttons were for beer products, there are several nice examples of whiskey and other alcoholic beverages.

1-1-G-B	2-2-I-B	3-2-C-B	4-2-D-C	5-2-I-B
6-3-C-C	7-3-W-B	8L-5-A-B	9-2-D-C	10-1-D-B
11-4-M-C	12-1-B-B	13-2-D-C	14-2-D-D	15-4-I-B
16-2-D-C	17-2-E-B	18-3-G-B	19-2-D-D*	20-3-E-B	21-3-I-B

22-2-C-B   23-2-D-C   24-3-J-B   25-1-D-C   27L-5-E-A

26-2-D-D

28-3-G-A   29-1-D-C   30-2-D-C   31-2-K-B

32-4-D-C*   33-4-D-C*   34-5-J-B   35-2-D-D   36-2-D-D

37-2-N-C*   38-2-D-D   39-2-D-D*   40-2-D-D   41-2-D-D*

42-2-D-D*   43-2-D-D*   44-2-D-D*   45-2-D-D*   46-2-D-D*

47-2-D-D* 48-2-D-D 49-1-D-D 50-1-D-D

51-2-D-C*

52-2-D-D 53-2-I-B 54-5-E-B 55-2-D-E

56-1-A-C 57-2-D-D 58-2-D-D* 59-1-D-E

60-1-D-C 61-1-A-B 62-1-D-B 63-1-K-C 64-2-T-B 65-1-D-D

66-2-D-E 67-2-D-C* 68-2-D-C 69-2-D-C 70-1-D-E 71-2-C-C 72-4-G-B

110

BAKED GOODS: BREAD, BISCUITS, CAKES, COOKIES, CRACKERS, DOUGHNUTS, PIES, WAFERS

A basic staple in every household, bread accounted for a prolific number of advertising buttons from local manufacturers. The first completely automatic bread plant was opened by the Ward Baking Company, Chicago, in 1910 and most bread buttons were produced after that, particularly in the 1930s. Additional baked goods contributed to the great variety in this category. Buttons usually pictured a child or child-interest subject, or simply an illustration of the product. Rarely was an adult depicted. Bond Bread and others issued 'airplane' buttons (see Aviation sections in Transportation category).

73-3-D-B   74-3-D-B   75-2-D-G   76-4-D-E*   77-5-J-C

78-5-A-B   79-5-C-A   80-4-J-B

81-2-D-C   82-2-C-C   83L-5-I-B   84-3-C-B   85-2-D-C

86-2-A-C   87-2-D-B   88-5-J-A   89-5-R-B   90-4-D-E

91-5-E-B   92-5-M-A   93-5-J-A   94-5-D-B   95-2-M-A

111

96-5-C-C

97-5-C-A

98-5-G-A

99-5-E-B

100L-5-E-A

101-3-C-C*

102-5-G-A

103-5-M-A

104-5-O-A

105-1-J-A*

106-5-G-A

107-4-C-B

108L-5-O-A*

109L-5-E-B

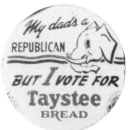

110L-5-E-B

111-5-J-A

112-4-C-B

113-4-J-B

114-3-D-C

115-5-C-B

116-2-J-C

117-6-D-B

118-2-D-D

119-2-T-A

120-2-D-C

121-2-C-A

122-2-D-A

123-3-E-B

124-2-E-A

125-2-C-A

126-1-T-A

127L-5-C-A*

128-5-E-A*

129-5-M-A

130-5-M-A

131-5-G-A

132-5-C-B

133-2-D-D

134-3-D-B

135-2-D-B*

BAKING INGREDIENTS: FLOUR, BAKING POWDER, YEAST, SALT, SEASONINGS, SPICES

Flour was the housewife's basic baking need, a fact not lost on flour manufacturers which advertised with buttons. A large number of flour buttons were produced with nice detail and choice color, hopefully for the lady of the house to keep as a reminder of her wisdom in purchasing the particular brand. There is also a large assortment of related baking buttons, many examples with nice design and color.

136-2-D-B

137-2-D-C

138-2-M-A*

139-3-M-A

140-3-C-B

141-2-D-D

142-2-D-B

143-2-D-F

144-3-D-B

145-3-D-B

146-2-C-E

147-4-C-A

148-2-D-C

149-2-R-B*

150-2-R-A

151-2-A-A

152-5-C-A

153-1-D-D

154-2-D-B

155-2-D-D

156-2-D-D

157-2-E-A

158-3-G-A

159-1-E-A

160-2-D-D

161-5-C-B

162-2-I-A

163-1-D-B

164-1-D-C

165-1-D-C   166-1-C-B   167-1-D-A   168-1-D-A   169-1-D-B   170-2-D-A

171-2-J-A   172-2-H-B   173-2-A-B   174-2-E-A

175-4-J-A

176-3-D-A   177-2-D-A*   178-2-D-E   179-2-D-C   180-1-Y-A

CANDY, CONFECTIONS, CHEWING GUMS, PEANUTS & PEANUT BUTTER, POPCORN, POTATO CHIPS

Snacks and candy treats have always appealed to youngsters, who were commonly illustrated on buttons for these products. There is not a great number of buttons for any individual product in this category, but a nice assortment is available in total.

181-2-C-C   182L-5-E-A   183-5-I-A   184-1-C-A   185-5-E-B   186-2-D-C

187-2-E-C   188-3-D-D   189-2-D-D   190-2-C-C*   191-1-B-B

192-2-D-D

193L-5-E-A

194-4-D-B*

195-2-D-B

196L-5-G-A

197-5-C-B

198-2-D-B

199-3-M-B

200-2-D-B

201-4-C-A

202-4-E-A

203-1-A-C

204-1-C-B

205-1-G-A

206-2-I-A*

207-1-A-C

208-1-G-B

209-2-D-C

210-2-E-C

211L-5-E-E

212-5-E-C*

213-4-E-B

214-1-E-B

215-1-D-D

216-1-T-B

217-2-A-B

218-2-A-B

219L-5-J-C

220L-6-J-C

221-2-E-C

222-3-C-A

223-5-C-A

224L-5-E-A

225-5-D-B

226L-5-D-A

116

CEREALS, BABY FOOD

'Ready-to-eat' breakfast cereals appeared about the same time as celluloid buttons in the late 1890s. Probably the earliest cereal manufacturer was C.W. Post, although the company's early products were not button-advertised. Later cereals depicted on buttons included Cream of Rye, H-O, and Force. Quaker Oats was an early button advertiser and Kellogg's followed in the 1930s.

227-5-G-A

228-2-D-D

229-2-D-C

230-4-D-B

231-4-G-A

232-5-J-B

233-4-D-C

234L-7-C-A

235-3-C-A

236L-5-E-A

237-5-I-A

238-3-D-C

239-2-D-B

240-2-B-C

241-2-D-C

242-1-D-D

243-7-N-B

244-5-G-B

COFFEE, TEA, COCOA & MALT PRODUCTS

Some examples of early coffee buttons rate with the choice elite of all advertising buttons. The "Dutch Java" variations are quite beautiful and there are several buttons with very nice 'container' illustrations. Many different coffee buttons were produced. Tea buttons are not as common.

245-2-D-D

246-2-C-A

247-2-D-C*

248-2-C-A

249-2-C-B

250-2-A-B

251-3-G-A

252-5-Y-A

253-3-I-A

254-2-D-C

255-2-D-C

256-2-I-A

257-3-D-C

258-4-I-A

259-3-D-D

260-2-D-B

261-3-D-B

262-2-D-B

263-2-D-B

264-2-D-A

265-2-D-A

266-2-D-A

267-2-E-B

268-2-E-B*

269-4-J-A

270-3-J-A

271-5-E-A

272-3-D-B

273-4-E-B

274-3-J-A

275-1-D-A

276-3-G-A

277-1-D-C*

278-3-C-A

279-2-G-A

280-3-K-A

281-4-C-A

282-3-D-B

283-3-E-A

284-5-L-A

285-2-C-A

286-2-D-A

287-5-L-A

288L-6-G-A

289L-6-I-A

290-2-D-B

291-1-K-D

292-2-D-B

293-2-D-C

294-2-D-C

295-1-D-C

296-1-D-B

COLAS, SODAS, JUICES

The soda and cola manufacturers vied for popularity in the 1920s-30s much as they do in present times. Several very colorful button examples were issued by Cherry Smash, Grape Smash, Satenet and others. Today's 'giants'— Coke, Pepsi, 7up—issued buttons in the 1930s but any earlier from these companies is considered a rarity. There is not a great number of fruit juice button examples.

297L-5-N-A

298-2-I-A

299-2-C-A

300-3-D-B*

301-3-D-C

302-4-D-C

303-4-E-B

304-2-J-F

305-5-D-E

306-5-D-D

307L-7-C-B

308-1-M-A

309-5-C-A

310-2-F-C

311-2-B-E*

312L-5-I-A

313L-5-G-A

314L-5-A-A

315-2-J-B

316L-5-X-A

317-3-D-B

318-5-J-B

319-6-M-B

320-5-G-A

321-1-D-E*

322-4-E-B

323-5-M-A*

324-3-D-C

325-2-D-B

326-2-E-A

327L-5-Y-B*

328-6-E-B

329-7-Y-B

330-6-I-B

331-5-C-B

332-6-I-B

333-3-D-C

334-3-D-C*

335-5-C-A

336-2-D-E

337L-7-Q-A

338-5-C-B

339-5-J-B

340-3-J-A

341-5-N-A

342-2-D-D

343-3-D-D

344-3-E-C

345-1-A-B*

346L-5-I-A

347L-5-G-A

348-3-A-B

349L-5-O-A*

350-3-D-C

351-5-J-B

CONDIMENTS, RELISHES, SAUCES, SYRUPS, SOUPS, MACARONI, GELATINS, BAKED BEANS

A nice assortment of colorful or nicely-designed buttons was issued for table foods in this category. The H.J. Heinz Co. and the Campbell Soup Company were the principal button advertisers but nice examples exist from other smaller companies.

352-2-D-C

353-3-D-B

354-3-D-C

355-2-D-C

356L-5-P-A

357-3-D-B

358-2-D-F*

359-2-J-B

360-4-D-B

361-3-D-B

362-2-R-A

363L-5-G-B*

364-1-D-C

365-1-J-C

366-2-D-D

367-3-D-B

368-5-E-B

369-5-C-B*

370-2-B-B

371-3-D-B

372-3-D-C

373-4-D-C

374-4-D-C

375-4-D-C

376-4-D-C

377-4-D-E

378-1-B-C

379-3-C-A

380-1-D-D

381-1-C-B

382-1-D-B

383-1-D-B

384-5-J-A

DAIRY PRODUCTS: MILK & CREAM, BUTTER, ICE CREAM, CHEESE

Milk, like bread, was a basic food staple throughout the years of button making. Hundreds of milk-related buttons were produced, usually depicting a youngster with the product, the product bottled, or the product source—the cow. Similarly, many buttons promoted butter and "butter color" oleomargarines. Although these buttons frequently had only the name of the product, several beautiful examples picture a cow, or the butter itself. There are several choice early ice cream buttons, particularly from the "Telling Company" and other very nice, but isolated, examples from other companies plus the popular 1930s "Good Humor" safety series. Illustrated buttons usually depict the product or children enjoying the product. Adult ice cream-eaters were seldom depicted.

385-1-D-C

386-5-E-C

387-5-G-A

388-2-D-B

389-3-A-B

390-2-D-B

391-2-D-B

392-4-D-B

393-5-K-A

394-5-I-A

395-3-D-B

396-2-E-A

397-5-G-A

398-4-E-A

399L-5-Y-A

400L-6-I-A

401-5-E-A

402-5-E-B

403L-5-A-B

404-6-E-A

405-3-E-B*

406-1-D-C

407-2-D-C

408-4-J-A

409-2-D-C

410-5-D-C

411-3-J-B

412-2-D-D

413-1-D-C

414-2-D-B*

415-2-D-B*

416-2-D-C*

417-2-D-C

418-2-D-C

419-3-D-B

420-5-G-A

421-1-E-A

422-4-D-A

423L-5-D-A

424L-7-Y-A

425L-8-D-A

426-2-Y-B

427-2-D-D*

428-3-D-B

429-3-F-D

430-2-D-B

431-3-D-A

432-5-A-A

433-5-A-B*

434-5-I-B*

435-3-D-B

436-3-D-B

437L-5-G-A

438-5-E-B

439L-5-C-A

440-5-M-B

441-5-M-B

442-6-C-A

443-6-E-A

FRESH FRUITS & VEGETABLES

Fresh produce, although commonly home-grown in earlier years, was still the subject of several buttons. Many colorful buttons were issued by tree nurseries, and local fruit carnivals accounted for an additional selection of nicely-colored button examples.

444-6-D-A

445-2-D-A

446-2-D-A

447-3-D-A

448-3-D-A

449-3-D-A

450-3-D-A

451-3-D-A

452-3-D-A

453-3-D-A

454-3-D-A

455-3-D-A

456-2-D-A

457-3-D-A

458-2-C-A

459-2-D-B

460-2-D-A

461-2-D-A

462-4-L-A

463-4-D-A

464-4-D-B

125

MEAT, SEAFOOD, POULTRY

Several excellent button examples were produced by early meat processing companies. A delectable-appearing, wrapped or unwrapped whole ham was a frequent motif. Pork products were widely advertised by buttons, beef was not. There were not many seafood or poultry food buttons; those issued were typically illustrated with lobsters or turkeys.

465-2-D-D   466-2-C-A*   467-2-D-B   468-3-D-B   469-5-C-B

470-2-D-E   471-3-J-B   472-3-J-A   473-5-C-A   474-5-C-A

475L-5-Y-A   476-3-D-C*   477-2-D-C*   478-1-D-A   479-3-J-A*   480L-5-E-A

481-2-C-A   482-2-D-B   483-2-D-B   484-2-D-B   485-2-D-B   486-5-D-B

487-2-J-B   488-2-D-B   489-5-I-A   490-5-C-A   491-5-D-A

FOOD STORES, CANNED GOODS BRANDS, FROZEN FOODS, FOOD PRODUCTION

A number of nicely-designed or quite colorful buttons promoted various canned goods lines before the beginning of 'supermarket' grocery shopping. Grocery stores and wholesale market buildings were commonly illustrated on buttons.

492-5-E-B

493-5-E-A

494-5-E-A

495-5-E-A

496-5-P-A

497-5-I-B

498-3-D-A*

499-5-E-A

500-2-B-A

501-2-C-B

502-5-E-B

503-4-D-B

504-4-D-B

505-2-D-C

506-1-D-A

507-2-A-A

508-3-C-A

509-3-C-B

510-1-D-A

511-5-E-A

TOBACCO

Tobacco buttons usually were directed to the sale of cigars, although there are also several early cigarette ad buttons and an occasional example for chewing tobacco and snuff. Buttons which depicted people usually illustrated males, but several exist that used an attractive female as a product inducement.

512-5-A-E   513-4-I-A   514-2-D-B   515-1-C-B   516-2-D-A   517-2-D-B   518-1-D-B

519-3-J-C*   520-1-F-B*   521-2-K-A   522-1-D-B   523-3-C-B

524-1-A-B   525-1-A-B*   526-2-D-B   527-2-D-C   528-2-G-C*   529-2-D-B*

530-1-I-B   531-2-D-C   532-2-G-B   533-2-T-B   534-1-D-C   535-5-D-B

536-5-J-B   537-1-D-C*   538-2-D-B   539-1-D-B*   540-2-D-B   541-2-D-D

542-1-D-B   543-1-D-A   544-2-D-B   545-3-D-A   546-1-J-A   547-1-E-A

NOTES

VI. FOOD, BEVERAGES, TOBACCO

ALCOHOLIC DRINKS
19. BACK PAPER: "DRINK SPECIAL BREW 'IMPERIAL' FRANCISKANER"
27. BACK PAPER: "Over 75 years ago Metz Brothers started manufacturing Metz Beer, which has become famous for its uniform quality and fine flavor. Today the great popularity of Metz Beer has automatically created the slogan, 'Glad To Metz You."
32. MULTICOLOR DIECUT CELLULOID HANGER W/"MILLER HIGH LIFE" TEXT ON REVERSE.
33. MULTICOLOR DIECUT CELLULOID HANGER W/BLANK REVERSE.
37. BACK PAPER HAS BLACK/WHITE "VAN NOSTRAND'S/OWL MUSTY/BUNKER HILL BREWERIES" OWL ILLUSTRATION.
39. BACK PAPER: "Brewed/A.G. Van Nostrand/Bunker Hill Brewery/Charlestown, Mass."
41. BACK PAPER HAS "VAN NOSTRAND'S" TEXT. BUTTON EXISTS IN MULTICOLOR VARIATIONS.
42.-46. FROM A SET. ALL BUT TWO ILLUSTRATED HERE HAVE "VAN NOSTRAND'S" TEXT ON BACK PAPER.
47. BACK PAPER: "P.B. Ale, Porter, Lager"
51. BACK PAPER: "PABST MALT EXTRACT/THE BEST TONIC"
58. BACK PAPER: "COMPLIMENTS OF THE NEEF BREWING CO./DENVER"
67. BACK PAPER: "Hunter/Baltimore Rye/M. Lanahan & Son/Baltimore"

BAKED GOODS
76. INSET MOVABLE EYEBALLS.
101. BACK PAPER: "This bread is only made by SKILLMAN. Take no substitute."
105. BACK PAPER INCLUDES: "SKILES BAKERY CO./MILWAUKEE"
108. SEEN IN VARIOUS SOLID COLOR BACKGROUNDS.
127. BACK INSCRIPTION: "NATIONAL BISCUIT COMPANY/2-36"
128. SIMILAR DESIGN TO A LARGE SERIES OF BUTTONS W/RISQUE INSCRIPTIONS.
135. BACK PAPER: "NEW ENGLAND PIES. ASK YOUR GROCER OR YOUR BAKER/DETROIT"

BAKING INGREDIENTS
138. BACK PAPER: "WHEN EVERYTHING ELSE FAILS/USE CERESOTA/TELL MOTHER ABOUT THIS."
149. GOLD/BLACK DIECUT CELLULOID RIBBON ATTACHED.
177. BACK PAPER: "HOFFMAN'S RICE STARCH/ABICHT, BRAUN & CO./CHICAGO, ILL."

CANDY, ETC.
190. BACK PAPER: "Montague & Co./Croft & Allen Co./Makers Confections and Chocolates"
194. RIM INSCRIPTION: "MADE IN ENGLAND"
206. BACK PAPER: "Chew Sterling Gum"
212. A NEWSPAPER ISSUE, BUT POSSIBLY RELATED TO THE CRACKER JACK CO.

COFFEE, TEA
247. BACK PAPER: "THE TOLEDO COFFEE & SPICE CO."
268. BACK PAPER: "CLARK & HOST COMPANY/Importers of Coffee and Tea/Milwaukee, Wis."
277. BACK PAPER: "THRICE A DAY/EVERY DAY/'WHITE HOUSE COFFEE' IS THE MAINSTAY OF THE INNER-MAN. DWINELL-WRIGHT CO. BOSTON-CHICAGO."

COLAS, SODAS, ETC.
300. GREEN STRING ATTACHED TO RESEMBLE CHERRY STEM.
311. HOLE ON RIM FOR METAL CLICKER ATTACHMENT.
321. BACK PAPER: "LIMETTA/BEWARE OF SUBSTITUTES/PUT UP ONLY BY DREWRY & SONS, ST. PAUL" POSSIBLY AN ALCOHOLIC DRINK.
323. ORANGE CRUSH.
327. REVERSE: "SPONSORED BY PEPSI-COLA OF NEW ORLEANS"
334. BACK PAPER: "SATAN-ET WILL GET YOU YET"
345. "SELTZER" BOTTLE.
349. 1933-1934 CHICAGO WORLD'S FAIR GIVE-AWAY.

CONDIMENTS, ETC.
358. BACK PAPER: "Any lady who receives this badge, if she will write me where she got it and inform me if she uses KNOX'S GELATINE or not, I will send her FREE my cookbook, 'Dainty Desserts for Dainty People,' which costs 25¢. KNOX'S is the purest GELATINE made. It's not like pie, it's healthy. Address, KNOX of Johnstown, N.Y."
363. 1933-1934 CHICAGO WORLD'S FAIR GIVE-AWAY.

369. BACK PAPER: "QUIMBY MFG. CO. 'IVOLOID.' "

DAIRY PRODUCTS

405. RIM INSCRIPTION: "By STANLEY/TORONTO"

414. BACK PAPER: "IT LEADS THEM ALL IN STRENGTH, UNIFORMITY, BRILLIANCY./THE HELLER & MERZ CO. NEW YORK"

415. BACK PAPER: "ALDERNEY BUTTER COLOR MANUFACTURED BY THE HELLER & MERZ CO., SOLD BY C. RICHARDSON & CO./ST. MARY'S, ONT."

416. BACK PAPER: "SWIFT'S JERSEY BUTTERINE/SWEET, PURE, CLEAN"

427. HOLE ON RIM FOR METAL CLICKER ATTACHMENT.

433.-434. CANADIAN.

MEAT, SEAFOOD, POULTRY

466. "AK-SAR-BEN" IS THE REVERSE SPELLING OF NEBRASKA.

476. CANADIAN, BACK PAPER: "THOS. WIBBY, TORONTO"

477. BACK PAPER: "The Products of SWIFT & COMPANY are sold in every country on the GLOBE."

479. EARLY SWIFT & CO. LOGO.

FOOD STORES

498. HOLED AT BOTTOM FOR CLICKER ATTACHMENT.

TOBACCO

519. BACK PAPER: "Gustav A. Moebs & Co., Makers of Fine Cigars/Detroit, Mich."

520. IN TYPE AT THE TOP: "WELLERETTES" AND AT BOTTOM: "RICHARDSON DRUG CO./OMAHA, NEB."

525. PICTURES PAUL KRUGER OF SOUTH AFRICA.

528. "ATHLETICS" REFERS TO THE PHILADELPHIA (AMERICAN LEAGUE) BASEBALL TEAM.

529. BACK PAPER INCLUDES: "PURE TOBACCO/NOTHING MORE"

537. BACK PAPER INCLUDES: "The Purest Form in which tobacco can be Smoked" and "LONDON LANCET"

539. BACK PAPER INCLUDES: "LUPFERT SCALES & CO. TOBACCO MFRS./WINSTON, N.C., U.S."

BRIDGES, PARKS, PLACES, LANDMARKS

Buttons depicting "places" in the United States are frequently historic or travel-related and many were likely obtained in tourist shops across the nation. Many examples are available from lesser-known locations and they are frequently quite colorful with a pleasing scene.

1-1-A-A

2-2-A-A

3-2-C-A

4-2-A-A

5-1-A-A*

6-2-B-A

7-4-I-A

8-4-G-B

9-1-A-A*

10-1-F-A

11-5-A-A

12-5-D-A

13-5-D-A

14-2-D-D*

15-5-E-A

16-5-A-A

17-3-D-A

18-4-C-A*

19-5-D-A

20-5-D-A

21-2-F-A

22-2-B-A

23-2-D-B

24-3-A-A

25-5-D-A

CITIES & CITY DISASTERS

Hometown pride often resulted in a button, particularly for blossoming market centers and communities steeped in a particular local tradition. Local celebrations also produced thousands of city or village-related buttons. Many collectors enjoy finding and saving buttons from their hometown if the town was sufficiently large to have accounted for an adequate number of buttons over the years. City disaster buttons are quite scarce.

26L-5-D-B

27-2-A-A

28-2-D-B

29-2-D-D*

30-3-D-B

31-3-C-A

32-2-D-B

33-3-D-A

34-5-G-A

35-3-D-A

36-2-D-B

37-3-D-A

38-2-B-B

39-3-D-A

40-2-D-C

41-4-D-B

42-2-D-B

43-2-D-C

44L-5-C-A

45-3-D-A

46-2-A-A

47-4-E-A

48-3-C-A

49-2-B-C

50-2-J-C

51L-8-A-A

STATES

States—particularly those noted for a specialty product—have been commemorated to some extent for many years. Various sets were issued at the turn of the century. The sets included depictions of state seals, flowers, birds and state maps. These were mostly issued as premiums with chewing gum, candy or tobacco products.

52-2-D-C

53-4-D-B

54-2-D-B

55-4-D-B*

56-2-B-B

57-4-D-A

| 58-1-B-A | 59-3-D-A | 60-1-Y-A* | 61-3-C-A | 62-2-D-A |

COUNTRIES

Although there are exceptions, the bulk of buttons related solely to countries was produced as early premium sets picturing either the country's flag or seal. Examples of these series are still common at many flea markets, antique shows and shops, and offer an excellent opportunity for the beginning collector.

| 63-3-D-A | 64-2-D-B | 65-3-D-A | 66-1-D-A* | 67-1-D-A* | 68L-5-D-A* |

TOURISM & TRAVEL AGENCIES

Travel buttons were never issued in great numbers, partially because the concept of mass tourism is relatively new since World War II. Earlier travel buttons usually were directed toward trips to offshore U.S. possessions or major U.S. parks or historic sites.

| 69-2-D-B | 70-5-N-5 | 71-4-C-A | 72-5-C-A | 73-5-G-A | 74L-7-E-A |

NOTES

VII. GEOGRAPHIC AREAS

BRIDGES, PARKS, PLACES, LANDMARKS
  5. BACK PAPER: "CABIN JOHN HOTEL. Popular Prices."
  9. BACK PAPER: "A.S. BURBANK, SOUVENIRS, PLYMOUTH, MASS."
  14. BACK PAPER: "For another button and information about YAZOO VALLEY write to E.P. SKENE, Room 212, Central Sta., Chicago, Ill."
  18. DIECUT RED/WHITE/BLUE CELLULOID RIBBON ATTACHED.
CITIES, CITY DISASTERS
  29. BACK PAPER IN LARGE TYPE: "LET IT BE CHICAGO FOR 1908"
STATES
  55. BACK PAPER: "Compliments of HAWAII PROMOTION COMMITTEE/HONOLULU, HAWAII"
  60. FROM A SET. SEE *BUTTONS IN SETS,* PAGE 22. (VERSIONS ALSO SEEN IN DOMINANT PINK.)
COUNTRIES
  66. PART OF A SET. SEE *BUTTONS IN SETS,* PAGE 21.
  67. PART OF A SET. SEE *BUTTONS IN SETS,* PAGE 21.
  68. PART OF A SET. SEE *BUTTONS IN SETS,* PAGE 23.

VIII. MILITARY

WAR OF INDEPENDENCE

America's struggle for independence was commemorated at various times by 20th century button makers. The most common motif was the fife and drummers.

1-4-N-A

2-1-D-B

3-2-D-A

4-4-D-A

5-3-D-B

WAR OF 1812

Commemorative buttons were issued for the various centennial celebrations of American victories or achievements in the country's 'second war of independence' for unfettered maritime trade and land expansion.

6-3-D-C

7-3-C-A

8-3-D-C

9-5-G-A

10-4-D-A*

11-3-E-A

12-3-C-A

13-3-E-A

14-3-A-A

15-3-D-A

16-3-D-A

CIVIL WAR: GRAND ARMY OF THE REPUBLIC/CONFEDERACY

The War Between The States ended in 1865 but was not forgotten by its Union veterans. Veteran reunions were held at innumerable locations and those held after the mid-1890s were often accompanied by a commemorative button. The buttons had drawn depictions of Union valor or contemporary scenes with veterans in dress uniforms. Others pictured drawings of gravesite tributes or columns or monuments erected in the intervening years. The graphic and color quality of many GAR buttons is splendid, and this is a frequently-collected category. Similar, but usually less colorful and fewer, buttons were issued for Confederate veterans.

17-1-R-B

18-1-D-C

19-2-R-C

20-3-D-B

135

21-3-F-B

22-1-D-B

23-2-D-B

24-2-D-C*

25-2-D-C*

26-3-D-C

27-3-D-C

28-1-C-C

29-2-D-C

30-1-D-C

31-2-A-B

32-2-C-A

33-2-A-A*

34-2-D-B

35-3-D-C*

36-3-D-A

37-1-E-A

38-2-D-B

39-3-A-A

40-2-B-A

41-6-E-A

42-2-C-C

PREST. JEFF. DAVIS

GEN. ROBERT E. LEE

43-2-E-B

46-2-D-C

44-1-B-C

45-1-B-C

47-2-D-E

48-2-D-E

49-2-D-E

50-3-A-B

51-3-F-C

52-1-B-B

53-2-A-B

54-1-B-C

55-2-J-C

56-1-A-B

57-2-F-B

58-3-D-B

59-1-A-B

60-2-F-C

61-2-E-A

62-2-D-C*

63-8-E-A

64-8-E-A

65-8-E-A

137

BOER WAR

The 1899-1902 conflict between the Boers (descendents of Dutch settlers of South Africa) and victorious British resulted in several pro-Dutch buttons in the United States.

66-1-A-D   67-1-C-A   68-1-A-C   69-1-C-A   70-1-C-B

71-1-C-C   72-1-D-B   73-1-D-C   74-1-C-B

SPANISH-AMERICAN WAR

The United States was becoming an international power by the 1890s and the latter part of the decade gave the country its first test of military strength. With much popular support for Cuba against land-owner Spain, Americans were incensed by the 1898 destruction of the U.S. battleship Maine in Havana Harbor with the loss of 260 men. In a short-lived war, Admiral Dewey led the win over the Spanish fleet in Manila Bay and the Spanish fleet was destroyed off Santiago approximately five months after the Maine sinking. The Maine and Admiral Dewey were depicted on a wide variety of buttons along with other U.S. heroes and Cuban motifs. Several buttons were issued with comic/caricature depictions of Uncle Sam mauling the upstart Spaniard.

75-1-F-C   76-1-D-B   77-1-D-B   78-1-D-C   79-1-F-B

80-1-G-B   81-1-F-B   82-1-B-B   83-1-F-B   84-1-F-B   85-1-H-B

86-1-F-C

87-1-A-B*

88-1-F-B

89-1-F-B

90-1-D-B

91-1-D-B*

92-1-J-C

93-1-A-B

94-1-F-D

95-1-F-B

96-1-F-B

97-1-F-B

98-1-F-B

99-1-F-B

100-1-F-D

101-1-F-C

102-1-A-C*

103-1-F-B

104-1-A-C

105-1-F-C

106-1-F-B

107-1-F-C

108-1-E-A

109-1-E-A

110-1-E-A

111-1-E-A

112-1-D-A

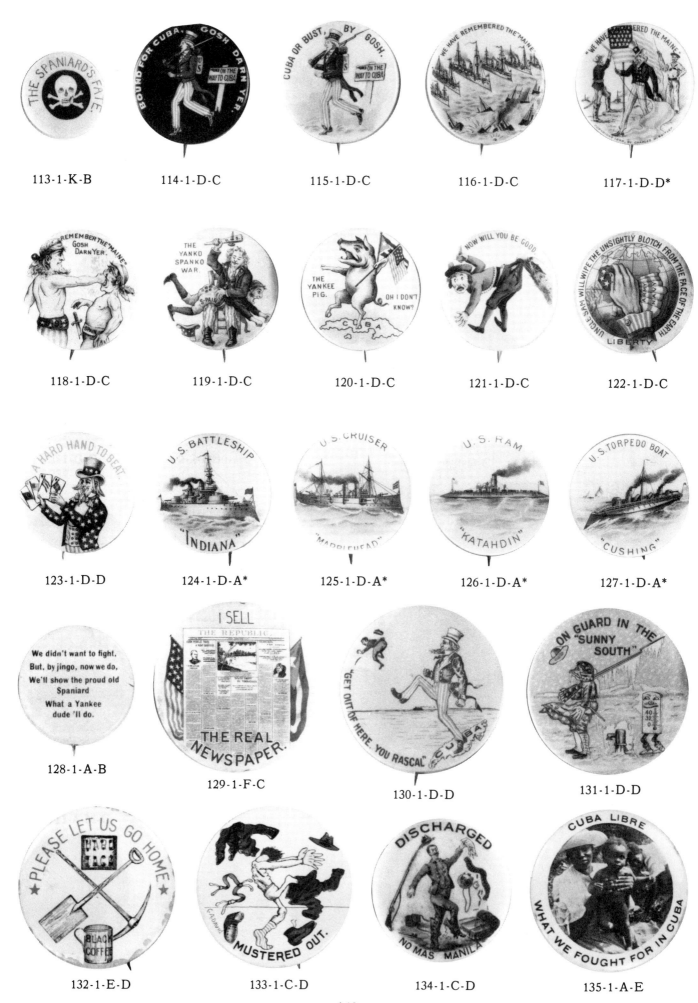

113-1-K-B

114-1-D-C

115-1-D-C

116-1-D-C

117-1-D-D*

118-1-D-C

119-1-D-C

120-1-D-C

121-1-D-C

122-1-D-C

123-1-D-D

124-1-D-A*

125-1-D-A*

126-1-D-A*

127-1-D-A*

128-1-A-B

129-1-F-C

130-1-D-D

131-1-D-D

132-1-E-D

133-1-C-D

134-1-C-D

135-1-A-E

EARLY U.S. PACIFIC OPERATIONS; MEXICAN BORDER CONFLICT

Following the Spanish-American War, the United States took steps to defend territories and demonstrate naval readiness in the Pacific and Far East. One display was the around-the-world dispatching of a portion of the U.S. fleet, led by Capt. Robley "Fighting Bob" Evans, Spanish-American War hero at the battle of Santiago. In 1914 tense relations between the U.S. and Mexico erupted into U.S. occupation of Mexican soil after an incident involving unarmed American sailors in Tampico. The harbor at Vera Cruz was bombarded by the U.S. Navy but disagreements were mediated short of actual war.

136-2-E-B

137-2-F-B

138-2-D-C

139-2-A-B

140-3-F-C

141-3-J-E

WORLD WAR I

Unlike the Spanish-American War less than two decades earlier, the United States in 1917 found itself in a war on a distant continent. Buttons were numerous and reflected the patriotism and dedication of a nation in its first overseas war. There was an underlying seriousness to WW I buttons as opposed to some flippancy on several Spanish-American War buttons. "Kick The Kaiser" was the height of WW I bravado. A number of very colorful buttons occured during and following World War I but the majority were more somber in design, color and message reflecting the gravity of "The War To End All Wars" for the United States and its citizens.

142-3-F-D

143-3-F-B

144-3-D-C

145-3-D-C

146-3-E-C

147-3-E-B

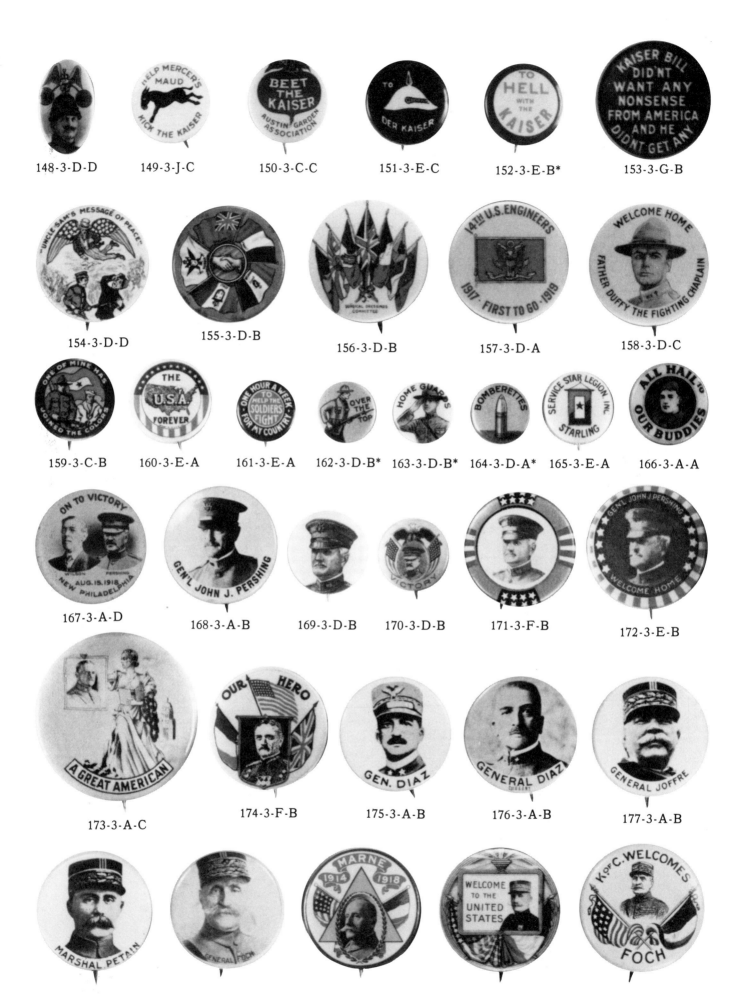

148-3-D-D 149-3-J-C 150-3-C-C 151-3-E-C 152-3-E-B* 153-3-G-B

154-3-D-D 155-3-D-B 156-3-D-B 157-3-D-A 158-3-D-C

159-3-C-B 160-3-E-A 161-3-E-A 162-3-D-B* 163-3-D-B* 164-3-D-A* 165-3-E-A 166-3-A-A

167-3-A-D 168-3-A-B 169-3-D-B 170-3-D-B 171-3-F-B 172-3-E-B

173-3-A-C 174-3-F-B 175-3-A-B 176-3-A-B 177-3-A-B

178-3-A-B 179-3-A-B 180-3-F-B 181-3-D-B 182L-3-E-B

183-3-E-B

184-3-D-D

185-3-C-C

186-3-E-C*

187-3-D-C

188-3-D-C

189-3-E-C

190-3-E-B

191-3-C-A

192-3-G-A

193-3-E-A

194-3-E-A

195-3-E-A

196L-3-E-A

197L-3-E-A

198-3-C-A

199-3-C-A

200-3-E-A

201-3-E-A

202-3-E-A

203-3-F-B

204-3-E-A

205-3-C-C

206-3-D-B

207-3-C-A

208-3-C-A

209-3-C-A

210-3-A-C

211-3-D-D*

212-3-D-D*

213-3-J-A*

214-3-A-C*

215-3-C-B*

216-3-C-C

217-3-C-C

218-3-C-B

219-3-D-B

220L-3-D-A

221-3-D-A

222-3-C-A

223-3-O-A

224-3-D-A

225-3-D-C

WORLD WAR II

World War II began in Europe in 1939 and in 1941 the United States entered world conflict for the first time in two hemispheres. No other war produced as many buttons, more remarkable since buttons were generally on the decline up until wartime. There was no doubt in World War II who the enemy was, and why. Hatred of enemy leaders was apparent in caricature and slogan Hitler, Mussolini and Tojo buttons. ''Remember Pearl Harbor'' was an oft-recuring slogan and U.S. generals and admirals, particularly McArthur and Eisenhower, were depicted on various buttons. War effort buttons to promote ''home front'' production in plants and conservation in the home were issued by thousands of companies and institutions. Most WW II buttons were done in patriotic red/white/blue and many were lithographed metal. Among the favorite buttons is a ''mechanical'' and colorful depiction of Uncle Sam hanging Hitler from a tree limb.

227L-6-A-D

229-6-E-A

228-6-A-D*

226-6-A-C*

230L-6-E-B

231L-6-F-B

232L-6-E-B

233L-6-D-D*

234L-6-G-A

144

235-6-E-C

236-6-G-C

237-6-E-B

238-6-E-B

239-6-E-B

240-6-A-C

241-6-J-B

242L-6-I-C

243-6-A-B

244-6-E-B

245-6-E-A

246-6-F-C

247-6-F-A

248-6-E-C

249-6-A-B

250-6-E-C

251-6-E-C

252-6-E-B

253-6-R-C

254-6-E-B

255-6-E-B

256-6-I-B

257-6-E-A

258-6-F-A

259-6-F-A

260-6-F-A

261-6-F-A

262-6-A-B

263-6-E-B

264-6-E-A

265-6-E-B

271-6-E-A*

266-6-E-A

267-6-C-A

268-6-I-A

269-6-C-A

270-6-E-A

272-6-E-A

273-6-E-A

274-6-E-A

275-6-E-A

276-6-E-B*

277-6-E-B*

278-6-E-A

279-6-E-B

280-6-E-B

281-6-E-B

282-6-E-A

283-6-E-A

284-6-E-A

285-6-C-C

286-6-E-B

287-6-D-A

288-6-E-A

289-6-F-A

290-6-E-B

291L-6-E-A

292-6-C-A

293-6-G-B

295L-6-I-A

296L-6-G-A

297L-6-G-A

298L-6-E-A

294-6-E-B

299-6-D-D* 300-6-G-B 301-6-G-B 302-6-G-B 303L-6-E-A

304L-6-E-B

305-6-C-B 306-6-E-B 307-6-C-A 308-6-E-B 309-6-E-B

310-6-E-A 311-6-E-A 312L-6-C-A 313-6-G-A 314-6-E-A 315-6-E-A

316-6-E-B 317-6-F-B* 318-6-E-B 319-6-I-B 320-6-E-A

VIETNAM WAR

The Vietnam Conflict, lasting from 20-25 years depending on the definition of starting and ending dates, was the longest—and likely most ''unpopular'' war in U.S. history. Caricature returned to war buttons, but the caricatures were of U.S. presidents and military advisors conducting the War. Virtually all buttons were anti-war; nearly two decades after the war, collectors have yet to find any significant number of pro-war buttons. Of the anti-war buttons, many were designed with creative flair in striking ''day-glo'' color breaking with the traditional red, white and blue norm of the 1940s and 1950s.

321-8-C-A 322-8-A-A 323-8-N-A 324-8-A-A

NOTES

CIVIL WAR

    24. BACK PAPER: "24TH ANNUAL REUNION/66th O.V.V.I./SEPT. 30TH, 1909. Compliments of J.S. RUHL"

    25. U.S. GRANT LIKENESS.

    33. RIM INSCRIBED: "BALLS R.R. WATCHES/CLEVELAND, O./1901"

    35. BACK PAPER: "C.D. KENNY CO./TEAS, COFFEES, SUGARS"

    62. HOLE ON RIM FOR METAL CLICKER ATTACHMENT.

WAR OF 1812

    10. GIVEN TO SCHOOL CHILDREN AND OTHERS WHO CONTRIBUTED TO THE "SAVE OLD IRONSIDES FUND." BACK PAPER HAS BRIEF HISTORICAL TEXT.

SPANISH-AMERICAN WAR

    87. BACK PAPER: LIFE INSURANCE POLICY DATA.

    91. BACK PAPER: "COMPLIMENTS OF RUTCHER & STARKS/ADMIRAL DEWEY IN LIFE SIZE WAX IN SHOW WINDOW."

    102. BACK PAPER: "HIGH STANDARD 5c CIGAR."

    117. BACK PAPER HAS LENGTHY TEXT ABOUT COMMEMORATIVE FUND FOR NAVY GUNNERS IN THE WAR.

    124.-127. PART OF A SET. SEE *BUTTONS IN SETS*, PAGE 44.

WORLD WAR I

    152. MOVIE BUTTON. BACK PAPER: "At Your Theater/SCREEN CLASSICS Inc./Metro Pictures"

    162.-164. SUNDAY SCHOOL BUTTONS. #162 FOR RALLY DAY. #163-164 FOR "TEAMS."

    186. "LLLL" STANDS FOR SOMETHING LIKE: LOYAL LEAGUE OF LOGGERS AND LUMBERMEN.

    211. CANADIAN BUTTON W/"THOMAS WIBBY/TORONTO" BACK PAPER.

    212. AUSTRALIAN BUTTON W/"A.W. PATRICK/MAKER /3 UNLEY RD./ADELAIDE" RIM INSCRIPTION.

ENGLISH BUTTONS

    213.-214. ENGLISH BUTTONS.

    215. AUSTRALIAN BUTTON.

WORLD WAR II

    226. UNCOMMON LARGE SIZE.

    228. WHITE NOOSED CORD ATTACHED.

    233. MECHANICAL BUTTON W/ORIGINAL CARD AND LEVER STRING.

    271. W/CLOTH BLUE/GOLD RIBBON ATTACHED.

    276.-277. PART OF A SET.

    299. INSCRIBED: "©1940 T.B.W."

    317. UNMARKED, BUT PROBABLY AUSTRALIAN OR ENGLISH MANUFACTURED.

COLOR SECTION

The following 16 pages of full color plates exemplify the superb color and design achieved by early button makers. The section also includes several examples to suggest the variety of popular "character" buttons from early and more recent eras.

All buttons in the color section are shown actual size.Buttons were grouped according to size to allow the maximum number of illustrations.

Each button in the color section is repeated in the black and white photo pages where it is described by age and value range. The number assigned to each color section button is the page number where that button is pictured with its description.

105   304   175   193   193   194   199   210   210

1   7   7   15   16   22   24

29   29   33   35   37   41   42

45   45   46   47   53   54   57

63   65   68   69   71   72   73

78   79   91   91   94   97   97

97   97   98   98   98   101   103

105   106   108   109   109   110   110

110 110 111 111 114 114 114

115 115 116 116 116 117 118

119 119 120 120 121 121 121

122 122 122 122 122 122 122

123 123 123 123 124 124 126

128 128 128 128 128 128 128

128 134 135 138 139 141 141

142 145 146 167 168 171 173

151

175   175   176   176   176   176   177

177   177   178   180   180   181   181

182   182   187   188   188   188   188

188   188   191   192   193   193   193

194   196   196   197   199   200   206

206   208   208   209   210   210   210

210   212   220   222   222   222   223

224   224   224   224   224   225   226

226   226   226   229   237   239   243

27   41   57   89   94   98

98   99   112   125   126   142

169   175   179   182   189   190

195   219   223   229   230   236

1   1   1   7   9

10   15   16   17   17

153

17   17   18   18   21

21   23   23   23   24

24   24   25   25   27

27   27   29   29   33

35   35   35   35   36

38   41   44   45   45

47

47

47

48

52

56

57

69

69

71

71

89

89

89

90

95

97

97

98

98

98

99

99

100

101

102

102

104
155

104

105

105

106

108

108

109

109

110

111

113

113

114

114

114

114

115

115

116

118

118

118

119

119

119

119

120

121

122

123

124

124

124

124

126

127

128

131

132

136

140

140

140

140

142

143

143

144

145

146

147

170

171

173

176

176

176

176

177

179

157

181

183

223

227

227

227

229

231

234

235

243

246

7

8

10

11

17

17

22

26

28

42

45

49

54

63

89

91

100

101

102

111

111

118

122

125

135

136

169

175

180

180

180

184

187

195

195

196

203

224

227

243

BAER FAMILY REUNION
KUTZTOWN PARK AUG. 6TH 1904

2

4

OKLA. CATTLEMEN'S MEET
Guthrie, Feb'y 14, 15, 16, '05.

5

LARGEST IMPORTERS OF PERCHERON, BELGIAN, GERMAN COACH, SHIRE & HACKNEY STALLIONS & MARES.
LAFAYETTE STOCK FARM, J. GROUGH & SON, PROPRS. LAFAYETTE, IND.

6

FOR A GOOD SALE AND FILL—MY PAPA SHIPS TO IOWA COMMISSION CO., SOUTH OMAHA

11

13

TO FALL IN LOVE IS AWFULLY SIMPLE TO FALL OUT OF IT IS SIMPLY AWFUL.

15

16

WELCOME TERRITORIAL PIONEERS
R.E. DOWDELL   A.L. VAN OSDEL

19

CARNIVAL AND STREET FAIR
A HOT TIME IN THE OLD TOWN

20

BELLEVILLE. 1900.
GO AS   YOU PLEASE
STREET FAIR

20

HELLO BILL, MEET ME AT THE BELLEVILLE STREET FAIR
SEPT. 10TH-15TH 1900.

20

WICHITA CARNIVAL AND FALL FESTIVAL WICHITA. OCT. 1 TO 6, 1900. FAIR

20

TOPEKA'S THIRD ANNUAL CARNIVAL
TOPEKA
K   K

20

SOUTH CAROLINA, INTER-STATE & WEST INDIAN EXPOSITION
MY-PAL-MET-HER
1901 - CHARLESTON - 1902

21

21

MEET US AT THE CEDAR RAPIDS CARNIVAL, OCT. 7TH TO 12TH 1901.
SEE DER RABBITS

21

FORT WAYNE CARNIVAL AND STREET FAIR.
Oct. 4, 5, 6, 7, 1898.

21

CLYDE MERCHANTS' STREET FAIR AND INDUSTRIAL EXPOSITION
SEPT. 25-26-27-28-29-30

21

THE LAND OF THE MIDNIGHT SUN.
THE LAND OF THE MIDNIGHT SUN
Ed. M. Bayliss, Jno. G. Marchand Concessionaires.
PAN-AMERICAN EXPOSITION 1901.

24

25

26

28

35

35

39

42

62

79

90

94

98

99

100

104

106

109

110

110

113

162

DULUTH IMPERIAL FLOUR
ASK YOUR GROCER
IMPERIAL MILLS 49 DULUTH IMPERIAL PATENT DULUTH MINN.
FOR SALE EVERYWHERE
114

USE HUNTER'S CREAM
THE HUNTER MILLING CO.
WELLINGTON, KANSAS.
114

FLEISCHMANN'S
IN STORM, IN SUNSHINE, RAIN OR SLEET, YOU SEE OUR WAGONS ON THE STREET.
YEAST
115

THE FINEST YET.
RED INDIAN CUT PLUG
IT WILL NOT BITE YOUR TONGUE OR GIVE YOU HEARTBURN.
128

1910
WHERE LIFE IS WORTH LIVING
DETROIT
132

OLD HOME WEEK
JULY 28 AUG. 3 1907
THE SHOE CENTRE
LYNN, MASS.
132

CONFEDERATE REUNION APRIL 22-24, 1902.
ROBERT E. LEE.
J.I. CASE THRESHING MACHINE CO. RACINE, WIS. U.S.A.
DALLAS, TEXAS.
137

"GET OUT OF HERE, YOU RASCAL"
CUBA.
140

MUSTERED OUT.
C. ADANE
140

WE'RE BEHIND THE MAN BEHIND THE GUN
143

6th ANNUAL BOY SCOUT MEET, SCHUYLKILL COUNTY
SEPTEMBER 3, 1923.
166

PLUMBAGO CLUB
167

ASCALON COMMANDERY Nº 59
KNIGHTS TEMPLAR
I BELONG TO ASCALON, WHERE YOU FROM?
YOU SHOULD BELONG TO ASCALON.
PITTSBURGH PA. 1906.
167

BOUND FOR WASHINGTON.
Morocco Temple 1900.
FROM THE HOT SANDS OF FLORIDA.
169

INTERNATIONAL CONVENTION CHRISTIAN CHURCHES
DELEGATE
OMAHA THE GATE CITY
OMAHA, OCTOBER 16-23, 1902.
170

COMFORT SOAP.
SAVE THE WRAPPERS
IT'S ALL RIGHT
177

PYRAMID SOAP POWDER
MADE BY THE CUDAHY PACKING CO. SOUTH OMAHA U.S.A.
177

Pears' Soap
"You dirty Boy"
Pears' Soap
177

Bry's
SCHOOL
BILLY BRY
DOROTHY BLOCK
SHOES
2824
181

WEAR PURITAN HOSIERY
BURNHAM HANNA MUNGER D.G. CO., KANSAS CITY, MO.
182

163

185

185

198

202

202

209

212

230

232

243

244

245

16

19

19

133

122

133

168

168

168

190

194

196

215

237
165

243

IX. ORGANIZATIONS, ASSOCIATIONS

Probably no other single category resulted in as many buttons as organizations and clubs. From the outset a button was almost synonomous with membership or meeting of lodges, associations, conventions, civic groups, trade groups and an endless list of other organizations. A button collector could pursue this category for a lifetime unless a strict specialization is imposed. Organization buttons range from very ordinary appearance to splendid examples of color, design and wry humor.

BOY SCOUTS/GIRL SCOUTS

The Boy Scouts of America, incorporated in 1910 and granted federal charter in 1916, resulted in a steady, but not large, quantity of buttons over the years with many nicely-colored examples appearing as recently as the 1960s. President Teddy Roosevelt's association with Boy Scout founding is a recurring motif. The Girl Scouts, although coming into being during 1912-1915, never enjoyed the same button popularity as its counterpart organization.

1-4-D-D* 2-4-A-B 3-3-D-D 4-5-E-A 5-5-A-B 6-5-D-B

7-5-D-A 8-5-B-B 9L-5-E-B 10L-6-N-B 11-5-C-B 12-5-C-B

13-5-G-B 14-6-L-B 15-5-H-B 16-5-M-B 17-5-M-B

18-6-M-B 19-6-N-B 20-6-L-B 21-6-G-A 22-5-O-B 23-6-D-B

24-6-D-B 25-6-D-B 26-6-D-A 27-6-J-A 28-6-E-A 29-6-E-A

166

30-4-D-B   31-5-A-A   32-5-L-A   33-6-I-A   34-6-E-A   35-6-I-A

CLUBS

Buttons were issued for numerous hobby, social and professional groups, although the nature or purpose of some of these groups has become uncertain over the years.

36-5-G-A   37-1-D-A   38-5-E-A   39-5-J-B   40-6-A-A   41-9-E-A*

LICENSES

Countless buttons have been issued over the years for factory identification, vending, and other certification purposes. The variety of such buttons and the numerous points of origin make this an almost unlimited collectible category.

42-4-N-A   43-5-A-A   44-5-I-A   45-5-I-A

LODGES, FRATERNAL GROUPS

Many cleverly-designed and quite colorful buttons were issued for lodge groups and their conventions. Numerous examples exist for all major lodge orders, both church-related and secular.

46-1-D-C   47-2-D-D   48-2-D-C   49-2-D-B

50-1-D-C*

51-1-D-C

52-1-D-C*

53-2-E-B

54-4-D-A

55-2-D-B

56-4-C-A

57-1-A-A

61-2-A-B

58-1-A-A

59-3-E-A

60-3-D-A

62-2-I-A

63-3-D-A

64-1-D-A

65-3-D-A

66-3-G-A

168

"RAJAH IN EASTON"
DEC. 1ST. 1915

67-3-J-A

BOUND FOR WASHINGTON.
Morocco Temple 1900.
FROM THE HOT SANDS OF FLORIDA.

68-1-D-C

POTENTATE

69-3-D-B

SAHARA
AL AMIN
JOINT CEREMONIAL
HOT SPRINGS, ARK
MAY 12, 1921

70-4-D-B

FLIGHT OF LOCUSTS TO KANSAS CITY 1901
Isis Temple
FROM GREAT AMERICAN DESERT

71-2-D-C

HANG ON TO THE ROPE

72-1-A-C

GRAND RAPIDS MICHIGAN
SALADIN TEMPLE

73-1-F-A

LU LU
IS IN TOWN

74-5-C-A

MARSEENEH TEMPLE 91
A.A.O.N.M.S.
BUFFALO, N.Y.

75-3-D-A

Der Hermanns Söhne

76-3-D-A

YAMATO SANCTORUM No. 96. O.O.H.d.P.

77-1-A-A

PIKE'S PEAK COMMANDERY No 6
COLORADO SPRINGS COLO.
K T

78-2-D-B

TOLEDO COUNCIL Nº 10

79-2-D-A

11th BIENNIAL CONVENTION
W M A D P S
JUNE 6-10 1899
KANSAS CITY, MO

80-1-D-A

DIE TAGET CLANK

81-2-D-A

FOE
CLEVELAND 1912

82-3-D-A

THE ROYAL ORDER
OF THE
YELLOW DOGS

83-5-N-A*

169

RELIGION

Buttons for religious purposes were issued in great quantity. Several 1920s ministers, particularly Bill Sunday, were depicted on buttons and there is a large assortment of buttons which trace the succession of the Papacy in modern times. There are a sizeable number of "Rally Day" Sunday School buttons which often are splendid examples of design and color.

84-4-A-A   85-5-B-A   86-4-A-A   87-1-C-A   88-2-B-A   89-1-F-C*

90-2-D-A   91-3-D-A   92-3-D-A   93-3-D-A   94-2-E-A

95-4-A-B   96-4-A-B   97-4-A-B   98-4-A-A   99-5-A-A

100-6-A-A   101-8-L-A   102-2-A-A   103-3-A-A   104-5-A-A

105-6-R-A   106-7-A-A   107-6-A-A*   108-9-E-A   109-9-E-A

110-4-D-A 111-4-D-A 112-4-D-A 113-4-D-A 114-4-D-A 115-4-D-A 116-4-D-A

SCHOOLS, COLLEGES, UNIVERSITIES

Although the button was rarely used to advertise the academic status of educational institutions, an endless number of buttons have been issued for local and secondary school events.

117-1-H-A 118-6-A-A 119-5-P-A 120-1-D-A 121-3-D-A

122-2-D-A 123-2-C-A 124-3-D-A 125-4-C-A 126-2-D-A 127-2-D-A

YMCA, YWCA

These organizations offer the collector an assortment of buttons dating from the turn of the century until the present day.

 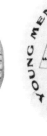    

128-2-E-A

129-2-E-A

130-5-E-A

131-5-G-A

132-6-A-A

133-3-E-A 134-3-I-A 135-5-E-A 136L-6-G-A 137-5-P-A 138-3-G-A

171

NOTES

IX. ORGANIZATIONS, ASSOCIATIONS

BOY SCOUTS
       1. BACK PAPER: "Compliments of DOUTRICH'S Boy Scout Outfitters."
CLUBS
     41. AMERICAN POLITICAL ITEMS COLLECTORS.
LODGES, FRATERNAL GROUPS
     50. BACK PAPER HAS BLACK/WHITE LOGO ILLUSTRATION FOR "International Armor Brand Shirt Collars and Cuffs/Noble goods for 'Nobles' wear"
     52. BACK PAPER SAME AS #50.
     83. ALSO SEE "DOGS" IN SECTION I.
RELIGION
     89. BRIGHAM YOUNG, FOUNDER OF MORMONISM.
    107. BACK PAPER: "Blessed Julie Billiart/Sisters of Notre Dame DeNamur/First American Foundation 1840 at Cincinnati"

X. PRODUCTS, SERVICES

Thousands of products and services have been advertised by buttons from the late 1890s to the present. It is unlikely that any imaginable product or service has escaped without at least one button on its behalf.

ADVERTISING MANUFACTURERS

Surprisingly, not a great number of buttons were issued to self-advertise the button manufacturers. Of the major manufacturers, Whitehead & Hoag produced the most 'self-advertising' buttons. Other companies produced buttons for themselves, but these examples are relatively scarce.

1-1-A-B   2-1-A-C   3-3-C-B   4-2-I-B   5-1-D-B   6-3-C-B

7-2-G-B   8-2-A-C   9-2-A-C   10-6-E-B

11-3-C-B   12-5-Y-B   13L-5-D-B

BANKS, SAFES, SAVINGS

Buttons issued by banks were often quite nicely colored and designed. The button illustrations frequently included a vault door, locked storage or other symbols of security. Prevailing interest rates were also a common motif.

14-3-E-B   15-2-A-A   16-2-D-B*   17-2-D-B   18-1-A-B

19-3-I-A

20-3-G-A

21-1-G-A

22-4-D-A

23-5-J-A

24-4-D-A

BUSINESS MACHINES, SUPPLIES, OFFICE AIDS

A nice assortment of buttons were issued in the early 1900s-1920s for business and office machines, particularly typewriters. These usually are not colorful, but are extremely well-detailed.

25-1-A-B   26-2-J-A   27-2-J-B   28-3-J-A   29-4-E-A

30-3-I-A   31-5-M-A   32-2-E-A   33-1-A-A   34-3-N-A   35-4-G-A

36-2-I-A   37-2-A-B   38-2-A-B   39-5-J-A   40-5-J-A*

41-2-C-B*   42-2-D-B*   43-2-R-B   44-4-E-A   45-1-J-A

BUILDING PRODUCTS, CLEAN-UP/PAINT-UP, PAINTS, VARNISHES, SHELLACS, ENAMELS, CEMENTS, ROOFING; ROAD CONSTRUCTION

A nice assortment of buttons was issued to promote products associated with the building trade. The most commonly-advertised products were house paints, interior varnishes and enamels. Several paint buttons are quite nicely-designed and very colorful; often the paint can itself was illustrated in nice detail since the product itself was difficult to depict. Other building products were also nicely done on buttons, although not as frequently as paint products. ''Clean Up/Paint Up/Fix-Up'' buttons flourished in the 1930s. Road building equipment appeared on several early buttons as the automobile boom created a vast need for better streets and roadways.

46-2-D-C   47-1-D-A   48-5-Y-A   49L-5-E-A   50-5-A-A

51-5-E-A   52-2-G-A   53-2-D-B   54-2-D-E   55-2-D-E

56-2-E-A   57-1-J-B*   58-2-J-A   59L-5-D-A   60-1-N-A   61-2-D-A

62-2-D-A   63-2-D-B*   64-2-D-A   65-2-D-A   66-2-D-B   67-2-D-A

68-2-D-A*   69-2-D-A   70-2-D-A   71-3-D-A   72-3-E-A   73-3-J-A   74-2-D-B

75-5-M-B 76-3-D-B 77-2-C-B 78-3-L-A 79-3-D-B

80-3-D-A 81-3-D-A 82-3-D-B 83-5-E-A 84L-5-N-A 85-5-G-A

86-5-C-A* 87-1-J-C 88-2-A-B 89-1-I-C

90-3-J-C 91-2-J-A 92-2-A-B 93-2-D-D 94-5-J-A

CLEANING AGENTS

Soaps and lye were among the earliest and most common button topics, continuing a ''trade card'' tradition spanning backward nearly to Civil War days. ''Premiums for wrappers'' was a common motif for early soap buttons as were dirty children and black-skinned Negro caricatures. There are a number of very nicely-designed and colorful early soap buttons and the total number over the years is virtually endless.

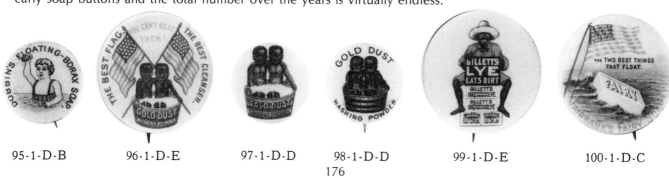

95-1-D-B 96-1-D-E 97-1-D-D 98-1-D-D 99-1-D-E 100-1-D-C

101-2-D-E

102-2-D-D

103-1-D-E

104-1-D-C

105-1-D-B

106-1-G-A

107-1-D-B

108-1-D-B

109-1-C-A

110-1-D-B

111-1-C-A

112-1-D-E*

113-2-D-B

114-2-D-C

115-1-D-C

116-1-D-C*

117-1-J-C*

118-3-M-B

119-3-D-B

120-2-J-A

121-2-D-A

122-3-D-B

123-2-D-A

124-2-D-B

125-3-I-A

126-1-C-A

127-3-E-A

128-5-A-B

129L-5-J-B*

130-3-C-B

131-5-C-B

132-5-J-A

133-5-T-A

134L-5-E-A

CLOTHING: HATS & CAPS, SUITS, SHIRTS, MISC. APPAREL

A vast number of clothing buttons exist from the earliest button era through the 1930s. Many have excellent color and design, and most depict clothing for youngsters and men. During the 1930s, youngsters of radio or movie fame were often pictured on buttons for children's clothing. There is a nice variety of buttons in this category.

135-1-J-A

136-6-G-A

137-2-E-B

138-3-J-B

139-2-D-A

140-2-D-B

141-2-B-B

142-2-K-B

143-2-D-C

144-5-M-A

145-2-D-A

146-2-J-B

147-4-G-A

148-5-A-B

149-5-A-A

150-4-A-A

151-3-D-B

152-3-D-B

153-1-A-A

154L-7-N-A

155-2-D-C*

156-2-A-B

157-6-J-A

158L-5-E-A

159-5-E-A

160-1-N-A

161-6-E-A

162-2-E-A

163-2-K-B

164-1-D-D

165-5-J-A

166-3-Y-A

167-2-D-B

168-5-C-A

169-1-B-B

170-3-J-A

171-5-J-B

172-1-A-A

173-6-A-A

174-2-D-D

175-2-A-B

176-1-G-A*

177-1-A-A

178-2-H-A

179-3-D-B

180-3-D-B

181-2-D-C

182-1-D-B

183-2-A-A

184-2-D-B

185-3-E-A

CLOTHING: HOSIERY, SHOES, BOOTS, MISC. FOOTWEAR

This category offers an excellent assortment for the collector. Both child and adult shoes were advertised extensively by buttons, with a good number of nicely-designed and colorful examples. "Buster Brown" buttons were issued in great numbers and varieties, and several early Buster Brown variations are considered among the best advertising buttons. Hosiery and boots were not button-advertised as extensively as shoes, but still there is a nice assortment of clever or colorful examples for these products.

186-2-D-D   187-2-D-F   188-2-D-E   189-2-D-E

190-2-R-A*   191-2-D-C*   192-2-D-D*   193-1-B-C   194-1-B-C*   195-1-B-C*

196-3-D-B   197-3-D-B   198-4-D-B   199-4-E-C   200-4-N-B   201-4-J-C

202-2-D-B   203-2-D-B   204-2-D-B   205-2-D-B   206-2-D-B   207-2-D-B   208-2-D-B

209-2-D-B   210-2-D-B   211-2-D-B   212-2-D-B

213-2-D-B   214-2-D-B   215-1-B-C*

216-2-D-A

217-4-F-A

218-2-L-A

219-2-F-A

220-2-D-E

221-3-D-C

222-3-J-A

223-2-D-C

224-2-C-B

225-2-D-C

226-2-D-B

227-3-L-B

228-1-D-C

229-3-D-B*

230-2-R-A

231-1-J-A

232-2-J-B

233-6-I-A

234-2-D-C*

235-1-E-A

236-2-G-A

237-1-D-C

238L-5-D-A

239L-5-Q-A

240L-5-Q-A

241L-6-Q-B

242-2-D-C*

243-2-G-A

244-4-E-C   245-3-J-A   246-3-C-A   247-2-D-A*   248-1-B-B   249-2-J-C

250-3-D-B   251-5-C-A   252L-5-J-A   253L-1-A-B*   254-2-D-C   255-2-D-B

256-2-D-B   257-2-D-C   258-2-A-B   259-3-C-B   260-5-N-A   261-4-J-A

262-1-J-A   263-3-C-A   264-2-C-A   265-2-M-A   266-3-D-B

267-2-D-E

DEPARTMENT STORES, RETAILERS

Department store buttons frequently pictured the building exterior, particularly if the building was of considerable size. Buttons are known for many of the ''big name'' stores from 1900 into the 1930s including Marshall Field, Montgomery Ward, Wanamaker. The buildings were sometimes depicted in nice colors but hundreds of examples have simply the store name inscribed.

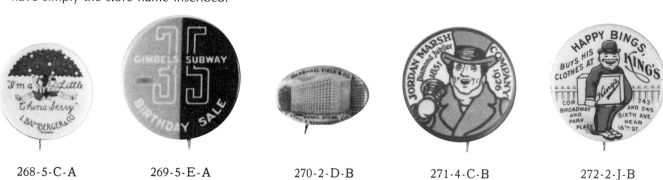

268-5-C-A   269-5-E-A   270-2-D-B   271-4-C-B   272-2-J-B

273-7-I-A   274-2-D-B*   275-2-D-B*   276-2-D-B   277-2-D-B

278-5-N-A   279-5-E-A   280-5-E-A   281-4-G-A

282-2-D-B   283-5-J-A   284-5-E-A   285-5-I-A   286-4-O-A

287-5-E-A   288-1-B-A   289-2-F-B*   290-2-C-A   291-5-A-A

FACTORIES, FACTORY EQUIPMENT, MISC. MANUFACTURING

Buttons depicting factories and equipment were frequently quite detailed but seldom brightly colored. This category offers a varied collectible opportunity.

292-2-H-A   293-3-E-A   294-2-G-A   295-1-A-A   296-2-D-C

297-1-J-B

298-1-B-A

299-2-T-A

300-3-G-A

301-1-B-B

302-2-A-A

303-2-A-A

304-2-A-A

305-2-A-A

306-2-C-C

307-2-D-B

308-2-B-A

309-2-J-A

FERTILIZER, SEEDS, GARDENING, FLOWERS, TREES

   The earth was rich and good, but fertilizer made it better. There is not a large assortment of early fertilizer buttons. Most examples either depicted a bag of the product or a perhaps-exaggerated illustration of its nutritional influence on crop growth. There are many examples of beautifully-colored flower buttons.

310-2-D-B

311-1-C-B

312-2-C-A

313-1-T-A

314-5-C-A

315-2-D-A

316-2-B-A

317-4-A-A*

318-1-D-E

319-1-A-B*

320-4-D-A

321-3-D-A

322-2-D-A

323-3-D-A

324-4-D-A

325-2-D-A   326-4-D-A   327-5-Y-A   328-3-Y-A   329-5-P-A   330-5-R-A   331L-5-C-A

FIREMEN, POLICEMEN

Since the beginning of buttons until the late 1940s the fireman, his acts of valor, and his equipment have been adulated with button depictions. Curiously, this adulation never spread to the policemen, whose depiction on an early button is quite rare. Firemen, nevertheless, are pictured on a number of early, extremely colorful and well-designed buttons depicting firefighting or blazing rescue missions. The various fire wagons and hand apparatus used by firemen over the years were invariably a source of community pride and were often button-pictured in conjunction with a local fair or homecoming celebrations.

332-1-D-C   333-1-D-C   334-2-D-C   335-2-D-C

336-1-D-C   337-1-D-C   338-2-F-B

339-2-B-C   340-1-A-B   341-2-D-B   342-1-A-B*

343-2-D-C   344-2-E-B   345-1-B-A   346-1-A-A   347-1-B-A

348-2-D-C   349-2-D-A   350-1-H-B   351-5-A-A   352-5-G-A

GROOMING AIDS, COSMETICS, BEAUTY PRODUCTS

One's appearance has always been the source of advertising fervor but, surprisingly, there are not a great number of buttons devoted to grooming products. Early examples, in particular, are quite rare.

353-1-G-A   354-3-D-A   355-5-G-A   356-5-G-A   357-5-G-A

358L-5-G-A   359L-5-I-A   360-6-O-A   361-5-R-A   362-6-I-A

GUNS, AMMUNITION, FIREARMS, PRODUCTS & EVENTS

Gunpowder and firearm buttons are one of the favorite collecting categories due to the excellent assortment of well-designed, extremely colorful examples from a number of early munitions manufacturers. Beautiful buttons related to field hunting and trap shooting were issued by Winchester, Peters, DuPont, and other arms companies to a lesser degree. Hunters and hunting dogs, hunting prey, and rifles, shotguns and ammunition are depicted either individually or in series.

363-2-D-D

364-2-A-C

365-2-D-D

366-2-A-B

367-2-D-E   368-2-E-C   369-2-C-F   370-1-C-C

371-3-D-G

372-3-D-E   373L-6-E-A

374-2-B-F*   375-2-D-D   376-2-D-E   377-2-D-E   378-2-D-D

379-2-D-D*   380-2-D-D*   381-2-D-D*   382-2-D-D   383-3-C-D   384-3-E-B

385-3-E-D   386-2-D-D   387-2-D-D   388-2-W-C   389-2-A-D   390-2-E-C

| 391-2-D-C | 392-2-D-C | 393-2-D-D | 394-2-D-D | 395-2-D-D | 396-2-D-D |

| 397-2-D-D | 398-2-D-D | 399-2-D-D | 400-2-D-D | 401-2-D-D | 402-2-D-D |

| 403-2-D-C | 404-2-D-C | 405-2-D-C | 406-2-D-C | 407-2-D-C | 408-2-D-D |

| 409-2-D-D | 410-2-D-D | 411-2-D-E | 412-2-R-E | 413-2-C-F* |

| 414-2-D-E | 415-2-D-E | 416-2-D-E | 417-2-E-D | 418-2-E-D | 419-2-E-D |

| 420-2-I-C | 421-2-I-C | 422-2-I-C | 423-2-I-C | 424-2-I-C | 425-2-R-C* |

| 426-1-A-B | 427-2-D-C | 428-2-C-D | 429-2-D-D | 430-2-C-D | 431-2-C-C |

432-3-C-I   433-3-C-F   434-3-C-F   435-3-C-F   436-3-C-E

437-3-D-F 438-3-D-F   439-3-D-E   440-2-C-B   441-2-J-C   442-2-J-C   443L-5-J-C*

HOME APPLIANCES, EQUIPMENT, FURNISHINGS, MUSICAL INTRUMENTS, RADIOS, PHONOGRAPHS, TV

Dozens of appliance manufacturers offered the housewife their wares with button advertising from the turn of the century through the 1930s. "Labor saving" improvements advanced from kitchen wood ranges to coal ranges to gas ranges; from ice boxes to gas and electric refrigerators; from washboards to manual wringer machines and from hand rug beaters to vacuum sweepers. Pianos, beds, furniture, radios and phonographs were advertised to some degree, but home decor buttons are scarce.

444-1-I-A   445-1-C-B   446-4-G-A   447-2-D-B   448-2-C-A

449-4-C-D   450-1-B-A   451-1-A-A   452-2-D-B   453-2-D-C

454-5-G-A   455-3-E-A   456-3-D-D   457L-5-Y-A   458-4-Y-B

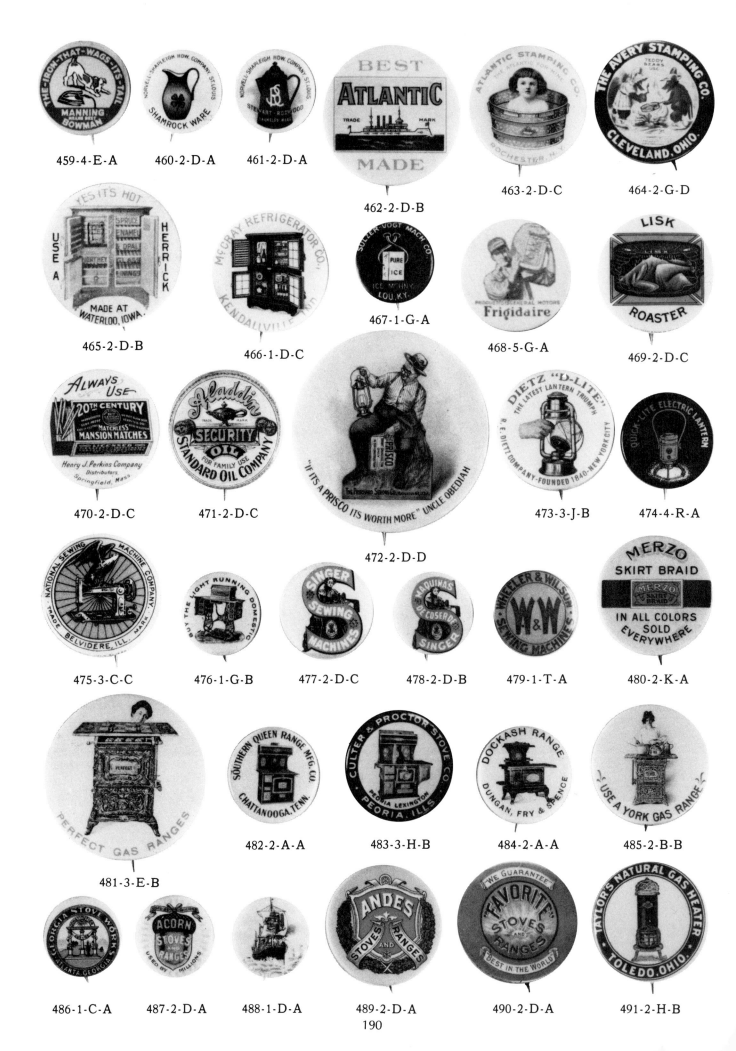

459-4-E-A

460-2-D-A

461-2-D-A

462-2-D-B

463-2-D-C

464-2-G-D

465-2-D-B

466-1-D-C

467-1-G-A

468-5-G-A

469-2-D-C

470-2-D-C

471-2-D-C

472-2-D-D

473-3-J-B

474-4-R-A

475-3-C-C

476-1-G-B

477-2-D-C

478-2-D-B

479-1-T-A

480-2-K-A

481-3-E-B

482-2-A-A

483-3-H-B

484-2-A-A

485-2-B-B

486-1-C-A

487-2-D-A

488-1-D-A

489-2-D-A

490-2-D-A

491-2-H-B

492-5-G-B

493-5-C-B

494-2-A-A

495-4-D-C

496-2-C-C*

497-2-D-C

498-2-D-C

499-2-D-B

502-2-D-F

500-1-D-B

501-1-I-B

503-2-D-E

504-2-D-A

505-2-C-A*

506-2-C-A

507-5-G-A

508-5-E-B

509-2-D-A

510-1-D-B

511-2-D-B

512-5-A-A

513-4-C-B

191

514-4-G-D

515-4-A-D*

516-1-D-D

524-2-A-E

517-2-D-F*

518-2-A-C

519-3-G-D

520-6-G-C

521-5-C-B

522-5-C-B

523-5-Y-C

525L-5-P-A

526-4-M-A

527-4-C-A

528-5-K-A

532-5-G-A

529-6-I-A

530-7-V-A

531-7-I-A

533-7-Q-A

534-7-N-A

535-7-M-A

536-7-J-A

HOTELS, RESTAURANTS

There is not a great number of buttons in this category, perhaps due to the transient nature of these businesses or the more practical gift of advertising matchbooks. Hotel buttons generally date from the pre-motel era. Several pre-1920 New York City hotel buttons offer free transportation and appear to be directed to newly-arrived tourists or immigrants.

537-3-G-A

538-1-A-A

539-3-L-A

540-1-B-A

541-1-B-A

542-3-G-A

543-3-T-A

544-3-E-A

545-3-I-A

546-3-E-A

547-5-C-A

548-3-L-A

549-1-A-A

550-2-D-A

551-1-A-A

552-5-C-A

INSURANCE

As a group, early insurance company buttons were done in nice detailed style and color, frequently in less than 1″ diameter. The eagle was a motif adopted by many companies, but there is an excellent assortment of other symbols.

553-3-D-A

554-2-E-A

555-2-J-A

556-2-D-A

557-2-D-A

558-2-D-A

559-2-D-B

560-2-D-A

561-2-D-A

562-2-D-A

563-1-C-A

564-2-D-B 565-2-C-A 566-3-C-A 567-3-C-B* 573-1-A-B

568-2-D-A 569-2-D-A 570-2-D-A 571-2-D-A 572-2-G-A

574-2-D-A 575-1-D-A 576-5-M-A 577-2-D-A 578-2-D-A 579-2-D-A 580-2-D-A*

MEDICINE & HEALTH, OPTICAL, DENTAL

There was no lack of imagination by early medicinal manufacturers or their button makers. Buttons advertised cures and remedies for bad blood, liver ailments, coughs and colds, to name a few. This is a very interesting category with several very nicely-done examples.

581-2-C-C 582-2-C-C 583-1-A-B 584-2-D-C 585-2-B-C

586-2-N-A 587-2-D-B 588-2-E-C 589-2-D-C 590-2-D-C

593-2-C-E* 591-2-J-C 592-1-A-A 594-2-I-B* 595-2-D-C 596-1-J-D

194

597-2-D-D

598-1-A-B

599-1-A-B

600-2-D-B

601-2-D-C

602-1-E-D

603-3-N-B

604-2-D-D

605-1-D-D*

606-1-B-C

607-4-E-B

608-2-G-A

609-3-I-A

610-3-N-E

611-2-D-B*

612-2-E-B*

613-4-L-A

614-5-A-A

615-5-A-A

616-5-A-A

617-5-C-A

618-2-D-A

619-2-D-A

620-1-A-A

621-2-D-B

622-5-G-A

623-1-H-B

624-1-A-B

625-2-G-A

626-3-D-B

NEWSPAPERS, MAGAZINES, PERIODICALS, BOOKS

A generous assortment of newspaper buttons exist, usually associated with sales efforts of the news carrier or upcoming youth-oriented features to appear in the newspaper. Although a few very colorful examples are known, buttons in this category are usually noted more for nice typographic qualities. A small assortment of buttons exists related to magazines and periodicals, but frequently these are related to youthful sellers of the magazine rather than the publication itself.

627-2-D-D*

628-2-D-C

629-2-E-B

630-2-L-B

631-1-D-B

632-1-D-B

633-4-C-A*

634-2-D-A

635-4-E-A

636-3-D-C*

637-2-C-D*

638-1-D-A

639-2-J-A

640-3-D-B

641-1-A-A

642-2-C-A

643-2-J-B

644-2-D-A

645L-5-I-B

646-3-A-A

647-1-G-A

648-5-N-A

649-5-I-A

650L-5-J-A

651-2-D-C*

652-2-C-C*

653-2-C-C*

654-9-D-B*

655-9-D-D*

656-9-A-B*

PHOTOGRAPHY, PRINTING, PHILATELIC

There are few photography button examples, and those that exist depict either the 'box' or 'folding' camera. A button illustrating film or photo accessories is rare. Buttons related to printing and stamps are more common, but rarely very colorful.

657-1-C-C

658-1-B-D

659-1-D-C

660-1-D-D

661-2-L-A

662-5-G-A

663-1-A-A

664-3-A-C

665-1-B-B

666-2-C-A

667-1-B-B*

668-3-C-B*

669-3-A-A*   670-3-D-A   671-2-A-A   672-5-E-A

673L-5-E-A   674-3-C-A   675-5-G-A   676-7-G-A

REAL ESTATE

Real estate buttons are not a prolific category, although there are several examples depicting early 'Western land' openings or offerings. Other real estate buttons exist, but few before the 1930s.

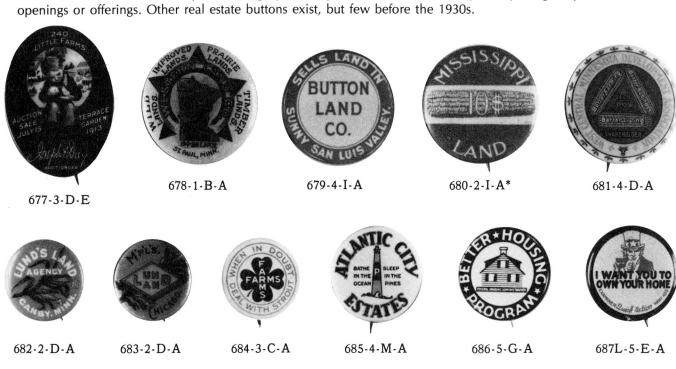

677-3-D-E   678-1-B-A   679-4-I-A   680-2-I-A*   681-4-D-A

682-2-D-A   683-2-D-A   684-3-C-A   685-4-M-A   686-5-G-A   687L-5-E-A

TEXTILES, MISC. PRODUCT SUBSTANCES

Buttons are not common for any particular product substance, but a limited assortment exists for textiles, leather and rubber.

688-2-D-B   689-3-E-A   690-3-G-A   691-4-E-A   692-2-I-A   693L-5-C-A

TOOLS, CUTLERY, WATCHES & TIMEPIECES

Early buttons in this category were directed toward the male buyer with an assortment of knives, saws and carpentry aids. Buttons for household serving cutlery or "feminine" kitchen tools are quite rare. Watch or watch-related buttons were produced in modest quantity, although frequently associated with the railroad industry. Several nice pocketwatch buttons exist, but a wristwatch or 'clock' button is rather scarce.

694-1-D-C* 695-1-A-B 696-2-D-A 697-2-F-A 698-2-J-A 699-2-D-A

700-2-D-A 701-2-C-A 702-2-J-C 703-2-D-A 704-2-C-D 705-2-J-A

706-2-C-B 707-2-I-A 708-3-D-A 709-3-C-A 710-2-C-A

711-1-C-A 712-2-R-B 713-2-J-A 714-3-D-A 715-3-A-A 716-2-A-C*

TOYS, DOLLS

Toys have long captured the imagination of youngsters and adults alike. Surprisingly, there were not a great number of toy buttons produced early in the century, although the number increased in the 1930s with the popularity of new character idols of movies and radio. Doll buttons particularly flourished during this time.

717-5-E-B* 718-5-D-C 719L-5-R-C* 720-5-R-B 721L-5-L-A 722-4-E-B

723-2-D-E*

724-4-C-C

725L-5-C-B

726-5-E-C

727-2-C-C

728-2-D-E

729-2-N-B

730-3-F-B

731-2-D-E

732-5-W-B

733-5-G-B

734L-5-K-B

735-5-A-B

736-5-A-B

737-5-C-B

738-5-E-B

739-5-J-B

740-5-G-B

741-3-C-C

742-5-G-C

743-5-D-B

744-5-R-B

745-5-R-B

746-5-R-B

747-5-J-C

748-5-A-B

749-5-A-D

750-5-C-C

751-5-R-C

752L-5-G-B

753-5-E-C

754-5-W-D

755-5-J-B

756-5-G-B

757-5-C-B

758-2-D-B

759-4-C-D

760-5-E-B   761-5-I-B   762-5-J-C   763-5-J-C   764-5-W-D

765-5-T-E   766-5-N-C*   767-5-B-C*   768-5-G-C*   769-5-A-C*

UTILITIES & FUELS: ELECTRIC, COAL, NATURAL GAS, POSTAL, TELEPHONE, TELEGRAPH

By the 1920s electricity in the home had become common, at least in urban areas. The "all-electric" home, however, was only a distant vision by a few, and electric appliances were steadily but slowly being developed for home use. Buttons in the 1920's-30's usually depicted the home's single basic need—the electric "lamp"(light bulb) or were aimed at the convenience of residential electricity. Telephone or telephone system buttons frequently depict a hand set or the early Bell System or "Independent" logo. Buttons advertised lighting and heating fuels, as well as the basic heat source for many early 20th century homes, coal.

770-5-C-B   771-4-G-B   772-2-D-B   773-5-L-A   774-2-E-B

775-5-M-A   776-5-M-A   777-5-H-A   778L-5-G-A   779-2-B-A   780-5-G-A*

781-5-E-B   782-5-Y-A*   783-5-A-A

784-5-E-A   785L-5-I-A   786-5-E-A   787-5-M-A

788-2-A-B

789-5-C-B

790-5-E-A

791-5-L-A

792-5-J-B

793-2-J-A

794-4-E-A

795-5-I-A

796-5-I-A

797-5-E-A

798-5-W-A

799-5-A-A

800-2-J-B

801-2-G-B

802-3-A-A

803-3-A-A

804-2-D-F

805-2-D-F

806-4-A-B

807-5-I-B*

808-2-G-C

809-3-G-B

810-3-G-B

811-3-G-A

812-4-G-A

813-5-G-A

202

814-2-A-A

815-3-E-A

816-3-E-A

817-3-E-A

818-3-E-A

819-3-E-A

820-3-E-A

821-2-E-A

822-5-G-B

823-3-E-A

824-2-A-B

825-2-D-E

826-2-D-B

827-1-J-B

828-4-E-A

829-4-E-B

830-5-K-A

831-1-D-C*

832-3-G-B

833-4-E-A

834-4-E-A

835-3-C-A

836-2-E-A

837-5-E-A

838-6-E-A

NOTES

X. PRODUCTS, SERVICES

BANKS, SAFES, SAVINGS
16. CANADIAN: "THOMAS WIBBY, TORONTO"
BUSINESS MACHINES
40. BACK PAPER: "THE MACHINE THAT DOES THINGS/DALTON/ADDING, LISTING AND CALCULATING MACH."
41. BACK PAPER: "FOR PARTICULARS REGARDING GOLDMAN'S ARITHMACHINE" AND COMPANY ADDRESS.
42. CANADIAN, THOS. WIBBY, TORONTO.
BUILDING PRODUCTS
57. SEEN W/VARIOUS SOLID COLOR BACKGROUNDS.
63. CANADIAN, THOMAS WIBBY, TORONTO.
68. BACK PAPER: "LACQUERET MAKES OLD FURNITURE, FLOORS AND WOODWORK LOOK LIKE NEW/STANDARD VARNISH WORKS/LONDON, NEW YORK, CHICAGO"
86. BACK PAPER HAS "CLEAN-UP BOOSTERS" TIPS AND "BE A CUB"
CLEANING AGENTS
112. BACK PAPER: "Many Beautiful Premiums are given for BEE SOAP WRAPPERS/MAIL ONE WRAPPER FOR 32-PAGE CATALOGUE/Read Directions on each wrapper."
116.-117. CANADIAN, "ADVERTISING NOVELTY MANUFACTURING CO.," TORONTO.
129. BACK INSCRIPTION: "A SUNDAY SHINE ALL THE TIME/CUB SHOE POLISH ONLY A DIME"
CLOTHING: HATS & CAPS, ETC.
155. CANADIAN, "ADVERTISING NOVELTY MANUFACTURING CO.," TORONTO.
176. TEXT RELATED TO SPANISH-AMERICAN WAR.
CLOTHING: HOSIERY, SHOES, ETC.
190.-195. BACK PAPER IN EACH W/EXCEPTION OF #193 FOR "THE BROWN SHOE CO., ST. LOUIS" MOST ALSO HAVE THE "5-STAR" LOGO.
215. BUSTER BROWN RESEMBLANCE IN CLOTHING, BUT NOT AN ASSOCIATED BUTTON.
229. BACK PAPER: "USE THIS PIN AS A BABY'S BROOCH" W/LOGO OF "BERLIN RUBBER MFG. CO."
234. BACK PAPER: "KALT ZIMMERS MFG. CO./CHILDREN'S SHOES/MILWAUKEE"
242. BACK PAPER: "FOR SALE BY ALL AMERICA SHOE SHOP, 620 OLIVE ST., ST. LOUIS, MO."
247. BACK PAPER: "TESS AND TED SCHOOL SHOES ARE MADE IN THE TWELVE BIG 'STAR BRAND' SHOE FACTORIES BY ROBERTS, JOHNSON & RAND SHOE COMPANY/ST. LOUIS"
253. EARLY LITHOGRAPHED METAL DIECUT.
DEPARTMENT STORES, RETAILERS
274. BACK PAPER: "SEND FOR OUR GENERAL CATALOGUE AND BUYERS' GUIDE/IT HAS 1,000 PAGES, 17,000 PICTURES AND GIVES YOU WHOLESALE PRICES ON 70,000 DIFFERENT THINGS. MONTGOMERY WARD & CO."
275. ON THE STORE FRONT IS "CROCKERY/LAMPS/GLASSWARE/HOUSE FURNISHING GOODS"
289. BACK PAPER: "The New Kind of Store/WANAMAKER/Originator."
FERTILIZERS, ETC.
317. ALSO SEEN LITHOGRAPHED METAL, C. 1930's.
319. CONTAINS ACTUAL SEEDS UNDER CLEAR CELLULOID. HAS LONG BRASS STICKPIN.
FIREMEN, POLICEMEN
342. BACK PAPER: "IN MEMORIAM/MERRIMAC ST. FIRE/FEB. 5TH, 1898"
GUNS, AMMUNITION, ETC.
374. ANNIE OAKLEY PICTURED.
379. BLACK RIM.
380. RED RIM.
381. BLACK W/WHITE TRIM RIM. SMALL 1897 COPYRIGHT AT BOTTOM OF PICTURE.
413. ANNIE OAKLEY PICTURED.
425. BRASS.

443. PICTURE INSCRIPTION: "SERVICE/QUALITY/WINCHESTER EXCLUSIVE AGENTS/THE WINCHESTER STORE"

HOME APPLIANCES, ETC.

496. BACK PAPER: "EVERY VANDERGRIFT ROTARY WASHER GUARANTEED SATISFACTORY OR MONEY REFUNDED. (ANY WRINGER CAN BE USED.)"

505. BACK PAPER: " 'CROWN' PIANOS AND ORGANS Made By GEO. P. BENT, CHICAGO, ILL./CATALOGUES FREE"

515. SOLID CELLULOID W/GROOVED DESIGN. "Columbia Phonograph Co." PAPER LABEL ON BACK W/MOUNTED PIN.

517. BACK PAPER: "VICTOR TALKING MACHINES/GOLD MEDAL 1901/MUSICAL INSTRUMENTS OF EVERY DESCRIPTION/THE R. WURLITZER CO./CINCINNATI, O."

INSURANCE

567. WHITEHEAD & HOAG 'CRYST-O-GLAS' DESIGN W/DIMENSIONAL REFLECTIVE BACKGROUND UNDER CELLULOID.

580. BACK PAPER: "American Mutual Aid Society/DETROIT, MICH./AGENTS WANTED"

MEDICINE & HEALTH, ETC.

593. 1" STRING TO RESEMBLE WAIST CORD IS ATTACHED ON THE BACK AND PASSES THROUGH HOLE IN THE FRONT.

594. "A ROARING SUCCESS" INSCRIBED AT ELEPHANT'S MOUTH.

605. CELLULOID COVER THAT WAS REMOVED FROM PRODUCT CONTAINER AND CONVERTED INTO A BUTTON.

611.-612. BACK PAPER: "MULFORD'S VACCINE ALWAYS TAKES. MULFORD'S ASEPTIC SHIELD PREVENTS SORE ARMS."

NEWSPAPERS, ETC.

627. ALSO SEEN IN 1¼" SIZE. VALUE B IN 1¼".

633. BACK PAPER: "THE AMERICAN BOY is the greatest Boy's Magazine in the world. 1000 illustrations, 400 pages a year. Costs $1.00 a year. THE SPRAGUE PUBLISHING CO. Detroit, Mich."

636. CANADIAN, THOS. WIBBY, TORONTO.

637. CHESTNUTS PICTURED AT THE TOP.

651. HOLE ON RIM FOR METAL CLICKER ATTACHMENT.

652.-653. FRANK BAUM ILLUSTRATIONS; BAUM AN EARLY 'WIZARD OF OZ' ILLUSTRATOR.

654.-656. MAURICE SENDAK ILLUSTRATIONS: #654 WAS USED BY A CHILDREN'S BOOK GROUP, CIRCA 1980; #655 WAS A HARPER & ROW PROMOTIONAL BUTTON; #656 WAS ISSUED IN 1982 TO PROMOTE CONNECTICUT LIBRARIES.

PHOTOGRAPHY, ETC.

667. EARLY 'X-RAY' PHOTOGRAPHY.

668.-669. ALOYS SENEFELDER, 'INVENTOR OF LITHOGRAPHY,' PICTURED.

REAL ESTATE

680. BACK PAPER: "Compliments/Martin Gauldin, Mgr. Land Dept./E.A. Cummings & Co./40 N. Dearborn St. CHICAGO"

TOOLS, ETC.

694. HOLE ON RIM FOR METAL CLICKER ATTACHMENT AND W/BACK PAPER WHITEHEAD & HOAG INSCRIPTION "DESIGN PATENTED DEC. 13, 1898"

716. REVOLVING DISC WHEEL TO DETERMINE TIMES AROUND THE WORLD.

TOYS, DOLLS

717. BACK PAPER: "I am an American and I play with only American-Made TOYS/That is why I am a member of this Club." A DEPRESSION-ERA BUTTON.

719. "LIONEL ENGINEERS CLUB" EMBOSSED BRASS BUTTON.

723. BACK PAPER: "SHERWOOD AUTO BOB Mfg'd by Sherwood Bros. Mfg. Co. Inc./Canastota, N.Y."

766.-769. BUTTONS FOR 'LOOK-ALIKE' DOLLS PATTERNED AFTER SHIRLEY TEMPLE.

UTILITIES & FUELS, ETC.

780. "BUY BULBS" REVERSED.

782. BACK PAPER: "Rochester Gas & Electric Corp."

807. "BELL TELEPHONE COMPANY OF CANADA"

831. BACK PAPER: "EL CAPITAN CHEWING GUM"

XI. SOCIAL CAUSES

AMERICANISM, PATRIOTISM, BUY AMERICAN

Patriotism buttons have emerged periodically over the years. "Buy American" was seen as one way of ending The Great Depression of the early 1930s and numerous buttons promoted this belief.

1-3-D-C 2-4-D-B 3-3-D-B 4-5-C-B 5-2-D-C 6-3-D-B

7-2-E-A 8-5-G-C 9L-5-I-B 10-5-E-B 11-5-F-B 12-5-G-B

13L-5-G-B 14-5-E-B 15-5-E-C 16-5-E-B 17-5-E-B 18-5-C-B 19-5-G-B

ANTI-ETHNIC, ETHNIC CARICATURES

Black citizens in the first third of the 20th century were occasionally subjected to caricature approaching ridicule on buttons and other mediums. Buttons deriding any other ethnic group are uncommon.

20-2-C-F 21-4-D-D 22-5-K-D 23-2-C-D* 24-5-A-D

25-3-D-A* 26-2-C-B* 27-4-E-D 28-4-F-D* 29-5-G-D*

CIVIL RIGHTS

Pre-1960's buttons advocating the rights of minorities are quite scarce, but flourished with the beginning and growth of the Black Movement. Civil rights buttons are unusual but do exist for other ethnic groups. Pre-1960 buttons with pictures of civil rights leaders are prized highly by collectors of this category.

30-3-B-E*   31-3-D-E*   32-3-D-E   33-4-A-E   34-4-C-C   35-5-A-E

36-5-A-C   37-7-E-B   38-8-A-B*   39-8-A-B   40-8-N-A

41-8-P-A*   42-9-C-A   43-9-E-A   44-8-A-A

ENVIRONMENT

Although there are isolated environmental buttons before the 1960's, this decade prompted an outpouring of buttons reflecting new public awareness and concern on this issue. Pollution and nuclear energy are the most common subjects of modern day environment buttons.

45-9-T-A*   46-9-T-A*   47-9-J-A   48-9-C-A

NO MORE HARRISBURGS

Washington May 6

49-9-A-A

50-9-C-A*

NO MORE HARRISBURGS!

MAY 6 MARCH ON WASHINGTON
May 6th Coalition

51-9-M-A

EQUAL RIGHTS, WOMEN'S SUFFRAGE

The right of women to vote, presented unsuccessfully to Congress since the late 1860's, finally gained momentum in the 1900's and became reality in 1920. A few pre-1920 buttons have a clever design, but most simply had a brief ''Votes for Women'' inscription without illustration.

52-4-G-C

53L-4-K-D

54-2-R-B

55-3-G-C

56-3-C-E

57L-5-G-B

58-5-C-B

HUMANITARIAN AGENCIES, RELIEF

The American desire to help his fellow man has created hundreds of causes since the early days of the button. Many buttons in this category are related to sympathies with the needs of people in foreign countries, although there are also a number of examples associated with domestic causes.

59-5-G-B

60-5-A-B

61L-5-G-B

62-5-C-C

63-6-A-B

64-6-A-D

65-5-E-B

66-6-E-B

67-6-E-B

68-5-A-B

69-4-H-B

70-5-J-B

71-2-A-B

72-2-D-B

73-3-D-B

74-3-D-B

75-3-D-B

76-3-J-B

208

LABOR, UNIONISM

Labor has rarely been staunch friends with management, and the labor cause for better working conditions has been a frequent subject of buttons. Many early buttons are quite beautifully done and attest simply to the pride of union organization or membership. Anti-labor buttons, although existing, are much fewer and a pure "pro-management" button is rare.

77-2-D-D

78-2-D-C

79-2-C-B

80-6-C-B

81-2-D-C

82L-4-F-F

83-2-A-D

84-4-A-D

85-4-C-C

86-5-E-C

87L-5-G-B

88-3-K-D

89-6-E-B

90L-6-A-C

91L-6-C-B

92-9-A-A

NATIONAL RECOVERY ADMINISTRATION

"NRA" was the acronym for the National Recovery Administration, a federal agency created in 1933 to combat the economic ravages of the Great Depression. The act intruded the federal government into private business and was judged unconstitutional and abolished January 1, 1936. In the interim, the public was urged to boycott businesses operating without the NRA "Blue Eagle" emblem which indicated support of the act. As a result, many NRA buttons with a product or service inscription were issued.

93-5-M-B

94-5-E-B

95-5-E-B

96-5-E-B

97-5-E-B

PEACE

Peace, never to be achieved through the history of mankind, nevertheless has been given a hopeful nudge from time to time by buttons from peace-aspiring individuals, groups or movements. Examples of peace buttons are known from the late 1890's to the present day and have flourished particularly in times when the country was on the verge of war.

98-3-D-C*   99L-5-G-B   100-5-G-B   101-6-E-B   102-6-F-C   103-6-E-B

104-5-E-B   105-6-E-B   106-6-E-B   107L-6-I-B   108-6-E-B   109-5-E-B   110-6-G-B

PROHIBITION, ANTI-TOBACCO

"Demon Rum" was conquered—legislatively, if not realistically—in 1920 with the enactment a year before of the 18th amendment. Several very nicely designed and colored temperance buttons preceded the enactment by as much as 20 years. Following enactment, most buttons were anti-prohibition—a sentiment borne out by the repeal of the amendment in 1933. Several clever cartoon or caricature buttons resulted from America's 13-year dilemma over "wet" or "dry." Buttons picturing early temperance leaders such as Carrie Nation are especially prized. Anti-tobacco proponents have existed from Colonial times to the present. Several anti-cigarette buttons have appeared over the years but other tobacco uses have seemingly escaped with no known anti-buttons.

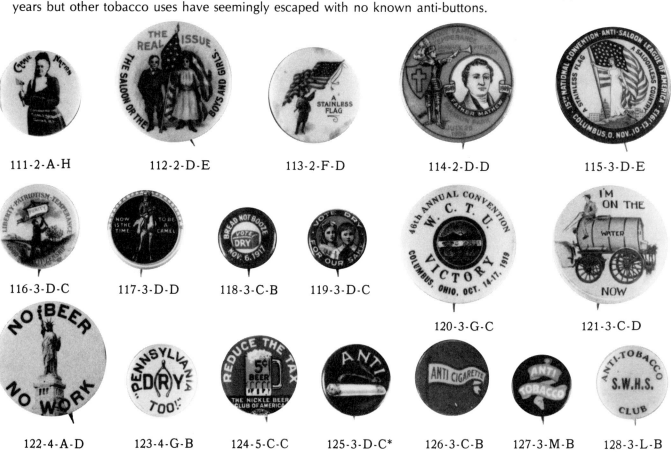

111-2-A-H   112-2-D-E   113-2-F-D   114-2-D-D   115-3-D-E

116-3-D-C   117-3-D-D   118-3-C-B   119-3-D-C   120-3-G-C   121-3-C-D

122-4-A-D   123-4-G-B   124-5-C-C   125-3-D-C*   126-3-C-B   127-3-M-B   128-3-L-B

210

NOTES

XI. SOCIAL CAUSES

ANTI-ETHNIC, ETHNIC CARICATURES
> 23. BLACK CARICATURE, CIRCA 1900. NO INSCRIPTION.
> 25. BACK PAPER: "TOKIO CIGARETTE." FROM A LARGE SET of CIGARETTE PREMIUM BUTTONS BY FAMOUS CARTOONISTS. THIS ONE IS BY "TAD" (THOMAS A. DORGAN). SEE *BUTTONS IN SETS*, PAGE 7.
> 26. BACK PAPER: "AMERICAN PEPSIN GUM CO." PART OF A SET.
> 28. BACK PAPER: "KLANHAVEN/THE ORPHAN HOME FOR CHILDREN/Should be on the Heart of Every/KLANSWOMAN AND KLANSMAN/Let us have a living Monument to the Cause/Send your gift to P.O.Box 411, Pittsburgh, Pa." ORIGINALLY CAME WITH A METAL BELL ATTACHED.
> 29. PICTURES FATHER COUGHLIN.

CIVIL RIGHTS
> 30. PICTURES LINCOLN AND FREDERICK DOUGLASS.
> 31. PICTURES FREDERICK DOUGLASS.
> 38. ISSUED BY STUDENT NON-VIOLENT CO-ORDINATING COMMITTEE.
> 41. INSCRIBED ON EDGE: "COPYRIGHT©1968 INDEPENDENT SOCIALIST CLUB/LISA LYONS." PART OF A SET.

ENVIRONMENT
> 45.-46. INSCRIBED ON EDGE: "ZPG, 367 State St. Los Altos, Calif."
> 50. INSCRIBED ON EDGE: "Mobilization For Survival, 1213 Race St. Phila. Pa. 19107."

PEACE
> 98. BACK PAPER: "ORDER FROM THE WORLD PEACE PROPAGANDA, CONNEAUT, OHIO/COPYRIGHTED"

PROHIBITION, ANTI-TOBACCO
> 125. BACK PAPER: "PRESBYTERIAN BOARD of TEMPERANCE/Pittsburgh, Pa."

XII. SPORTS

Sporting events and individual sport personalities are the subject of thousands of buttons from the late 1890's until the present day. The majority of sports buttons are baseball-associated with fewer, but still ample, quantities of buttons related to boxing, football, hockey, basketball plus public participation sports of bowling, golf, hunting and fishing. Early sports buttons are almost exclusively baseball-related, although there are several turn-of-the-century buttons depicting football teams and prizefighters. Sports buttons are a vast category, and are covered extensively in *Non-Paper Sports Collectibles* by Ted Hake and Roger Steckler, available from Hake's Americana & Collectibles.

BASEBALL

A virtually endless assortment of baseball buttons exists. Early buttons were often issued in sets picturing individual players from the different major league teams of the time. Such buttons were usually premiums given with chewing gum, bread and other common food products. Buttons were issued both in celluloid and lithographed metal, and baseball players are still depicted in team sets in modern times.

1-2-A-G	2-2-J-F	3-3-A-E	4-5-E-D	5-5-A-D	6L-5-D-B*
7-5-A-D	8L-5-J-D	9-5-L-D	10-6-A-D	11-6-A-B	
12-6-A-E	13-6-C-D	14-6-L-D	15-7-A-C		
16-6-J-D	17L-8-E-D	18-8-N-A	19L-8-H-A*	20L-8-H-A*	21L-8-J-A*

BASKETBALL

There is not a large number of basketball buttons although the sport has existed in America since the early 1890's. "Team Player" button series have emerged in recent years for professional teams, but early basketball buttons picturing individual players at any competition level are quite rare. Several early "team" buttons exist, but often the team is not adequately identified.

| 22-2-B-D | 23L-6-M-C | 24-6-R-C | 25L-7-E-D | 26L-6-G-B* | 27L-6-N-B* |

BOWLING

Bowling buttons were usually issued to commemorate a major tournament, professional or amateur, in metropolitan cities. A lesser number of buttons were issued for purely local purposes such as bowling alley promotion. Bowling motifs were used occasionally in product advertising buttons.

28-2-H-D

29-2-J-D

30-2-N-D

31-2-A-C

32-2-H-C

33-6-E-B

34-5-E-B

35L-5-E-D

BOXING

A good historical record of prizefight heroes exists on buttons from the late 1890's until the present, although quantities have perhaps waned somewhat since the early 1950's and closed-circuit performances. More buttons have been issued for the more popular weight classification boxers—heavyweights through middleweights—and boxing buttons are seldom colorful.

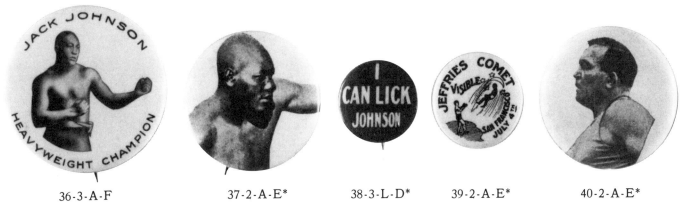

36-3-A-F

37-2-A-E*

38-3-L-D*

39-2-A-E*

40-2-A-E*

41-1-F-D*   42-1-A-D*   43-1-A-C*   44-1-A-C*   45-2-B-C   46-2-B-C

47-2-A-D   48-2-A-E*   49-5-B-D   50-5-K-C   51-6-I-C

52-6-A-C   53-6-A-D   54-6-A-B*   55-7-A-C   56-8-A-B

FISHING

Few buttons were ever issued for promotion of this sport, but a nice assortment exists of license buttons from various states. These usually date from the 1920s-1950s, before the wide use of paper licenses.

57-1-D-D   58-2-G-B   59-1-F-C   60-2-B-C   61-4-L-B

62-4-C-B   63-6-Y-A   64-6-B-B   65L-6-C-B

214

FOOTBALL

Football players did not enjoy the same button popularity as their baseball counterparts in the early days, although football series buttons have increased in recent decades with the growth of televised professional football. College football buttons are generally limited to "homecoming" or "big game" issues and these are often nicely-designed. Hundreds of buttons have been issued over the years for high school games. Early football buttons picturing an individual player at any level of competition are quite scarce.

66-2-B-D*

67-2-D-D*

68-5-J-E*

69-5-J-C

70-4-J-B

71-5-N-A

72-3-Y-C

73-5-N-A

74-5-A-C

75-5-A-D

76-5-N-C*

77-6-N-B

78-7-N-A

79-7-X-A*

80-7-N-A*

81-5-K-A

82-5-C-B

83-5-N-B

84-8-A-B

85-7-R-A

86-7-L-A

87-8-J-A

GOLF

Golf-related buttons are uncommon, possibly due to mass appeal of the sport occuring only in recent years. Few golfers are pictured on buttons, although there are a number of general tournament-issued buttons in the last two decades.

88-5-A-D

89-5-C-B

90-5-C-B

91-5-C-B

HORSE RACING

Champion race horses have been pictured on buttons sporadically since the 1890s although the total is not large. A colorful early "jockey" series was a premium by gum and cigarette manufacturers. Several commemorative buttons have resulted from the Kentucky Derby and other major annual races. Harness race buttons are less common.

92-1-D-B*

93-2-C-B

94-2-A-C

95-2-G-C

96-2-B-B*

97-2-B-C

98-2-B-B

99-2-B-C

100-2-B-B*

101L-5-K-B

102-5-K-A

103-7-A-A

104L-7-C-B

105-9-C-A

106-9-C-A

107L-9-L-A

108L-9-L-A

HUNTING

A nice assortment of ''sporting club/association'' buttons have appeared over the years and a few are quite nicely-designed or colored. ''Hunting license'' buttons were issued mostly in the 1920s-1950s but are not as common as fishing license buttons. A large number of hunting-related buttons were issued by arms and munitions manufacturers (see ''Guns, Ammunition'' section of Category X, ''Products, Services.'')

109-1-D-D

110-4-H-A

111-5-M-A

112-6-C-D*

MARBLE SHOOTING

Marble shooting was a major preoccupation of youth in simpler times. Championship tournaments were held to determine local or state winners, and a nice series of early 1930s annual buttons were issued in Pennsylvania to commemorate this particular tournament and its newspaper sponsor. Other marble shooting buttons are quite rare.

113-4-H-B

114-4-C-B

115-5-H-B

116-5-C-B

117-5-A-B

118L-5-I-B

119-5-A-B

OLYMPICS

Buttons have been issued as Olympic commemoratives although there is not a large total number. In earlier years, the button was usually associated with a product endorsement. Several colorful and nicely-designed buttons have resulted from more recent Olympic years but still not in large quantity.

120-4-E-B   121L-4-E-B   122-4-E-B

124-5-G-E

125-5-E-B

123-5-L-F

126-5-I-B

127-5-E-C

218

SPORTS MISC.

Minor sports, in terms of participant numbers, have prompted only a few buttons although it is doubtful if any sport has escaped button use entirely. Examples are known for swimming, track and field events, fox chases, yo-yo tournaments, skiing, ice skating, polo, billiards, log rolling, car and boat racing and others.

128-4-A-E*

129-7-A-C

130L-7-D-C

131-7-G-B

132-6-G-C

133-6-G-A

134-7-G-A

135-5-I-C

136-5-C-B

137-4-E-C

138-5-R-C

139-4-E-B

140-7-E-B

141-6-L-A

142-5-Y-B

143-5-N-B

144-7-E-B

145-2-B-B

146-5-G-A

147-4-M-E*

148-4-B-D

149-5-A-B

150-5-E-A

151-5-C-B

152-5-G-A

153-5-A-B

154-2-H-C

155-2-E-C

156-2-B-C

157-5-C-B

158-8-R-B

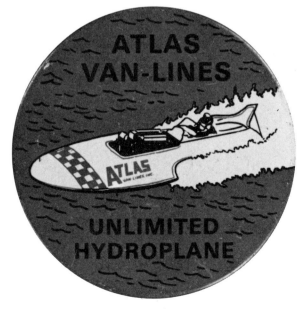

159L-8-F-B

NOTES

XII. SPORTS

BASEBALL

      6. PART OF A SET. SEE *NON-PAPER SPORTS COLLECTIBLES,* PAGES 16-18.

    19. PART OF A SET. SEE *NON-PAPER SPORTS COLLECTIBLES,* PAGES 10-11.

    20. PART OF A SET. SEE *NON-PAPER SPORTS COLLECTIBLES,* PAGE 20.

    21. PART OF A SET. SEE *NON-PAPER SPORTS COLLECTIBLES,* PAGE 20.

BASKETBALL

    26.-27. PART OF A SET. SEE *NON-PAPER SPORTS COLLECTIBLES,* PAGE 93.

BOXING

    37. JACK JOHNSON, 1910. MATCHES #40.

    38. BACK PAPER: "OBAK CIGARETTES" CIRCA 1910.

    39. PRE-FIGHT BUTTON DEPICTS JEFFRIES KNOCKING JOHNSON INTO OUTER SPACE, BUT ACTUALLY JOHNSON WON IN FIFTEEN ROUNDS.

    40. JAMES J. JEFFRIES, 1910. MATCHES #37.

    41. ROBERT L. FITZSIMMONS, CIRCA 1897.

    42. JAMES J. CORBETT AND ROBERT L. FITZSIMMONS, 1897.

    43. ROBERT L. FITZSIMMONS, 1897. "HIGH ADMIRAL CIGARETTES" ON EDGE.

    44. MATCHES #43. UNIDENTIFIED BOXER. THE BUTTON IS FROM 1897 AND JACK JOHNSON'S PROFESSIONAL CAREER DID NOT BEGIN UNTIL 1899.

    48. THERE IS A MATCHING "GENE TUNNEY".

    54. PART OF A SET. SEE *NON-PAPER SPORTS COLLECTIBLES,* PAGE 99.

FOOTBALL

    66. HAS ORANGE AND BLACK RIBBONS ATTACHED. CIRCA 1900.

    67. ALTHOUGH IN COLOR, APPEARS TO BE A MATE TO #66. POSSIBLY A UNIVERSITY OF PENNSYLVANIA BUTTON AS THE RIM IS RED AND BLUE. THE TIGER IS BW/YELLOW WITH A RED MOUTH. HIS TAIL IS IN THE BEAK OF A BW EAGLE.

    68. HAS DIECUT BRASS HANGER AT TOP DEPICTING AN INDIAN IN A CANOE. THE CANOE IS INSCRIBED "IMP'D O.R.M." (IMPROVED ORDER OF REDMEN-A FRATERNAL ORGANIZATION) WITH "FREEDOM FRIENDSHIP & CHARITY" BELOW. THE ONLY KNOWN BUTTON PICTURING JIM THORPE.

    76. ONE OF A SERIES OF "IOWA HOMECOMING" BUTTONS.

    79.-80. PART OF A SET. SEE *NON-PAPER SPORTS COLLECTIBLES,* PAGE 107.

HORSE RACING

    92. PART OF A SET. SEE *BUTTONS IN SETS,* PAGE 56.

    96. INSCRIBED: "THE ABBOT 2:03¼" (HELD ONE MILE TROTTING RECORD IN 1900).

   100. OWNER OF DAN PATCH.

HUNTING

   112. PART OF A SERIES. ALSO SEE SECTION I, #58.

SPORTS, MISC.

   128. WEARING BELT INSCRIBED: "WORLD'S CHAMPION WRESTLER." JOE STECHER, FAMOUS FOR HIS "SCISSORS HOLD," WON THE WORLD'S HEAVYWEIGHT CHAMPIONSHIP FROM CHARLES CUTLER AT OMAHA, NEBRASKA, CIRCA 1920's.

   147. "OFFICIAL" 1928 SOUVENIR BUTTON OF L.A. to N.Y. RACE WITH 199 ENTRANTS WON BY NINETEEN YEAR OLD ANDREW PAYNE OF OKLAHOMA IN 573 HOURS, FOUR MINUTES AND THIRTY-FOUR SECONDS.

XIII. TRANSPORTATION

BUGGIES, CARRIAGES, HORSE-DRAWN VEHICLES

Although U.S. carriage manufacturers flourished long before the introducing of advertising buttons, buggies were still the nation's leading form of family transportation well into the early 1900's until the eventual acceptance of the "horseless carriage." Buggy and carriage builders were legion and many advertised their product on a button, a few quite beautifully. A beautiful button, perhaps, was considered an advantage for a product which otherwise had a very similar appearance to all other market competitors.

1-2-J-D*	2-2-D-D	3-2-D-D	4-1-B-D

5-2-C-C	6-2-C-C	7-2-C-C	8-2-D-D	9-2-D-D

10-2-D-E	11-2-G-D	12-2-D-E	13-2-D-D*	14-2-D-D*	15-1-B-D

16-2-J-C	17-1-F-C*	18-2-D-C	19-2-D-B	20-2-F-B*

21-2-H-D 22-2-D-D 23-2-C-D 24-2-E-C

25-2-D-D 26-2-E-B 27-2-G-C* 28-1-H-C 29-1-D-C 30-2-D-D

BICYCLES: COMPANIES, BICYCLISTS, RACES & EVENTS, PRODUCTS

Although the popularity of bicycles remains to the present day, there is no parallel to the avid mass enjoyment the two-wheeler provided in the late 1890's and into the early 20th century. The bicycle was the sole means of short distance personal transportation without the expense of a horse and before the emergence of the automobile. There were dozens, perhaps hundreds of bicycle and bicycle accessories manufactured and many chose the button or the celluloid stud as an advertising medium. Many interesting designs emerged to promote different manufacturers.

31-1-E-D 32-1-A-D* 33-1-X-B 34-1-D-B 35-1-M-A

36-1-D-B 37-1-D-D 38-1-J-B* 39-1-D-B 40-1-L-A 41-5-C-C

42-1-G-A 43-1-K-B 44-1-D-B 45-1-D-B 46-2-E-D

47-1-D-C   48-1-D-D*   49-1-G-B   50-1-D-D   51-1-D-B   52-1-J-B

53-2-J-B   54-1-D-B   55-2-D-C   56-1-D-B   57-1-C-C   58-1-D-B

59-1-C-B   60-1-D-D*   61-1-G-A   62-1-A-B   63-1-E-B   64-1-G-A

65-1-G-A   66-1-G-A   67-1-C-D   68-1-F-B   69-1-G-A   70-1-G-A

71-1-D-B   73-1-D-B   74-1-C-B   75-1-M-A   76-1-M-A

72-1-C-C

77-1-D-D   78-1-D-B*   79-1-A-A   80-1-J-A   81-1-G-C   82-1-M-A

83-1-D-B 84-1-D-C 85-1-F-B

86-1-M-C

87-1-G-C

88-1-D-D 89-1-G-A 90-1-D-B

91-1-E-A

92-1-G-B

93-1-E-C 94-1-B-C 95-1-B-C 96-1-A-B

97-1-C-D* 98-1-F-D 99-1-F-C 100-1-C-D 101-1-B-D

102-1-A-D 103-1-A-C 104-1-B-D 105-1-E-C 106-1-G-C

107-1-E-C 108-1-D-C 109-1-A-C 110-1-D-C 111-1-L-A

112-2-D-B   113-3-D-B   114-3-D-B   115-3-D-D*   116-2-D-C

117-1-G-B   118-1-A-A*   119-1-A-A*   120-1-A-A*   121-1-A-A*

MOTORCYCLES

With the introduction of the internal combustion engine, motorcycles were a logical and quick next step from the popular bicycle. Early motorcycle manufacturers that advertised with buttons included Armac, Yale, and Merkel. Several nice 1920's and 1930's buttons were issued by the Harley-Davidson and Indian companies. Most buttons that depicted the product itself usually featured the "lightweight" cycle; buttons for the classic large motorcycles of the late 30's and 40's are quite scarce.

122-3-J-D   123-3-G-D   124-3-I-D   125-3-A-D

126-3-A-D   127-3-D-C   128-2-D-C   129-2-E-D   130-2-D-C

131-3-C-C   132-3-C-C   133-3-C-D   134-2-E-B   135-2-D-C   136-2-A-D

137-2-D-D   138-2-G-D   139-2-A-D   140-3-G-B

RAILROADS

By the turn of the century, the railroads had reached every state of the union, and by 1910 rail service spanned the nation. Rail service is said to have peaked about 1916 with more than 254,000 miles of lines. Buttons were used by several railroad lines in the promotion of new land development in the Western states and, to some extent, railroad tours. There were many buttons issued for various rail ''Brotherhood'' lodge and union purposes. Some early buttons with smoke-blowing coal engines are quite colorful. Railroad buttons began to wane after World War II along with the industry itself.

141-2-D-D   142-1-D-C   143-3-D-C   144-2-H-B   145-1-A-C

146-1-D-D   147-2-E-C   148-2-C-B   149-4-D-B

150-2-D-C   151-3-C-C*   152-4-C-C   153-2-A-B

154-5-A-C*   155-5-C-C   156-6-E-B

157-4-C-A   158-2-I-A   159-2-J-A*   160-4-K-A   161-5-G-A   162-4-E-A

163-6-E-C

164-2-C-B

165-5-J-A

166-3-C-A

167-2-C-B*

168-3-Y-B

169-3-X-C*

170-2-J-B

171-3-D-B*

172-2-A-B

173-2-A-A

174-2-K-B

175-2-D-C

176-5-R-C

177-6-E-A

178-7-C-B

179-5-Y-A

180-5-N-A*

181-5-I-A

182-7-C-A

SUBWAYS & TROLLEYS

By the turn of the century, the railroads had opened "long lines" between most major metropolitan areas, at least in the eastern United States. The development of underground subway transportation began in the larger cities (Boston's was completed in 1895, New York's in 1904) and would continue for several decades. The first trackless trolley system with two auto buses began on the West Coast in 1910 by the Los Angeles Pacific Electric Railway Co. No matter what conveniences resulted from subways and trolleys, dissatisfaction with fares, comfort and timeliness are the dominate button theme.

183-2-A-D

184-2-D-B

185-2-G-B

186-2-E-A

187-2-G-A

188-1-A-A

189-2-G-A

190-2-D-D*

191-1-J-D

192-2-H-C

193-2-A-B

194-3-C-B

195-1-D-D

196-2-C-B

197-2-G-A

198-2-I-A

199L-5-C-A

200-2-K-B

201-2-D-C

202-2-D-C

203-2-D-C

204-2-D-C

SHIPS, BOATS, MARINE-RELATED

Until commercial trans-ocean air flights began in the 1940's, the majestic seagoing ocean liners were the only transportation between continents (and, in many cases, across large lakes of the United States). Several beautiful buttons and numerous black/white buttons from shipping lines promoted foreign and domestic water travel. The flag standard of the various lines was also a common theme. Most major ocean liners are represented by a button although, ironically, a *Titanic* button has never been seen. Representations of early warships are depicted on several button sets or series. Early yacht races prompted a series of "cup winners" buttons and several beautiful individual examples.

205-1-B-D

206-1-D-B

207-2-C-D

208-1-B-C

209-3-J-C

210-3-D-C

211-1-D-A*

212-3-D-D

213-3-D-C

214-3-D-A

215-3-D-A

216-2-D-D

217-2-A-B

218-3-I-A

219-2-C-A

220-2-C-A

221-1-D-B

222-3-D-A

223-3-G-A*

224-2-G-B

225-2-D-D

226-2-J-B

227-1-E-B

228-3-J-B

229-5-A-A

230-5-A-A

231-1-F-B

232-3-C-B

233-1-E-A

234-2-B-B

235-2-C-B

236-3-G-A

237-1-D-A*

238-1-B-A

239-2-D-C

240-2-D-C

241-2-D-C

242-2-D-B

AUTOMOTIVE: RACES & SHOWS, TOURS, PRODUCTS, FUELS

Once the automobile established itself as more than a fool's pastime, competitive and commercial uses flourished. Buttons were widely used at auto shows and to promote tires, oil and gasoline and auto accessories.

243-2-I-D

244-2-Q-E

245-3-A-B

246-4-I-B

247-3-I-C

248-3-G-A

249L-5-M-A

251-6-A-B*

252-5-C-C

250-5-C-C*

254-3-A-A

255L-5-H-A*

256-6-E-A

253-5-E-A

257-2-J-B

258-2-D-C

259-3-D-E

260-4-J-B

261-2-C-C

262-4-A-B

263-2-E-A

264-2-O-A

265-2-G-A

266-3-G-A

267-5-Y-A

232

268-2-D-D

269-3-M-A

270-1-B-C

271-2-D-C

272-2-G-C

273-2-D-D

274-2-D-D

275-2-C-C

276-4-N-B*

277-5-G-B

278-2-M-B

279-2-N-B

280-2-C-C

281-4-N-B

282L-5-G-A

283-2-C-B

284L-5-C-A

285L-5-F-A*

286-6-C-A*

287-6-E-A

288-6-E-A*

289-3-D-A

290-3-E-B

291L-5-J-A

292L-5-J-A

293-5-G-A

294-4-C-B

295-2-D-C

296-2-A-C

297L-3-D-B

298-3-D-A*

299-2-D-B

300-2-D-B

301-3-D-A*

302-3-Y-B

AUTOMOTIVE: COMPANIES & MAKERS

Whether powered by steam, "stove gasoline" or electricity, the horseless carriage began to rule the roads in the first decade of the 1900's. The Duryea Motor Wagon Company is generally considered to be the first auto manufacturer (and advertiser) in the 1890's, although at least one other company—Haynes—claimed on their buttons the distinction of "America's First Car." Other now-scarce, early buttons were issued for "The Steam Car," "The Montgomery Ward Electric Horseless Carriage" and the "Detroit Electric." By the 1930's many better-known (and lesser-known, short-lived) automakers were advertising their vehicles by buttons. Included in the more successful manufacturers were Ford, Reo, Velie, Durant, Pierce-Arrow, Cadillac, Overland, Maxwell and Buick.

AUTOS CIRCA 1900-1920'S

303-1-G-E

304-1-B-E

305-2-D-E*

306-2-A-E

307-3-H-E

308-3-E-E

309-2-R-B

310-3-A-C

311-4-C-A*

234

312-3-D-F

313-3-N-C

314-3-A-C

315-3-A-B

316-2-E-F

317-2-E-B

318-2-E-B*

319-4-G-B

320-3-A-F

321-4-I-B

322-3-C-C

323-3-C-C

324-3-C-B

325-3-G-B

326-3-A-D

327-3-A-D

328-4-G-B

329-4-O-B

330-2-A-B

331L-4-E-A*

332-3-A-E

333-4-C-B

334-4-G-E

335-3-A-D

336-4-G-B

337-4-E-B

338-3-J-D

339-3-J-E

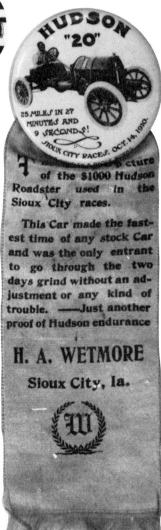

340-2-A-F

235

341-3-M-C

342-4-I-B

343-2-A-E

344-2-A-E

345-2-D-F

346-2-E-B

347-2-A-B

348-3-D-C

349-2-J-D

350-2-D-F

351-3-C-C

352-2-E-C

353-2-A-D

354L-4-N-A

355-2-I-E

356-3-D-A

357-3-G-C

358-3-E-C

359-4-A-B

360-4-E-C

361L-4-O-B*

362-2-D-B

363-4-G-E

236

364-3-H-C

365-3-I-B

366-3-E-C

367-4-E-C

368-3-E-B

369-4-H-A

370-3-C-B

371-3-D-B

372-3-D-B

373-2-A-D

374-2-B-D

375-2-A-D

376-2-C-B

378-2-D-G

377-4-I-A

380-3-C-B

379-2-C-F

381-2-A-A

382-4-C-C

383-4-M-C

384-2-J-C

385-5-L-D

386-5-A-E

387-5-G-A

391-5-J-D*

388L-5-G-B

389L-5-I-B

390L-5-E-B

392-5-I-C

393L-6-E-C

394L-6-E-B

395L-6-E-B

396L-6-E-B

397-6-G-B

398-6-I-B

399-6-I-B

400-5-C-D

401L-5-G-B

402-5-G-B

403-5-G-B

404-5-G-B

405-5-I-D

406L-5-M-C

407L-5-M-B

408L-5-A-B

409L-5-E-B

410L-5-D-B

411L-5-O-B

412L-5-E-B

413L-6-M-B

414L-6-D-B

415L-6-E-B

416L-6-D-B

417L-6-E-B

418L-6-E-B

419-5-D-C

420-5-N-B

421L-7-N-B

422L-7-G-B

423L-7-G-B

424L-7-G-B

425L-5-M-B

426-6-I-B

428-5-R-C*

427-6-Y-B

429L-6-I-B

430L-6-G-B

431L-6-G-B

432L-6-N-B

433-5-C-C

434L-5-E-A

435L-5-E-C

436L-5-D-B

437L-5-M-B

438L-5-D-B

439L-5-D-B

440-5-R-C*

441-6-G-D

442L-6-G-B

443-6-G-D*

444-6-G-B

445L-6-E-B

446L-6-E-B

447-5-G-B

448L-6-N-C

449L-6-E-B

450L-6-C-B

451-6-C-B

452L-5-J-C

453-6-E-B

454-6-A-A

455-5-G-B*

456-6-G-C

457-6-J-C

458L-6-I-A

459-6-I-B

460L-7-M-C*

462-6-C-C

463-6-I-B

461L-6-C-C

PONTIAC
A GENERAL MOTORS MASTERPIECE

464-5-E-C

465L-5-D-B

466L-5-D-B

467-5-E-B

468-6-Y-C

469L-5-E-C

470L-6-V-B

471L-6-I-B

WARNING
LOOK BOTH WAYS BEFORE
CROSSING THE STREETS–
THIS TOWN IS FULL OF
STUDEBAKERS

472L-6-J-C

473L-6-J-B

474-5-I-B

475-4-G-B

476L-5-C-D

477-6-E-B

1942 CHRYSLER
PREVIEW MEETING

478-6-E-C

BUG ME
JAY WEAVER
MOTOR Co.

479-7-G-A

AVIATION: BALLOONS, DIRIGIBLES, ZEPPELINS, HELICOPTERS, PLANES, RACES & EVENTS

The centuries-old dream of man flying like a bird became reality in the early 20th century. From the earliest flights of a few hundred feet, the concept of air flight grew steadily if not rapidly. Early air show buttons indicate the progress of aircraft structure, but flight was still rather a local novelty until Lindbergh's daring solo trip across the Atlantic moved the country into the air age.

480-2-D-C*

481-2-D-E

482-2-M-E*

483-2-D-E

484-2-A-D

485-2-H-D

486-2-J-D

487-2-G-D

488-2-D-D

489-2-C-D*

490-2-E-D

491-3-E-D

492-3-D-D

493-4-G-D*

494-2-A-A*

495-3-C-C

496-3-H-E

497-3-D-E

498-3-D-C*

499-3-E-C*

500L-4-E-C

501-4-C-C

502-4-A-C

503L-5-O-B*

504-5-O-B*

505L-4-E-B

506-5-C-D

507-5-E-D

508-5-M-C

509-5-D-C

510-5-N-B

511L-5-E-A

512-5-G-A

513-5-E-A

514-5-J-A

515L-5-O-A

516L-5-G-A

517L-5-E-A

518-5-G-A

519-5-E-A

520-5-N-B

521-5-G-B

522-5-M-B

523L-5-W-A*

524L-5-W-A*

525-5-E-A

526L-5-E-C

527L-5-E-C

528-6-E-D

529-5-Y-B

530-6-G-B

531-5-D-B*

532-5-D-B*

533-5-D-B* 534-5-D-B* 535-5-D-B* 536-5-D-B* 537-5-D-B*

AVIATION: LINDBERGH

Captain Charles A. Lindbergh amazed and stunned the world with his 1927 trans-Atlantic flight in his single engine "Spirit of St. Louis." His feat prompted a large variety of commemorative buttons and opened the door to commercial air service. The number of different Lindbergh buttons is equal to any other individual event in the history of buttons.

538-4-E-F

539-4-F-F

540-4-E-D

541-4-A-F

COMMITTEE

WELCOME TO CAPT. CHARLES A. LINDBERGH 1927

548-4-F-I*

542L-4-E-E

543L-4-E-D

544L-4-O-D*

545-4-A-C

546-4-F-D

547-4-E-C

549-4-F-C*

550-4-O-C*

551-4-F-C*

552-4-F-B

553-4-F-B

554-4-F-C

555-4-E-C

556-4-E-C

557-4-F-D

558-4-J-C

559-4-F-D

560-4-A-C

561-4-A-C

562-4-G-D

563-4-A-C

564L-4-A-B

565L-4-G-B

566-4-B-C*

567L-4-G-C

568-4-A-D   569-4-F-D   570-4-F-D   571-4-F-D   572L-4-A-C

573-4-F-C*   574-4-F-C*   575-4-D-C*   576-4-E-C   577-4-A-D*

578-4-H-D   579-4-A-D   580-4-F-D   581-4-A-E   582-4-A-B

AVIATION: PILOTS, FEATS

Although buttons have recorded a few individual flight achievements before 1927, the Lindbergh flight touched off a flurry of "higher and faster" personal endurance and distance attempts. Continents as well as oceans were crossed before the inevitable first "round the world" solo flight by Wiley Post in 1933.

583-2-J-D   584-3-A-D   585-5-A-D*

586-4-A-F*   587-4-F-C   588-4-A-C*   589-3-F-E*

590-4-F-C*

591-4-A-C*

592-4-A-B*

593-4-C-B*

594-4-A-B*

595-4-F-A*

596-4-A-C*

597-4-C-B*

598-4-A-B*

599-4-A-B*

600-4-C-B*

601-4-C-C*

602-4-A-C*

603-4-F-C*

604-5-N-C

605-5-A-B

606-5-A-B

607-4-E-D

608-5-A-C

609-5-E-D

610-5-N-C

611-5-E-C

612-5-A-D

613-5-C-C

614-5-A-B

615-5-A-B

616-5-F-B

617-5-A-D

618L-6-E-C*

619-6-E-C*

620-5-J-B*

621-5-N-B*

622-5-H-B*

623-5-P-B*

624-5-P-B*

625-5-M-B*

626-5-T-B*

SPACE: FLIGHTS, MISSIONS, ASTRONAUTS

Even a nation jaded by almost two centuries of technical accomplishments could not take its eyes from the television screen July 20, 1969 as an American first stepped on the moon. The Apollo XI lunar landing peaked the nation's interest in space exploration programs that scarcely had begun only 10 years earlier. The U.S. space program from the outset to the present has been well-documented by commemorative buttons and this is a category of growing interest for collectors.

627-8-A-C*

628-8-F-A*

629-8-F-B*

630-8-J-C*

631-8-G-C*

632-8-F-B*

633-8-F-B

634-8-F-B

635-8-E-C

636-8-F-B

637-8-E-B

638-8-F-B

639-8-E-B

640-8-F-B

641-8-F-C

642-8-F-B

643-8-E-B*

644-8-J-B

645-8-J-B

646-8-D-A

648-8-M-B

649-8-E-C

647-8-E-A

650-8-F-A

651-8-F-A

652-8-F-B

653-8-F-B

655-8-G-A

654-8-F-B

656-8-D-A*

657-9-D-A*

658-9-D-A*

659-9-D-A*

660-9-D-A*

661-9-D-A*

662-9-D-A*

NOTES

XIII. TRANSPORTATION

BUGGIES, ETC.

1. ALSO SEEN 1¼" W/SIMILAR DESIGN.
13. BACK PAPER: "Made only by FRANK C. SCHERER & SONS, 27th & BROWN STS. PHILA. PA."
14. BACK PAPER: "FULTON & WALKER CO./WAGONS FOR BUSINESS/PHILA., U.S.A."
17. BACK PAPER: "JOHN J. HOOVER'S SON/BUILDER OF FINE CARRIAGES, 242-244 W. ORANGE ST., LANCASTER, PA."
20. TOP RIM: "WE DO REPAIRING WHILE YOU WAIT"
27. BACK PAPER: "Use only ½ as much MICA as any other Axle Grease. FOR SALE EVERYWHERE."

BICYCLES

32. W/PURPLE LETTERING.
38. "1896" ON PENNANT DEPICTION.
48. DEPICTED CYCLIST WAS AMERICAN SPRINT CHAMPION 1898-1900.
60. PART OF A SET.
78. "SUNOL" HELD ONE MILE TROTTING RECORD IN 1891.
97. PICTURES: EDDIE McDUFFIE (TOP), JIMMY MICHAEL(left) and LUCIEN LESNA(right).
115. RIDER ILLUSTRATED IN BOY SCOUT UNIFORM.
118.-121. PART OF A SET. SEE *BUTTONS IN SETS,* PAGE 38.

RAILROADS

151. WHEEL SPOKES INSCRIBED WITH NAMES OR INITIALS OF RAILROADS.
154. BACK PAPER: "Compliments of Chessie/CHESAPEAKE & OHIO RAILWAY."
159. BACK PAPER: "HOMESTEADS, FARM LANDS, TOWNSITES IN WESTERN CANA-DA . . .WRITE DAVIDSON & McRAE, GENERAL AGENTS, WINNEPEG, CANADA."
167. ALSO SEEN IN MULTICOLOR. VALUE D.
169. HOLE ON BOTTOM RIM FOR ATTACHMENT.
171. BACK PAPER: "FOR INFORMATION REGARDING THE LOOP TRIP, SEND 2¢ STAMP TO B.L. WINCHELL, GEN. PASS'R AGENT, DENVER, COLO."
180. BACK PAPER: "I Pledge That I will STOP, LOOK & LISTEN Every time I Cross a Railroad crossing."

SUBWAYS, TROLLEYS

190. BACK PAPER: "If you want the Subway Demand that a Franchise be Granted"

SHIPS, BOATS, ETC.

211. PART OF A SET. BACK PAPER FROM "HIGH ADMIRAL CIGARETTES"
223. BACK PAPER: "Printed in Germany" IN THREE LANGUAGES.
237. PART OF A SET. SEE *BUTTONS IN SETS,* PAGE 42.

AUTOMOTIVE: RACES, SHOWS, ETC.

250. NAZI FLAG AMONG THOSE DEPICTED.
251. WITH ATTACHED RACING CAR AND RWB CLOTH RIBBONS.
255. SUNDAY SCHOOL "TEAM" BUTTON.
276. FRONT METAL CLIP HOLDS ACTUAL AUTO FUSE.
285. "AMERICAN OIL COMPANY" BACK INSCRIPTION.
286. ART BY DR. SEUSS. BACK PAPER: "Happy Motoring! 'STANDARD' ESSO DEALER".
288. DEPICTS FLYING RED HORSE 'PEGASUS,' SYMBOL OF MOBILGAS/SOCONY VACUUM OIL CO.
298. SEEN W/VARIOUS MILEAGE NUMBERS AND COLORS.
301. AUTO TIRE MANUFACTURER.

AUTOMOTIVE: COMPANIES & MAKERS

305. BACK PAPER HAS MONTGOMERY WARD TEXT, BUT NOT RELATED TO THE ELECTRIC HORSELESS CARRIAGE.
311. POSSIBLE REFERENCE, BUT UNCERTAIN, TO 'STUTZ BEARCAT' AUTO.
318. BRASS RING HELD DIECUT CELLULOID SPARKPLUG.
331. ESSEX. ALSO SEEN IN SMALLER BLUE/WHITE.
361. SUNDAY SCHOOL "TEAM" BUTTON.
391. EMBOSSED PAPER W/BLUE/GOLD RIBBON.
428. ACTUAL FOUR-LEAF CLOVER UNDER CELLULOID.
440. EMBOSSED SILVERED BRASS BUTTON FROM 1939 NEW YORK WORLD'S FAIR.

443. "FORD" AND "LINCOLN ZEPHYR" ON ATTACHED BLUE/WHITE RIBBONS.

455. FROM 1933 CHICAGO WORLD'S FAIR.

460. PICTURES ED WYNN FROM RADIO SPONSORSHIP.

AVIATION: BALLOONS, ETC.

480. PICTURES WRIGHT BROTHERS' AIRPLANE.

482. AMERICA'S FIRST INTERNATIONAL AIR MEETING HELD JANUARY, 1910 AT DOMINGUEZ FIELD, LOS ANGELES. GLENN CURTISS SET A NEW SPEED RECORD OF 55 MPH.

489. SEE NOTE #482.

493. 'BARNSTORMING' BUTTON.

494. IDENTITY OF "JOHNSON" IS UNKNOWN.

498.-499. AUSTRALIAN WORLD WAR I BUTTONS.

503.-504. SUNDAY SCHOOL "TEAM" BUTTONS.

523.-524. FROM A SERIES, EACH W/SOLID COLOR BACKGROUND.

531.-537. BUTTONS OBTAINED BY SENDING IN "SILVER WINGS LABELS." A BREAD COMPANY IS THOUGHT TO BE THE SPONSOR OF "SPECIAL UNCLE DON BROADCASTS" OVER NEW YORK CITY STATION W.O.R. EACH BUTTON HAS A BACK PAPER WHICH IDENTIFIES THE PICTURED AIRCRAFT AND OFFERS AN "AIRPLANE PICTURE BOOK" FOR 12 LABELS. THE PICTURED AIRPLANES ARE NO. 531, FOKKER 32 TRANSPORT; NO. 532, AUTOGIRO; NO. 533, LOCKHEED VEGA; NO. 534, BELLANCA MONOPLANE; NO. 535, STINSON DETROITER; NO. 536, FLEETSTER TRANSPORT; NO. 537, SIKORSKY S-38 AMPHIBIAN TRANSPORT.

AVIATION: LINDBERGH

544. LIGHT BLUE BACKGROUND/SILVER AIRCRAFT/BW PORTRAIT.

548. RWB RIBBON W/GOLD LETTERING, ALSO RIM IS PARTIALLY GOLD.

549. RIM IS PARTIALLY GOLD.

550. CLOTH-COVERED, DARK BLUE W/SILVER DESIGN.

551. RIM IS MOSTLY GOLD.

566. BRASS RIM.

573. PART OF RIM DESIGN IS GREEN, PORTRAIT OVAL IS GOLD.

574. HORSESHOE IS GOLD.

575. PORTRAIT IS BW.

577. RED RIM. IDENTITY OF OTHERS UNKNOWN.

AVIATION: PILOT, FEATS

585. FIRST WOMAN TO TRANS-ATLANTIC SOLO, MAY 20-21, 1932.

586. RWB RIBBON, BRASS RIM AND HANGER BAR. CHAMBERLIN PILOTED THE FIRST TRANS-ATLANTIC PASSENGER FLIGHT, JUNE 4-5, 1927. (SEE #603).

588. LIGHTLY-TINTED PORTRAIT.

589. NECKLINE INSCRIPTION: "I'M GLAD TO BE BACK IN THE U.S.A."

590.-591. SEAPLANE PILOT FROM NEWFOUNDLAND TO SOUTH WALES, JUNE 17-18, 1928.

592.-602. ISSUED FOR THE FIRST EAST-WEST TRANS-ATLANTIC CROSSING BY BARON GUENTHER VON HUENEFELD, PILOTED BY GERMAN CAPTAIN HERMANN KOEHL AND IRISH CAPTAIN JAMES FITZMAURICE. THE FLIGHT LEFT DUBLIN APRIL 12, 1928 FOR NEW YORK CITY. SOME 37 HOURS LATER, THEY CRASHED ON GREELY ISLAND, LABRADOR, AND WERE RESCUED.

603. FIRST TRANS-ATLANTIC PASSENGER (SEE #586).

618. POST-WORLD WAR II FOR CAPT. EDDIE RICKENBACKER.

619. FIRST ROUND-THE-WORLD NONSTOP FLIGHT COMMANDER, CAPT. JAMES GAL-LAGHER. (FEB. 27-MARCH 2, 1949)

620.-626. SET. SEE *BUTTONS IN SETS,* PAGE 1.

SPACE: FLIGHTS, MISSIONS, ASTRONAUTS

627. MAY 5, 1961.

628.-630. FEB. 20, 1962.

631. 1962.

632. FEB. 20, 1962.

643. DEC. 4-18, 1965.

656. NOV. 14-29, 1969.

657. JAN. 31-FEB. 9, 1971.

658. APR. 12-14, 1981.

659.-660. JUNE 18-24, 1983.

661.-662. AUG. 30-SEPT. 5, 1983.

XIV. "OTHER" CELLULOID ADVERTISING

In addition to buttons, celluloid was used either in pure form or as a thin cover in the manufacture of a fascinating variety of other 'giveaway' advertising items. Generally, the items had a useful purpose in addition to excellent color and attractive graphic design.

The era of beautiful "other" celluloid advertising pieces closely paralleled the 1896-1920's period of magnificent button production. Celluloid covered pocket mirrors and notepads were the most popular giveaway items and, like buttons, sufficient examples have survived to form modern-day collections.

A sampling of celluloid novelty items is shown on the following pages. Each item is numbered with a "C" prefix. Otherwise, the numbering code for age, color and value is the same as used for buttons in this book. Most items are shown actual size with exceptions noted in individual descriptions.

C1-1-D-E.	Celluloid covered Whitehead & Hoag sample ink blotter pad.
C2-2-D-D.	Celluloid covered Whitehead & Hoag 1908 sample notepad.
C3-2-D-D.	Celluloid covered Whitehead & Hoag 1906 sample two-page notepad.
C4-1-A-C.	Solid celluloid Whitehead & Hoag sample ruler and letter opener. Company ad on reverse.
C5-3-A-D.	Celluloid covered Pulver Co. sample ink blotter pad.
C6-3-D-E.	Celluloid covered notepad with mixed drink recipe pages and 1911-1912 calendar pages.
C7-3-D-D.	Celluloid covered notepad with Austin-Western Road Machinery Co. product illustrations and 1915 back cover calendar. Loose-bound with two brass rings.
C8-2-F-C.	Celluloid covered notepad.
C9-2-D-E.	Celluloid covered notepad with bw farm machinery illustration on back cover and inside 1906 calendar.
C10-2-A-C.	Celluloid covered notepad.
C11-3-K-C.	Celluloid covered notepad.
C12-2-D-E.	Celluloid covered notepad with full color front and back cover, inside farm equipment illustrations and 1906 calendar. Bound and edged in leather.
C13-3-D-C.	Celluloid covered table calendar on celluloid easel base. (Pictured reduced from actual 3¼" W x 4¼" T)
C14-5-C-B.	Diecut celluloid pocket calendar for 1930 with 12-month calendar back.
C15-3-D-B.	Celluloid pocket calendar for 1919 with "Wyandotte Cleaners" and 12-month calendar on back.
C16-3-D-E.	Celluloid pocket calendar for 1920 with front Maxfield Parrish "Prometheus" illustration and 12-month calendar on back. Advertises General Electric's "Edison Mazda" lamps.
C17-4-D-E.	Celluloid pocket calendar for 1921 with front Maxfield Parrish "Egypt" illustrations and 12-month calendar on back. Advertises General Electric's "Edison Mazda" lamps.
C18-2-D-D.	Celluloid brass back and stickpin. "Wear Billy Buster Shoes"
C19-3-D-C.	Celluloid with metal back and brass stickpin. "Indiana Ice Dealers Assn."
C20-3-D-E.	Celluloid with brass back and stickpin. "Victor"
C21-3-D-E.	Celluloid with brass back and stickpin. "Smith Guns"
C22-3-D-D.	Celluloid with brass back and stickpin. "Emerson Foot Lift Farm Implements"
C23-3-D-E.	Celluloid with brass back and stickpin. Reverse inscription for "Teddy Bear Bread"
C24-3-D-D.	Celluloid with brass back and stickpin. "Omega" Cream Separators
C25-3-D-D.	Celluloid with brass back and stickpin. "New Departure Coaster Brake"
C26-3-D-D.	Celluloid with brass back and stickpin. Reverse inscription for "Rumely Co.," farm equipment manufacturer.
C27-2-D-A.	Diecut celluloid with brass stickpin and advertising on reverse. Diecut flags such as this were issued for many different advertisers and purposes.
C28-2-D-B.	Diecut celluloid 'flipper' with loose-mounted small pin at the top. "Kingan's" meat ad on the back. A string (not shown) was pulled to flip up the celluloid, revealing the advertising copy.
C29-2-K-C.	Two-sided celluloid with metal cigar cutter and key holder combination.
C30-2-D-B.	Diecut celluloid bookmark with diecut page slot at top.
C31-2-L-B.	Celluloid stamp holder. Two-sided protective sleeve for carrying postage stamp booklet. Designed like an envelope.
C32-2-C-D.	Brass pill case with celluloid inset lid illustration.
C33-2-C-B.	Celluloid 'clicker' with metal spring clicker on back.
C34-2-D-F.	Celluloid inset metal watch fob with back inscription "THE SPARKLING GRAPE DRINK/VIN FIZ/AT ALL FOUNTAINS/5¢."
C35-2-A-D.	Celluloid-topped ink blotter with rounded bottom and embossed brass corners. (Photo reduced from actual 2¼" T x 4¼" W size)
C36-4-J-B.	Celluloid covered "Auction Bridge" score pad with aluminum edges.
C37-3-C-C.	Diecut slotted celluloid armband for World War I "Liberty Loan" bond sales.
C38-2-E-D .	Celluloid pen wiper with wiper layers of scalloped-edged felt.
C39-2-D-D.	Diecut celluloid lapel hanger with brass hanger bars. C.D. Kenny Co. ad on back.
C40-3-D-D.	Diecut celluloid two-sided baggage tag. The sides are riveted to swing apart with inside space for owner's name.

C41-3-D-D. Same as C40.
C42-3-D-D. Diecut celluloid card game scorekeeper. Inside celluloid discs revolve to produce a variety of different facial expressions as "points," "games," and "trumps" are revolved on the back.
C43-3-D-D. Diecut celluloid baseball score counter with revolving inside discs to change score entries. The obverse and reverse are designed to resemble a catcher's mitt.

C44—C75: Celluloid pocket mirrors with mirror backs. (Each photo is reduced about 10% from actual size unless indicated otherwise).

C49-3-T-D. The 'barrel' was a stock design used for various products with a company imprint on one end of the illustration.
C50-3-D-E. Uncommon 1¼" mirror (photo actual size).
C60-4-J-E. Pictures "Enrico Caruso." One of a series picturing "Victrola" recording stars with imprint of local music dealer.
C72-5-D-E. The colorful 'birthstone' border was used by many different advertisers, frequently jewelers.
C73-7-A-D. Issued for a 1957 movie starring Bob Hope.
C74-7-A-D. Jules Feiffer caricature of Judge Hoffman, who tried the "Chicago Seven" after the 1968 Democratic National Convention.
C75-4-A-D. Shows "Gutzon Borglum Inspecting Work At Rushmore Memorial."
C76-3-D-D. Paperweight-mirror combination.
C77-3-D-E. Paperweight-mirror combination.
C78-3-J-E. Celluloid covered whetstone.
C79-4-T-D. Celluloid covered whetstone.
C80-4-H-D. Celluloid covered whetstone.
C81-2-D-D. Celluloid inset hand mirror with metal handle.
C82-4-C-C. Celluloid hand mirror with swivel celluloid handle.
C83-2-D-D. Celluloid diecut badge with brass hanger bar and pendant on rwb fabric ribbon.
C84-2-D-D. Celluloid diecut slotted badge on silk ribbon with brass hanger bar.

C85—C99: Celluloid two-sided tape measures with retractable fabric tapes operated by center spring.

C86-2-D-D. (St. Louis) "World's Fair 1904"
C100-3-D-C. Celluloid pinholder with mirror back.
C101-4-G-C. Celluloid toothpick with rotating arms.
C102-5-R-B. Celluloid pencil clip with metal clip.
C103-3-A-D. Celluloid matchbox holder.
C104-3-D-D. Celluloid inset in metal matchsafe.
C105-3-D-D. Celluloid inset in metal matchsafe.
C106-5-E-E. Celluloid inset in metal matchsafe.
C107-3-D-E. Celluloid covered matchsafe with metal ends.
C108-2-D-E. Celluloid covered matchsafe with metal ends.
C109-5-E-D. Celluloid covered matchsafe with metal ends.

C110-3-D-D. Whitehead & Hoag celluloid 10-year calendar with revolving disc wheel to determine dates forward or backward for the years 1908 through 1918. Multicolor illustration and simulated appearance of molded frame with cardboard backing and easel. (Shown actual size.)

C1-1-D-E

C2-2-D-D

C3-2-D-D

C4-1-A-C

261

C5-3-A-D

C6-3-D-E

C7-3-D-D

262

C8-2-F-C

C9-2-D-E

C10-2-A-C

C11-3-K-C

C12-2-D-E

C13-3-D-C

C14-5-C-B

C15-3-D-B

C16-3-D-E

C17-4-D-E

C18-2-D-D

C19-3-D-C

C20-3-D-E

C21-3-D-E

C22-3-D-D

C23-3-D-E

C24-3-D-D

C25-3-D-D   C26-3-D-D

C27-2-D-A

C28-2-D-B

C29-2-K-C

C30-2-D-B

C31-2-L-B

C32-2-C-D

C33-2-C-B

C34-2-D-F

C35-2-A-D

C36-4-J-B

C37-3-C-C

C38-2-E-D

C39-2-D-D

C40-3-D-D

C41-3-D-D

C42-3-D-D

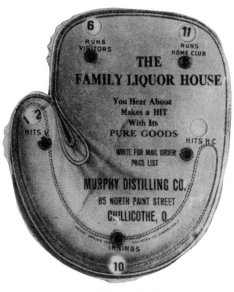

C43-3-D-D

C44-2-D-E

C45-2-D-E

C46-2-D-F

C47-2-D-E

C48-3-J-E

C49-3-T-D

C50-3-D-E

C51-3-A-D

C52-2-D-D

C53-3-C-F

C54-4-B-F

C55-2-D-E

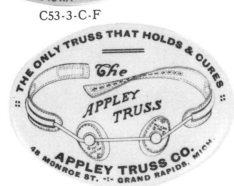

C56-2-A-D

C57-4-D-D

267

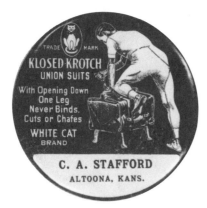

C58-3-A-D

C59-2-D-G

C60-4-J-E

C61-3-D-E

C62-4-A-D

C63-2-C-D

C64-3-D-E

C65-3-D-E

C66-3-D-E

C67-2-D-G

C68-2-D-G

C69-2-A-D

C70-4-A-E

C71-4-A-D

C72-5-D-E

C73-7-A-D

C74-7-A-D

C75-4-A-D

C76-3-D-D

C77-3-D-E

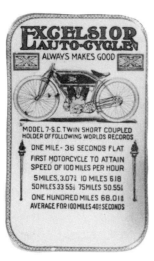

C78-3-J-E

C79-4-T-D

C80-4-H-D

C81-2-D-D

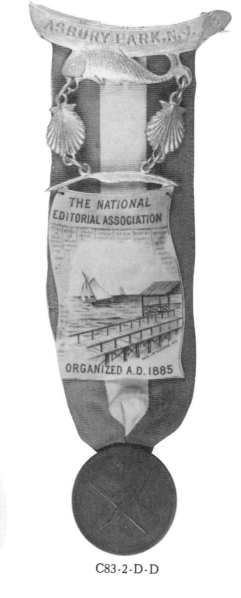

C83-2-D-D

C84-2-D-D

C82-4-C-C

C85-5-A-C

C86-2-D-D

C87-5-B-C

C88-2-J-D

C89-2-B-C

C90-2-J-D

C91-5-H-C

C92-4-A-D

C93-5-H-C

C94-4-A-D

C95-5-A-C

C96-5-H-C

C97-4-D-E

C98-4-D-D

C99-5-R-C

271

C100-3-D-C

C101-4-G-C

C102-5-R-B

C103-3-A-D

C104-3-D-D

C105-3-D-D

C106-5-E-E

C107-3-D-E

C108-2-D-E

C109-5-E-D

THE HISTORY OF THE WHITEHEAD & HOAG COMPANY
NEWARK, NEW JERSEY
by Gary Patterson

Benjamin S. Whitehead
1858-1940

Chester R. Hoag
1860-1935

Benjamin S. Whitehead was born in Newark, N.J. on January 24, 1858. His father was a deputy collector in the Dept. of Internal Revenue under Presidents Lincoln, Grant and Garfield.

In 1870, he decided to become a printer and completed his technical education at Cooper Union Institute in New York City. His first success came when his printing samples were exhibited at the 1876 Centennial Exposition in Philadelphia. Later he opened his own printing shop under the firm name of Whitehead & Clark. Whitehead first appeared in the Newark city directory as a book job printer in 1876.

A Republican in politics, he was a member of the Methodist Church, a member, trustee, and president of many Newark clubs and various state fraternal organizations.

Whitehead traveled extensively, visiting 22 countries as well as all parts of the United States. Wherever he went, he made photographs and gathered ideas for novelties to be manufactured in his plant.

He had a taste for good music and welcomed the opportunity to bring musical attractions before the Newark public. His hobby, fishing, led to his collection of over 2,000 rods and reels. He would spend his summers with regularity in the development of a summer estate on Whitehead's Island at Kezar Lake near Lovell, Maine.

Whitehead was married and had a son (Ray, who later was in charge of the branch office in New York City) and one daughter. He died at the age of 82 on April 16, 1940.

Chester R. Hoag was born November 28, 1860, in Wellsboro, Pa. He had no formal schooling beyond grammar school but read every book he could obtain. He came to Newark in 1882 to find work and covered Essex County on a high wheel bicycle for a paper and twine distributor, being paid $8 a week. Hoag first appears in the Newark city directories (Harrison & Hoag) as a paper merchant in 1886.

Hoag, active in vocational and religious education, was an elder in the Presbyterian Church and president of the Newark Museum. He was instrumental in producing exhibitions of medals, in particular "Medals Made in Newark." The museum's coin collection has a large number of medals made by the firm and donated by him.

His favorite sports were shooting and fishing. He did considerable shooting abroad and hunted and fished in every section of the states. He maintained a summer home at Clayton, N.Y. where he kept several speed boats. He was married and had one daughter and three sons.

Hoag died of heart ailment on February 28, 1935, after a long illness. In his will, he advised his children to retain his interest in the company and suggested that if anyone wanted to sell their share it should be offered first to the other children. One son, Phillip Hoag, was president of the company at the time of his death in 1953.

Note: The Whitehead & Hoag Co. was the first button manufacturer and remained the foremost throughout the early years of the industry.

"The Button is without question the best advertising Medium"—from late 1890's Whitehead & Hoag button sample card.

Although the Whitehead & Hoag Company (W&H) made over 5,000 different advertising novelty items, this article will focus on the history of the company and its contribution to button collectors.

Whitehead & Hoag 'Team Up'

In his shop, Whitehead was printing programs for local picnics and parties plus printing badges on silk, when Hoag began to sell him twine. A friendship developed and the two formed a new business partnership that was incorporated in 1892. It was soon to become the country's largest business in the manufacture of advertising novelties.

Early Patents

The company acquired three major button patents prior to its immediate step into button manufacture in 1896. A December 3, 1893 patent was filed by Amanda M. Lougee of Boston, Massachusetts. W&H apparently purchased rights to this patent to protect their other claims, although actually the patent was for a cloth and metal clothing button.
The second patent, filed December 6, 1895, established the reverse design of celluloid buttons. Issued as a "jewelry" patent to George B. Adams, assignor to W&H, it specified "a shell with a marginal rim to form a chamber and contain a continuous piece of wire with both a holding portion and a free end lying in the same plane."
The final patent was filed March 23, 1896, and issued July 21, 1896, again to George B. Adams. Six claims were made, each varying slightly from Claim 1 which reads:

In a badge pin or button, in combination, with a shell having a marginal rim or bead, a covering bearing an inscription, design, emblem, or the like, over said shell and having its edges turned down over said marginal rim, a ring or collet in said shell placed over the edge of said covering to hold or secure the latter in position, and a bar or pin having one of its ends bent to form a holding portion adapted to be secured in said ring or collet, substantially as and for the purposes set forth.

Adams was a Newark jewelry manufacturer who patented 49 different novelty articles.

The Factory

In 1892, the main office and factory was located at Washington & Warren Streets. As the company continued to grow and expand, a new factory was built at 272 Sussex Ave. & First Street in 1903.
The new factory had a complete printing and lithographing plant with over 50 modern presses, a complete art and photo engraving plant in which all the engraving sketches and plates were made, a complete button plant with a capacity of over one million buttons a day, and a machinery plant where the company made all its own tools, dies and special machinery.

Button Dept.

W&H was devoting its time to ribbon badges and making some with celluloid parts when the button was patented. Before their patents expired and the development of the small printing press, they would become the largest manufacturer of buttons in the world.

The success of the button idea was astonishing, and buttons swept the country in an avalanche. Advertising buttons such as the ones illustrated on a late 1890's sample card were innumerable (see next page). Their first big order went to the American Tobacco Co., at the rate of one million a day.

There were no machines at the time to place the pin and paper in the back of the buttons. W&H solved this problem by offering extra spending money to the families living around the factory to do it. Every night after school the children would walk over to the factory and pick up a box full of buttons, pins and back papers.

The company had always been non-partisan, accepting button orders not only from both major parties but from such minority groups as the Socialists, the Communists, Prohibitionists and others. A few of the artists that worked for W&H from time to time included Norman Rockwell, Maxfield Parrish and Harrison Fisher.

ADVERTISING BUTTONS.

THE
WHITEHEAD & HOAG CO.
NEWARK, N. J.

The Button is without question

the best Advertising

Medium.

WRITE FOR SAMPLES AND PRICES.

Branch Offices

In the late 1890's W&H set up a network of branch offices in many major cities across the United States. Argentina, Australia and England were just a few of the foreign offices opened. However, these were closed prior to 1940.

Although all the work was being done at the factory in Newark, the branch offices were supplied with samples to show the prospective customers. They also were given a list of all conventions to be held in that branch office city for the year. It was up to the branch office salesmen, working on a sales commission basis, to contact all the local churches, business and fraternal organizations.

Union Trouble

In 1919, an important reorganization took place and Whitehead left the presidency and became Chairman of the Board. It was at this time W&H became a non-union company. Prior to this, most of their items were marked with the union seal or listed the local unions which worked in the factory. Although W&H was no longer a union company they would still mark certain items to make it appear they were union made—especially political buttons.

War Years

During World War II, normal button production was shelved for a period of time at the factory. W&H then turned to the identification buttons which were worn by millions of workers in the war plants. At the peak of the war, W&H had over 400 employees making these buttons which were required to be worn by state and federal laws.

Sale to Bastian Bros. Co.

Bastian Bros. of Rochester, N.Y. (founded in 1895) was a long-time competitor of W&H. Bastian, being a union company, could not compete with W&H's prices and like many other agents and jobbers would subcontract out some of their work and buy parts from W&H.

There were several reasons why W&H sold out to Bastian Bros. When Phillip Hoag died in 1953, no member of the family was left on the board or in a policy-making role. Another reason was the company had a long history of making a great deal of money for one or two years and then operating at a loss for several years. A third reason was the company's insistence on making a top quality product and their refusal to advertise any other way than on their own product. In the early years, if a customer insisted that the W&H logo not appear on the item, the price was raised considerably.

W&H first offered the sale of the company to Bastian Bros. The sale took place and W&H closed its factory in May, 1959. The president of Bastian at the time of the sale came to Newark, ordered the factory to be sold and any unusable machinery, dies or tools to be scrapped. W&H kept records of every item they ever made and these records were ordered destroyed. Bastian continued to use W&H's name, finally phasing it out in 1964-65.

ADVERTISEMENTS OF BUTTON MANUFACTURERS

The following pages illustrate catalogues, brochures, and advertisements of various button manufacturers. Many of the illustrations are from *The Novelty News,* a Chicago based magazine, published and edited by Henry S. Bunting. The magazine began around 1906 and continued into 1916 and perhaps beyond. Advertising specialty salesmen were the primary audience and the magazine offered "new ways to build up business: unique and original advertising ideas: inducement methods to stimulate sales: novel things: souvenirs: emblems: post cards and convention dates." Surprisingly, Whitehead & Hoag was not one of the magazines' advertisers. The following are notes on the illustrations:

1. Whitehead & Hoag Co. catalogue cover from 1897. The catalogue was issued with an unillustrated black and white paper wrapper inscribed "Catalogue No. 25. Illuminated Edition/Ribbon Badges." Our illustration shows the full color cover under the paper wrapper. Actual size is 8½"x11".

2. This illustration shows the back cover of the paper wrapper described above. The text offers fifteen different "series" (Flags, Presidents, Warships, Little Pinkies, etc.) priced per set or as an assortment priced at $1.50 per 100. The plant's capacity is listed as "now about one million buttons per day."

3. St. Louis Button Co. *The Novelty News.* November, 1911.

4. The Peacock Company. *The Novelty News.* November, 1911.

5. Bastian Bros. Co. *The Novelty News.* November, 1911.

6. Parisian Novelty Co. *The Novelty News.* November, 1911.

7. American Badge Co. *The Novelty News.* February, 1912.

8. J.L. Lynch. June 1, 1923 four page brochure "announces the consolidation and absorption of the J.L. Lynch Co., the World's Largest Advertising Button Factory, by Green Duck Metal Stamping Co., The Foremost Manufacturer of Metal Advertising Novelties." The text claims Lynch's invention of "decorated metal button(s) was revolutionary and rendered celluloid buttons as obsolete as celluloid collars . . .''

9. Greenduck button price sheet from the 1930's.

10. Whitehead & Hoag sales sheet promoting the use of the "Membership Button" by World War II "Defense Bond Clubs."

ILLUSTRATION 1

BUTTON COLLECTIONS.

WE are having such a tremendous demand for buttons by those desiring to make collections that we have gone to a great expense in getting out special designs to meet the demand of those who are desirous of making elaborate and large collections. The illustrations on this page show a few of the different series that we now have in stock.

			PER SET
Flags of all Nations,	- -	68 in set,	$1.35
Presidents of the United States,	-	24 "	.50
American Generals,	- -	13 "	.25
Maps of Important States,	-	15 "	.30
Choice and Rare Flowers,	-	15 "	.30
Rare and handsome Birds,	-	21 "	.45
Ocean Steamships,	-	17 "	.35
Warships of the United States,	-	17 "	.35
Celebrated Men and Women,	-	59 "	1.20
Regulation College Buttons,	-	18 "	.35
Defenders of America's Cup,	-	5 "	.15
Governors of the States,	-	46 "	1.00
Athletes,	- - -	14 "	.25
Little Pinkies,	- -	20 "	.40
Crowned Heads,	- -	13 "	.25

We will furnish buttons from each variety assorted as desired, at 25 cents per dozen, net, or $1.50 per 100, net.

ADVERTISING BUTTONS.

We have manufactured these buttons for many of the largest advertising concerns in the United States, among them The American Tobacco Co., Colgate & Co., N. K. Fairbanks & Co., Faultless Chemical Co., Studebaker Bros. Mfg. Co., Davis Baking Powder Co., and thousands of others.

We have the largest plant in the world devoted to the exclusive manufacture of buttons, badges, flags, banners, etc., and our capacity is now about one million buttons per day, and is being continually increased.

THE WHITEHEAD & HOAG CO.
NEWARK, N. J., U. S A.

ILLUSTRATION 2

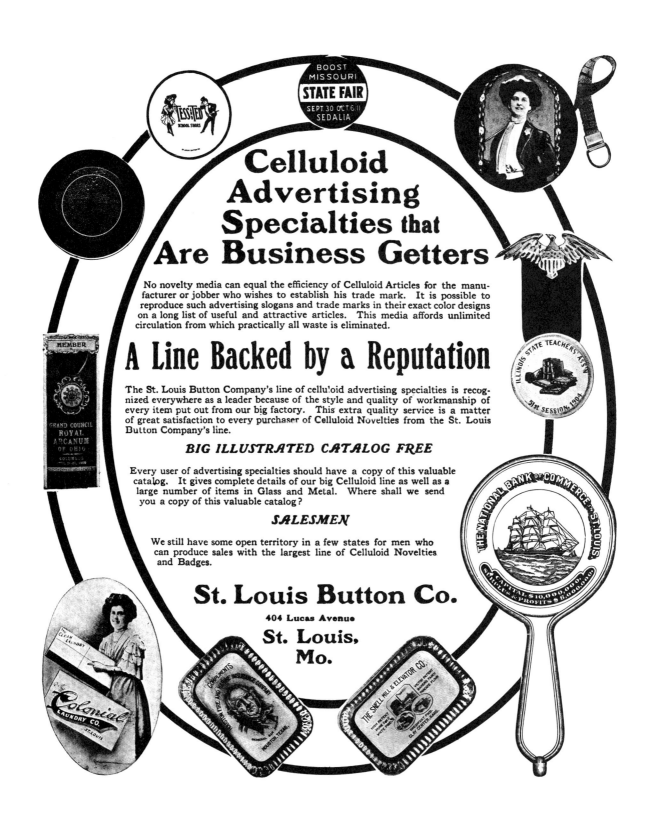

Celluloid Advertising Specialties that Are Business Getters

No novelty media can equal the efficiency of Celluloid Articles for the manufacturer or jobber who wishes to establish his trade mark. It is possible to reproduce such advertising slogans and trade marks in their exact color designs on a long list of useful and attractive articles. This media affords unlimited circulation from which practically all waste is eliminated.

A Line Backed by a Reputation

The St. Louis Button Company's line of celluloid advertising specialties is recognized everywhere as a leader because of the style and quality of workmanship of every item put out from our big factory. This extra quality service is a matter of great satisfaction to every purchaser of Celluloid Novelties from the St. Louis Button Company's line.

BIG ILLUSTRATED CATALOG FREE

Every user of advertising specialties should have a copy of this valuable catalog. It gives complete details of our big Celluloid line as well as a large number of items in Glass and Metal. Where shall we send you a copy of this valuable catalog?

SALESMEN

We still have some open territory in a few states for men who can produce sales with the largest line of Celluloid Novelties and Badges.

St. Louis Button Co.

404 Lucas Avenue

St. Louis, Mo.

ILLUSTRATION 3

ILLUSTRATION 4

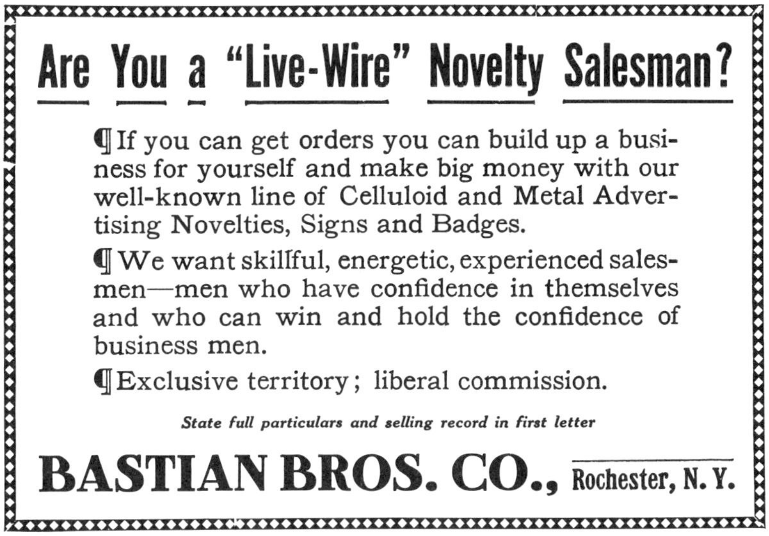

ILLUSTRATION 5

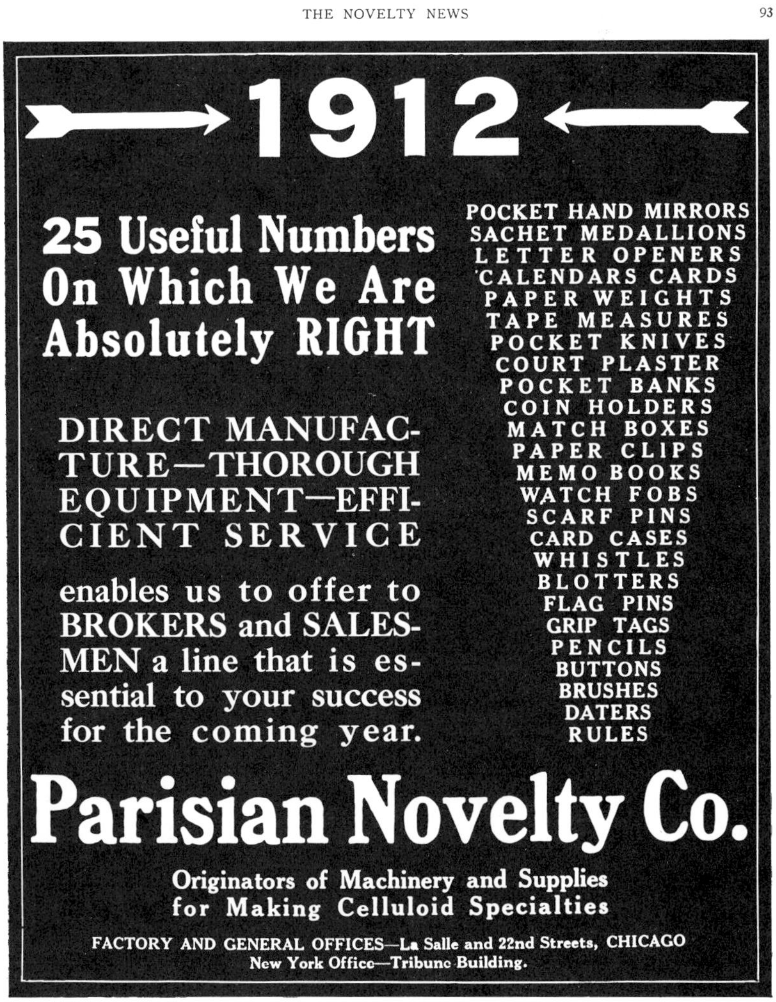

ILLUSTRATION 6

ILLUSTRATION 7

BUTTONS THAT MOULD PUBLIC OPINION

Address all mail to
the Main Office
Hoyne and Van Buren St.
Chicago, Ill.

J. L. Lynch

Manufacturer of
BUTTONS, BADGES, BANNERS, FLAGS.
325 W. MADISON STREET.
CHICAGO ILL.

THE GREENDUCK METAL
STAMPING COMPANY.

J.L.LYNCH BRANCH

WILLIAM U. WATSON
PRES.

June 1, 1923.

Gentlemen:-

This—announces the consolidation and absorption of the J. L. Lynch Co., the WORLD'S LARG-
EST ADVERTISING BUTTON FACTORY, by the Green Duck Metal Stamping Co., THE FOREMOST MANU-
FACTURER OF METAL ADVERTISING NOVELTIES.

This consolidation which involved thousands of dollars is considered the BIGGEST deal in
the novelty industry, making the GREENDUCK CO. second to none. Our two wonderfully
equipped factories stand SUPREME today to produce metal and celluloid buttons and novelty work, lithographed signs, etched name plates, metal stampings, fired enameled work
and badges at a price consistent with quality to BEAT competition.

The invention of J. L. Lynch was revolutionary and rendered celluloid buttons as obsolete as celluloid collars, as our decorated metal button is superior in appearance than
the celluloid-LOWER IN PRICE-of unequaled brilliance-hardness-permanence of coloring-a
button that doesn't peel, chip, soften, tarnish or become discolored.

Our buttons used exclusively by the U. S. in the Liberty Loan and War Saving Drives,
American Red Cross, Salvation Army, Republican and Democratic National Committees,
and EVERY great organization clearly demonstrate their TREMENDOUS SALABILITY.

Heretofore—the prodigious DEMAND for our buttons by AMERICA'S large institutions made it
unnecessary to use agents because production was taxed to capacity BUT NOW our TWO immense factories enables us to double SERVICE and make ONE MILLION buttons PER DAY. We are
now in a position to offer our agents a chance to solicit business on our complete line.

The Greenduck Co. JUST secured the ENTIRE American Red Cross order for this year amounting
to TWENTY MILLION-think of it-20,000,000 buttons-which was the FIRST time in history that
the entire order was given to ONE CONCERN--WHY?--because of OUR QUALITY-OUR PRICE-OUR
SERVICE as the best in the WORLD.

We have a U. S. Patent No. 1215675 on our metal buttons-which has been sustained in court
and is strongly protected against imitation and infringement.

ALL COMPETITORS throw up their hands when OUR metal buttons and products are shown and
prices quoted — they HAVEN'T A CHANCE. The demand for our buttons is increasing daily
and with the coming presidential and political campaigns the field is simply UNLIMITED.
If you are interested in representing us in a high class manner-we will give it our very
best consideration.

Financially yours,

Address Main Office
Hoyne and Van Buren,
Chicago, Ill.

GREENDUCK METAL STAMPING CO.

General Sales Manager

MAXIMUM RESULTS AT MINIMUM COST

ILLUSTRATION 8

SALES INFORMATION ON BUTTONS

Terms—30 days net—1% ten days—F. O. B. Chicago. Prices include any one colored lettering or design upon a white background, therefore, the color white is not counted as a color.

Prices below are per 1000 except under 1000 they cover the lot. Please note there is no drawing, electro, or plate charge on any quantity of 3000 or over.

SIZES	100	250	500	1000	3000	5000	10000	25000	50000	100000	250000
20-24-26-28 ligne size	$6.00	$7.00	$9.50	$12.50	$10.50	$8.00	$5.75	$4.50	$4.35	$4.15	$3.95
30–32 ligne size	7.00	7.50	10.00	13.00	11.00	8.50	6.00	4.75	4.60	4.40	4.20
36 ligne size	7.00	8.00	10.50	13.50	11.50	9.75	7.00	5.75	5.60	5.40	5.20
46 ligne size	8.00	9.25	13.00	18.50	14.00	12.00	9.50	8.00	7.60	7.15	6.95
56 ligne size	8.00	10.50	14.50	22.00	17.75	15.00	12.50	10.25	9.85	9.40	8.95
Extra colors per M under 1M per lot	2.25	2.50	3.00	3.50	3.50	2.00	1.50	.75	.50	.35	.25

On gold bronze coloring, charge the same as two colors. If we furnish printing plates add to the above prices for any quantity under 3000: Zinc Etchings $3.50; Half-tones, $5.00; Engraved designs, $6.00 for each color. No commission paid on cost of plates. THERE IS NO PLATE CHARGE ON ANY QUANTITY OF 3000 or OVER. If customer has printing plates, we make no charge.

ZINC ETCHINGS at $3.50 are based where the customer furnishes the correct copy, and if we are required to make drawings or changes in copy, they will be classified as engraved designs.

REVERSE PLATES at $5.00 are used when customer wants lettering to show white on a solid background and furnishes us with correct copy before reversing.

ZINC ETCHINGS at $3.50 are based where the customer furnishes the correct copy, and if we are required to make drawings or changes in copy, they will be classified as engraved designs.

HALFTONES at $5.00 are used when a customer wants a portrait, building, or work of similar nature reproduced, providing we are furnished with correct copy. If any retouching, painting out of background, or portions of building, etc., an additional charge is made which is usually double.

ENGRAVED DESIGNS at $6.00 per color, are made when we are required to make drawing and printing plate to reproduce customers' design, trademark, etc. Most buttons require the engraved design, charge of $6.00 per color, as customer seldom has his own cuts, nor furnishes correct copy.

IMPORTANT—Be sure and make ample charge for all cuts. It's a good rule to quote customer on the above standard prices plus the cost of any necessary cuts, placing confidence in us to charge net manufacturing price on same and use the most economical but still practical type. MANY TIMES WE CAN USE STANDARD TYPE FOR WHICH WE MAKE NO PLATE OR CUT CHARGE.

CHANGES—When changes in copy are required where customer wants the names of officers, salesmen or agents on the button, there will be a charge of $1.00 per change regardless of quantity.

CONSECUTIVE NUMBERS—On each button—for ⅜-inch numbers, charge for same as one extra color. On one inch numbers, charge same as two extra colors. This price prevails in quantities up to 5000. On consecutive numbers on quantities over 5000, ask for prices.

WE HAVE A UNITED STATES PATENT No. 1215675 ON OUR METAL BUTTONS, WHICH HAS BEEN SUSTAINED IN COURT AND IS STRONGLY PROTECTED AGAINST IMITATION AND INFRINGEMENT. INFRINGERS WILL BE STRONGLY PROSECUTED. DELIVERY SERVICE IS BEST IN THE WORLD. We can manufacture ONE MILLION BUTTONS PER DAY.

PRICES ON LINEN FINISH BADGES

Same size or smaller as our circular indicates. These linen badges have a tremendous sale for one day occasions, such as picnics, political drives, and campaigns. They are very attractive and present a rich appearance—although, very low in price.

100	250	500	1000	2500	5000	10000	
$7.00	$9.00	$11.00	$17.00	$15.00	$12.00	$10.00	Price per 1000 under 1000 per lot.

These prices cover any one color lettering upon a white background. Where cuts are required, an additional charge will be made.
These badges are generally attached to coat or waist by means of one of our attractive buttons. Thousands have been sold to political and labor organizations for officers with the canidates picture or ad on button.

They serve most satisfactorily in place of the expensive silk ribbon. These badges can bear the UNION LABEL approved by the American Federation of Labor, which is essential with any political or labor cause.

ILLUSTRATION 9

ILLUSTRATION 10

Confessions of a Button-Back Voyeur

It all began innocently enough a few years ago when I turned a button over to examine the back and discovered that it, too, along with the front, rendered information. It wasn't long before I was studying the back paper, curl, and any metal engravings as thoroughly as the front.

Unaware of having slipped into an abyss of minutiae, I started a list. Addictive buying in flea markets and auctions, not for a desired button face but because the back disclosed a new company or jobber, accelerated my descension. Later my life consisted of grubbing in library stacks and feeding ravenous xerox machines. Oh, for a Button-Back Voyeurs Anonymous Association. Alas, none existed.

The following information is printed, not because it is perfect or complete, but as a catharsis.

J. Scharre Thompson

P.S. In truth, my obsession hasn't waned at all (surprise!) and I look forward to receiving additional data or corrections from readers.

Button Manufacturers and Jobbers

The following list consists of button manufacturers and jobbers, the most recent addressess found, and the year or years in which they were active. When company names varied over the years, the most recent name is listed first, followed by earlier versions. More than one address is given only if there is a change in a company name and city of location.

Notations are made connecting companies either financially (e.g. Torsch & Lee and Baltimore Badge & Novelty Co.) and/or locationwise (e.g. Merit Co. and Kleer Co.).

Since many political artifacts originated in the last century with clothing button and badge manufacturers (e.g. Scovill Mfg. Co.) and because we have one word to indicate a clothing or a pin-back button, it is difficult to eliminate all clothing button manufacturers from a pin-back button list. As far as is known, no company solely producing civilian clothing buttons has been included in this list. Also excluded are companies believed to have made only medals, trophies, or identification buttons or badges.

No attempt to differentiate between jobbers (persons who negotiate sales between clients and manufacturers) and the manufacturers themselves has been made. There are many more jobbers than manufacturers. Some makers identify only the jobber on the button and not themselves. Others identify both (e.g. Whitehead & Hoag Co.).

Listing necessitates omitting much information that shows the breadth of these button manufacturers. Perhaps the colorful slogan of the Wm. H. Hoegee Co. put it best: "Everything from a celluloid button to a circus tent."

A few companies used distinctive lettering or logos to make their products recognizable (e.g. monograms: Gerraghty & Co.; signatures: V.H. Blackinton & Co. and Litchfield Corp.; logos: Green Duck Corp. and Lucke Badge & Button Co.).

Old forms of addresses can help to date buttons, whether there is a zone number between the city and state (e.g. East Hartford 8, Conn. - 1952) or whether there is or isn't a zip code after the state. Telephone numbers (area codes) can locate jobbers, and certainly a button noting a four digit New York City telephone number has to spell antiquity!

By far, the most difficult decision to make is whether "to assume or not to assume" relationships. When evidence indicated a likelihood, the leap was made. If doubts were dominant, assumptions were laid aside. Errors were made, no doubt, in both directions.

KEY:

F.	- Founded.
c.	- Circa, approximately.
. . . 1961 . . .	- Company or jobbers could have functioned before and after this year.
. . . 1930's OE . . .	- Functioned in the 1930's or earlier.
(date omitted)	- No specific year found.
Address	- Most recent one found. Many companies have had several addresses over the years.

Dictionary, not telephone directory, alphabetizing is used.

A.A.A. Nov. Co.
310—9th St., N.W.
Washington, D.C.
. . . 1961 . . .

A & M Assoc.
59 Middlesex Turnpike
Bedford, MA 01730

ABC Imports, Inc.
Pawtucket, R.I.
. . . 1981 . . .

A Bee M & M WKs.
New York

Aberer, O., Mfg. Co.
St. Louis, Mo.
. . . 1906-1912 . . .

Abingdon Cokesbury Press

Access Co.

ACCL
4803 Nicollet Ave. S.
Mpls., Mn.

Ace Banner & Flag Co.
107 W. 27th St.
New York, N.Y. 10001
. . . 1980-1985 . . .

Ace Rubber Stamp & Office
Cleveland, Oh. 44114

Ace Rubber Stamp Works, Inc.
12 E. Park
Newark, N.J.
. . . 1968 . . .

Achievement Badge & Trophy Co.
1511 W. 7th St.
Los Angeles, Ca. 90017

Achievement Products, Inc.
294 Route 10
East Hanover, N.J. 07936
. . . 1980-1985 . . .

Acorn Badge Co. Inc.
500 N. Michigan Ave.
Chicago, Il.
. . . 1945-1985 . . .

A.C. Press
U.S.A.

Ad-Aids Unlimited
Manchester, N.H. 03103
. . . 1982 . . .

Adams, S.G., Printing & Stationery Co.
920 Olive St.
St. Louis, Mo. 63101
. . . 1961-1985 . . .

Adams, S.G. Stamp & Stationery Co.
. . . 1921-1927 . . .

Adams, S.G., Co.
. . . 1928-1959 . . .

Adcraft Mfg. Co.
2700 Roosevelt Rd.
Broadview, Il. 60153
F. 1919-1985 . . .

Ad Factory, (The)
1587 Greg St.
Sparks, Nv.
. . . 1985 . . .

Adler and Son
Amsterdam, N.Y.
. . . 1930's OE . . .

Advance Supply Co.
Providence, R.I.
. . . 1930's OE . . .

Adver-Tek, Inc.
854 Angliana Ave.
Lexington, Kentucky 40508
. . . 1981-1985 . . .

Advertiser's Mart, Inc.
Kenilworth, N.J.
. . . 1961 . . .

Advertising Specialties Mfg. Co., Inc.
Max Shertzer & Assoc., Inc.
2301 Collins Ave.
Miami Beach, Fl. 33139
. . . 1980-1985 . . .

Adv. Premium Sales
St. Louis, Mo.

All Around Equipment and Novelty Co.
New York City
. . . 1930's OE . . .

Allied Printing
Newark, N.J.
. . . 1912 . . .

Aluminum Novelty Co.
. . . C. 1912 . . .

American Advertising Aids
P.O. Box 1101
New York, N.Y. 10163
. . . 1985 . . .

American Art Works, Inc. (The)
1938 Stull St.
Coshocton, Ohio
. . . 1904-1981 . . .

American Badge Co.
15537 So. 70th Ct.
Orland Park, Il. 60462
F. 1900-1985 . . .

American Baptist Publication Society
Philadelphia, Boston, Chicago, St. Louis
. . . 1930's OE . . .

American Baptist Publishing Society
Philadelphia

American Emblem Co., Inc.
Earle St.
Utica 1, N.Y.
. . . 1938-1961

American Gold Label & Printing Co.
509 N. 18th St.
St. Louis, Mo.
. . . 1985 . . .

American Gold Label Co.
. . . 1980 . . .

American Identification Products, Inc.
143 58th St.
Brooklyn, N.Y. 11220
. . . 1976-1981 . . .

American Novelty Adv. Co.
Kansas City, Mo.
. . . 1930's OE . . .

American Signs Company, Inc.
126 Baldwin Ave.
Jersey City, N.J.
. . . 1985 . . .

American Specialties Mfg. Co.
5112-14 4th Ave.
Brooklyn, N.Y.
. . . 1945 . . .

American Stamp & Novelty Mfg. Co.
1029 Richmond Ave.
Houston, Tx. 77006
F. 1896-1985 . . .

American Supply Co.
94 Arch St.
Boston, Mass.

Anderson & Sons, Inc.
216 N. Elm
Westfield, Ma. 01085
. . . 1931-1982 . . .

Angell Mfg. Co., Inc.
1250 E. Monument Ave
Dayton, Ohio
. . . 1942-1961 . . .

Animate Toy Co.
N.Y.
. . . 1930's OE . . .

Ann St. Badge & Novelty Co.
21-23 Ann St.
N.Y.
. . . 1909 . . .

Antioch Bookplate Co.
888 Dayton St.
Yellow Springs, Oh. 45387
. . . 1980-1982 . . .

Apollo Jewelry
N.Y.C.
. . . 1930's OE . . .

Armantrout Bros.
Guthrie, Okla.
C. 1900 . . .

Armen, A.H., Manuf'g Co.
47 Hanover St.
Boston
C. 1898 . . .

Arrow Publicity & Novelty Co.
Cleveland, Ohio
. . . 1925 . . .

Artcraft Mfg. Co.
1735 Elizabeth N.W.
Grand Rapids, Mich.
. . . 1961-1982 . . .

Art Guild Inc.
Richmond, Va.
. . . 1980-1985 . . .

Award Incentives, Inc.
160 Jay St.
Brooklyn, N.Y.
. . . 1950-1985 . . .

Bachrach & Co.
556 Market St.
S.F.
. . . 1909 . . .

Badge A Minit & R.P.M. Assoc.
P.O. Box 618
La Salle, Il. 61301

Badge & Button Corp.
33 Waugh Dr.
Houston, Texas
. . . 1974-1985 . . .

Badge & Specialty Co. Ltd.
P.O. Box 456
Montreal
. . . 1935 . . .

Bainbridge, Chas. J., (C.J.), Badges & Buttons
134 Seymour
Syracuse, N.Y.
. . . 1907-1959 . . .

Bainbridge, H.C.
1401 N. Salina St.
Syracuse, N.Y.
. . . 1961-1985 . . .

Baldwin & Gleason Co. Ltd.
61 B'way
N.Y.
. . . 1888-1897 . . .

Bale Co., Div. of Carnation Co.
222 Public St.
Providence, R.I.
. . . 1980-1985 . . .

Balfour, L.G., Co.
25 County St.
Attleboro, Mass.
. . . 1938-1985 . . .

Ballou Reg'd.

Baltimore Badge & Novelty Company
Baltimore, Md.
. . . 1901-1908 . . .
(Successor to: Torsch & Lee)

Baltimore Badge Supply Co.
Baltimore, Md.
. . . 1915 . . .

B & R Mfr.
N.Y.C.
. . . 1930's OE . . .

Barron, J.G., and Associates, Inc.
333 N. Michigan Ave.
Chicago, Il. 60601
. . . 1980-1981 . . .

Barstow & Williams
Prov. R.I.

Bastian Bros. Co.
1600 Clinton Ave.
Rochester, N.Y. 14601
F. 1895-1983 . . .
(See: Whitehead & Hoag Co.)

Bayes Mfg. Co., Inc.
22 W. 21st St.
New York, N.Y. 10010
. . . 1961-1980 . . .

Beckwith Co., (The)
Norwich, Conn.
. . . 1909 . . .

Bell Co., (The)
Nashville
. . . 1930's OE . . .

Benz, Geo. E., & Co.
310 Olive St.
St. Louis
. . . 1904 . . .

Benz, Victor E.
51 Maiden Lane
New York
. . . 1906 . . .

Benziger Bros.,
Cincinnati
. . . 1912 . . .

Bernard Creations
N.Y.

Berrie, Russ, & Company, Inc.
111 Bauer Drive
Oakland, N.J. 07436
. . . 1974 . . .

Best Seal Corporation
54 Greene St.
New York, N.Y. 10013
. . . 1971-1985 . . .

Big Store
112 MacDougal St. (Ave.)
N.Y.C. 10012
. . . 1967 . . .

Big Three Badge Novelty Co.
Cleveland, O.
. . . 1921 . . .

"Bim" The Button & Badge Man
10 & 12 East 23rd Street
New York
. . . 1920's . . .

Blackinton, V.H., & Co., Inc.
221 John L. Dietsch Blvd.
Attleboro Falls, Ma. 02763
. . . 1938-1985 . . .

Blanckensee, L., & Co.
Phila., Pa. 19107
. . . 1976 . . .

Blank, Arthur, & Co., Inc.
140 Braintree St.
Boston, Mass. 02134
. . . 1961-1985 . . .

Bleder, J.L., Co.
334 So. Clinton
Chicago, Il.
. . . 1909-1912 . . .

Boller, J.
N.Y.
. . . 1930's OE . . .

Boston Badge Co.
294 Washington St.
Boston, Mass.
. . . 1920-1927 . . .

Boston Regalia Co., (The)
Boston, Mass.
. . . 1908-1922 . . .

Bothe, M & J
Jersey City, N.J.
. . . 1930's OF . . .

Bradshaw, Harry C., Co.
60 River Rd.
Summit, N.J.
. . . 1968-1985 . . .

Brandon Printing Co.
Nashville, Tenn.
. . . 1900 . . .

Braxmar, Chas. G., (C.G.) Co.
216 E. 45th
New York City, N.Y.
. . . 1896-1985 . . .

Brookes, A.W.
Detroit, Mich.
. . . 1930's OE . . .

Brown and Bigelow
St. Paul, Minn.
. . . 1939-1941 . . .

Brown, Wm. R., Co.
33 Eddy St.
Providence, R.I.

Browning, George M.
105 W. 40th
New York, N.Y.
(Successor to: Napier-Browning Co.)
. . . 1923-1924 . . .

Brueckman Specialties
703 E. 8 Mile Rd. at I-75
Hazel Park, Mich. 48030
. . . 1980-1985 . . .

Brunt, Walter N., Co.
111 7th St.
San Francisco, California
. . . 1899-1939

Bryce Enterprises
20 Jerusalem Ave.
Hicksville, N.Y.
. . . 1974-1985 . . .

Buchlein, Div. of Quality Engraving Co.
1000 Broad St.
Newark, N.J. 07102
F. 1852-1985 . . .

Bullard & Moore
1116 Main St.
Kansas City, Mo.
. . . 1899 . . .

Bullard Button Co.

Bunting Stamp Co., Inc.
312 Blvd. of the Allies
Pittsburgh, Pa. 15222
. . . 1926-1983 . . .

Butaco Corp.
6051 S. Knox
Chicago, Il.
. . . 1980-1985 . . .

Button King
780 E. Trimble Rd.
San Jose, Ca.
. . . 1985 . . .

Button Works
300 Broad St.
Nevada City, Ca. 95959
. . . 1975-1982 . . .

Button Works
947 S. Robert St.
St. Paul, Minn.
. . . 1981-1985 . . .

Cada Zin Co.
. . . 1972 . . .

Cady, Roy Brewster
Detroit, Mich.

Cammall Badge Co.
Boston, Mass.
. . . 1926-1932 . . .

Campbell, Morin, Co.
. . . 1930's OE . . .

Canadian Stamp
A.R. Gillon & S.O. Berring
Winnepeg
. . . 1936 . . .

Carnes Stamp Co.
182 W. 7th
St. Paul, Minn.
. . . 1968 . . .

Carolan & Clark Co., (The)
Newark, N.J.
. . . 1905 . . .

Carroll, J.B., Co.
3053 Carroll Ave.
Chicago 12, Ill.
c. 1902-1952 . . .

Chattanooga Button & Badge Mfg. Co.
P.O. Box 4253
Chattanooga, Tenn.
. . . 1928-1985 . . .

Childs, S.D. & Co.
17 N. Loomis
Chicago, Ill.
. . . 1916-1938 . . .

CHP
Chicago
. . . 1969 . . .

Cincinnati Regalia Co.
139 W. 4th St.
Cincinnati, Ohio
. . . 1968-1985 . . .

City Button Works
New Jersey
1923-1955

City Button Works
New York
F.1875-1893,1895-1923

Clark, A.N., & Son
Clarke, A.N., & Sons
Plainville, Conn.
c. 1880-1907 . . .

Cleveland Metal Works Co.
1291 W. 6th
Cleveland, Ohio
. . . 1916-1927 . . .

Clover, F.G., Co.
160 Franklin Ave.
Rockaway, N.J. 07866
. . . 1937-1985 . . .
(Successor to:
American Railway Supply Co.)
. . . 1890's-1936 . . .

Club Supplies, Inc.
P.O. Box 8502
Chicago, Il.
. . . 1980 . . .

Collins and Collins
Philadelphia
. . . 1930's OE . . .

Colonial Adv. Co.
6510 W. Broad St.
Richmond, Va.

Colorado Badge & Novelty Co.
1435 Welton St.
Denver, Colo.
. . . 1931-1952 . . .

Colorado Badge & Trophy Co.
1115 Lincoln St.
Denver, Col. 80205
. . . 1980-1985 . . .

Colso Novelty Co.
698 N. High St.
Columbus, Ohio
. . . 1902-1905 . . .

Colson, U.O., Printing & Advertising Co.
Paris, Il.

Columbia Advertising Co.
13317 101st Ave.
Richmond Hill, N.Y. 11419
. . . 1968 . . .

Columbia Spec. Co.
Calif.
. . . 1964 . . .

Columbus Plastic Products, Inc.
1601 W. Mound
Columbus, Ohio
. . . 1942-1950 . . .

Concors and Zarino
U.S.A.
. . . 1930's OE . . .

Conquest Industries
15962 Downey Blvd.
Paramount, Ca.
. . . 1981-1985 . . .

Continental Press, Inc.
St. Cloud, Minn.

Cook, David B.
Elgin, Ill.
. . . 1930's OE . . .

Cook, David C., Publishing Co.
Elgin, Il.; Chicago; New York; Boston

Coshocton Specialty Co.
Coshocton, Ohio

Cosmo Mfg. Co.
Chicago

Crafters-Green Duck Div.
255 S. Elm St.
Hernando, Miss.
. . . 1975-1976 . . .

Crafters, Inc.
14 So. Jefferson St.
Chicago, Ill.
. . . 1950-1964 . . .

Cranley Mfg. Co.
Chicago
. . . 1898 . . .

Cranley Photo Button Mfg. Co.
Chicago, Ill.
. . . 1907-1910 . . .

Creative Hse.
Chgo. 60641
(See N.P.P. Inc.)
. . . 1966 . . .

Crowell Pubg. Co.
N.Y.

Cruver Mfg. Co.
Chicago, Ill.
. . . 1907-1945 . . .

Cunningham, M.E., Co.
100 East Carson St.
Pittsburgh, Pa.
. . . 1918-1938 . . .

Dalo Button & Emblem Co.
166 5th Ave.
New York, N.Y. 10010
. . . 1980-1985 . . .

Danisch, A.J.
Chicago, Ill.
. . . 1930-1935 . . .

Darco
Box 5553
Cleveland, Ohio 44101

Darling, J.C.
Topeka, Kansas
. . . 1930's OE . . .

Dawson Co. Mfrs.
2136 E. 19th St.
Cleveland, Ohio
. . . 1952-1985 . . .

Dayton Stencil Works Mfg. Co.
113 E. Second St.
Dayton, Ohio 45402
[Dayton Stamp & Stencil Works Co., (The)]
. . . 1936-1985 . . .

Dealer Aids
12910 Woodward Ave.
Detroit, Mich.
. . . 1980-1985 . . .

Decorative Poster Co.
2115 Bennett Ave.
Cincinnati, Ohio
. . . 1938-1968 . . .

DeMoulin Bros. & Co.
1018 So. 14th St.
Greenville, Ill.
. . . 1913-1955 . . .

Detroit Badge & Novelty
City Bank Bldg.
Detroit, Mi. 48776
. . . 1980 . . .

De Turk, A. Lewis
Allentown, Pa.
. . . 1915 . . .

Dieges and Clust
Chicago
. . . 1930's OE . . .

Dieges and Clust
230 Public St.
Providence, R.I.
. . . 1958-1981 . . .

Dietz, Wm. H.
10 So. Wabash Ave.
Chicago, Ill. U.S.A.
. . . 1930's OE . . .

Dismar Corp.
4415 Marlton Pike
Pennsauken, N.J.
. . . 1985 . . .

Dodge Inc.
702 N. Hudson Ave.
Chicago, Ill.
. . . 1945-1968 . . .

Dodge Trophies & Awards
3519 Church St.
Clarkston, Georgia
. . . 1980-1985 . . .

Donaldson Publishing Co.
543 Clay St.
San Francisco, Ca.
. . . 1921 . . .

Donnelly/Colt Buttons
Box 271
New Vernon, N.J. 07975

Dove Co.
Chgo.

Dukinfield Printing Co.
Seattle
. . . 1935 . . .

Dunne, Thos., Co.
520 Natchez
New Orleans, La.
. . . 1938-1945 . . .

Eagle Metalart Co.
7 Dey St.
New York City, N.Y. 10007
. . . 1968-1985 . . .

Eagle Regalia Co., Inc.
7 Dey St.
New York, N.Y. 10007
F. 1910-1985 . . .

E.B.I. Breakthru, Inc.
821 4th Ave.
Lake Odessa, Mich.
. . . 1981-1985 . . .

Economy Novelty & Printing Co.
227 W. 39th St.
New York City, N.Y.
. . . 1939-1968 . . .

EDI Graphics, Inc.
1352 Armour Blvd.
Mundelein, Ill. 60060
. . . 1980-1981 . . .

Eells and Frame
Toledo, Ohio
. . . 1930's OE . . .

Ehrman Mfg. Co.
Boston, Mass.
Milford, N.H.
Walden, Mass.
. . . 1906-1920 . . .

Elwar Ltd.
. . . 1960's . . .

Emeloid Co., Inc. (The)
289-293 Laurel Ave.
Arlington, N.J.
. . . 1938 . . .

Empathy Graphics
N.Y.C.
. . . 1972 . . .

Emress Specialty Co.
N.Y.C., N.Y. 10010
. . . 1930's-1950's . . .

Erisman's
Lancaster, Pa.
. . . 1930's OE . . .

Esser Bros.
233 Fifth Ave.
Pittsburgh, Pa.
. . . 1908 . . .

Esty, Austin S.
Boston
. . . 1930's OE . . .

Etched Products Corp.
3907 Queens Blvd.
Long Island City 4, N.Y.
. . . 1950-1961 . . .

Evans & Convery, Inc.
Benson East
Jenkintown, Pa. 19048
. . . 1948-1985 . . .

E.W. Novelties, Inc.
16120 Cohasset St.
Van Nuys, Ca. 91406
. . . .1984-1985 . . .

Faircraft Co.
P.O. Box 155
Rock Island, Il.
. . . 1968-1985 . . .

Fargo Rubber Stamp Works
64 N. 4th St.
Fargo, N.D.
(See: FRS Industries, Inc.)
. . . 1980-1981 . . .

Felsenthal, G., & Sons
4114 Grand Ave.
Chicago, Ill.
. . . 1931-1942 . . .

Felsenthal and Co.

Felt Crafters
Plaistow, N.H.
. . . 1930's OE . . .

Filene's
Boston

Fink Badge Co.
St. Louis, Mo.
. . . 1910 . . .

Fisher, L. Harvey, Novelty Co.
Brooklyn, N.Y.
. . . 1930's OE . . .

Flags International
Osceola, Ind.
. . . 1980-1985 . . .

Floding Co., (The)
684 Spring St., N.W.
Altanta, Ga. 30308
. . . 1938-1982 . . .

Floding, W.E.
. . . 1916-1932 . . .

Floersheim, J. Kunstadter and Co.
Chicago
. . . c. 1900 . . .

Four Word Industries Corp.
9462 Franklin Ave.
Franklin Park, Il.
. . . 1980-1985 . . .

Fox Co., (The)
3400 Beekman St.
Cincinnati, Ohio
. . . 1930-1953 . . .

Fox, Gustave, Co., (The)
. . . 1918-1927 . . .

Fox, Lou
Chicago
. . . 1930's OE . . .

Franklin Printing & Engraving Co., (The)
321 Superior Street
Toledo, Ohio
. . . 1902 . . .

FRS Industries, Inc.
64 N. 4th St.
Fargo, N.D.
. . . 1985 . . .

Fgo. Rubber Stamp
. . . 1930's OE . . .

Fargo Rubber Stamp Works
. . . 1980-1981 . . .

Fuller Regalia & Costume Co.
Worcester, Mass.
. . . 1938 . . .

Funds 'n Games
218 Franklin
Des Moines, Iowa
. . . 1980-1985 . . .

Gage, F.E.
Lincoln, Neb.
. . . 1896 . . .

Garland Advertising Co.
4702 18th Ave.
Brooklyn, N.Y. 11204
. . . 1980-1985 . . .

Gemsco, Inc.
551 Anderson Ave.
Milford, Conn.
. . . 1931-1985 . . .

General Identification Products Co.
222 W. 19th St.
N.Y., 11, N.Y.
. . . 1952 . . .

General Mfg. Co.
. . . c.1912 . . .

General Specialty Co., Inc.
255 Spring St., S.W.
Atlanta, Ga.
. . . 1942-1985 . . .

George Bros.
Lincoln, Neb.
. . . 1922-1933 . . .

Geraghty, Charles M., Inc.
1520 W. Montana
Chicago, Ill.
. . . 1945-1963 . . .

Geraghty & Co.
. . . 1909-1944 . . .

Gerber, M.
729 South St.
Phila., Pa.
. . . 1908 . . .

German-American Button Co.
. . . 1910 . . .

German Literary Board
Burlington, Ia.

G.H. Stamp Works
Aberdeen, Wash.
. . . 1930's OE . . .

Gibson, A.C., Co. Inc.
877 Englewood Ave.
Buffalo, N.Y.
. . . 1938-1981 . . .

Gleason, Thos. Jay, (T.J.)
Brooklyn, N.Y.
. . . 1912 . . .

Gogerty, Pat, Displays
Mount Vernon, N.Y.
. . . 1948-1950's . . .

Gogerty, Pat, Co.

Goodenough and Woglom Co.
19 Beekman St.
N.Y.C.
. . . 1930's OE . . .

Good H. H.
Bellefontaine, Ohio
. . . C. 1900 . . .

Govin's Inc.
P.O. Box 2271
Tampa, Florida
. . . 1985 . . .

Grammes, L.F., & Sons, Inc.
80 Union St.
Allentown, Pa.
. . . 1920-1953 . . .

Granley Photo Button
Chicago
. . . 1930's OE . . .

Green Duck Corp.
255 S. Elm St.
Hernando, Ms. 38632
. . . 1977-1985 . . .

Greenduck Co., (The)-Chicago, Ill.
. . . 1912-1925 . . .

Green Duck Co., (The)
. . . 1926-1949 . . .

Green Duck Metal Stamping Co.
. . . 1950-1964 . . .

Green Duck Co.
. . . 1965-1974 . . .

Crafters-Green Duck Div.
Hernando, Miss.
. . . 1975-1976 . . .

Greene Co., (The)
New York
. . . 1939 . . .

Greyer Mfr. Co.
Boston
. . . 1930's OE . . .

Griffith & Roland Press
Philadelphia, Boston, Atlanta, Chicago,
Dallas, St. Louis, New York

Guedon Co.
Box 123
Audubon, N.J.
. . . 1961 . . .

Guild Inc.
2634 Georgia Ave.
Washington, D.C. 20001
. . . 1980 . . .

Haerr & Rosenberry Mfg. Co.
Springfield, Ohio
. . . 1950 . . .

Hall, Henry C. Branch of
Henry Moss and Co.
Philadelphia, Pa.
(See: Moss Industries, Inc.)
. . . 1931 . . .

Hallmark Cards, Inc.
. . . 1970's . . .

Hamilton Button M'f'y
116 High St.
Hamilton, Oh.
. . . 1902 . . .

Hammond Pub. Co.
Milwaukee

Hannah, Frederick W., Ltd.
Honeyborne
Evisham, England

Harding Uniform and Regalia Co.
Boston
. . . 1930's OE . . .

Harris, Benjamin, Co., Inc.
117-20 14th Rd.
College Point, N.Y.
. . . 1920-1973 . . .

Hart, Leo
Rochester, N.Y.
. . . 1930's OE . . .

Hartman, Wm. L.
Cincinnati, O.
. . . 1908 . . .

Haskell, W.H.
St. Louis
. . . 1930's OE . . .

H.A.S. Novelties, Ltd.
Toronto 863-1190

Haywood, S.F., & Co.
39 Park Pl.
New York City, N.Y.
. . . 1912-1915 . . .

Heartland Ltd.
Toronto, Canada

Heidelberg; (The)
15th & Race Streets
Philadelphia

Helwig, Louis, & Co.
205 W. Madison
Chicago, Ill.
. . . 1938 . . .

Helwig, Wm., & Co.
434 Elm
Cincinnati, Ohio
. . . 1938 . . .

Henderson Lith Co.
Cincinnati
. . . 1930's OE . . .

Henderson, W.D.
Chicago
. . . 1930's . . .

Hendler and Co.
San Francisco
. . . 1930's OE . . .

Hennigar's
Philadelphia
. . . 1930's OE . . .

Herbstreith, C.F., & Co.
Nutley, N.J.

Herff Jones, Div. of Carnation Co.
226 Public St.
Providence, R.I. 02940
. . . 1985 . . .

Hetzberg Diamond Shops, Inc.

Hewig & Marvic, Inc.
136 E. 57th St.
New York, N.Y. 10022
. . . 1968-1985 . . .

Hill Advertising Specialties Co.
110 E. 42nd St.
New York City, N.Y.
. . . 1942-1950 . . .

Hipco
Chgo, Ill.

Hizer, Joe, Novelty Co.
224 N. 11th St.
Philadelphia, Pa.
. . . 1926 . . .

Hodges Badge Co., Inc.
Schoolhouse Ln.
Portsmouth, R.I.
. . . 1928-1985 . . .

Hoegee, Wm. H., Co., Inc.
Los Angeles, Cal.
. . . 1906-1920 . . .

Horn Co.
Phila., Pa. 19126
. . . 1968 . . .

Howard, Don, Associates, Inc.
N.Y. 10036
. . . 1930's OE . . .

Howard, F.J.
Boston
. . . 1930's OE . . .

Humphrys Flag Co.
238 Arch St.
Philadelphia, Pa. 19106
. . . 1980-1985 . . .

Hursen Bros.
Chicago
. . . 1900 . . .

Hyatt Mfg. Co.
1 N. Holiday
Baltimore 2, Md.
. . . 1907-1968 . . .

Imber, L.J., Co.
1639 W. Evergreen Ave.
Chicago, Offices in Detroit & N.Y.
. . . 1930's-1961 . . .

Indianapolis Badge & Nameplate Co.
25 W. McLean Pl.
Indianapolis, Ind. 46202
. . . 1980-1985 . . .

Indianapolis Photo Button Mfg. Co.
8½ E. Wash. St.
Indianapolis, Ind.
. . . 1901-1903 . . .

International Badge & Novelty Co.
Newark, N.J.
. . . 1905-1908 . . .

Irish-American Company
Philadelphia, Pa.
. . . 1930 . . .

Irvine & Jachens, Inc.
6700 Mission
Daly City, Cal.
(See: Jachens)
. . . 1915-1980 . . .

Irwin-Hodson Company (The)
Ninth & S.E. Woodward
Portland, Or. 97202
. . . 1912-1983 . . .

Jaad, Inc.
13965 Burleigh Rd.
Brookfield, Wi. 53005
(Wisconsin Badge-O-Matic)
. . . 1985 . . .

Jachens
2129 Market St.
S.F., Cal.
(See: Irvine & Jachens, Inc.)
. . . 1910 . . .

Jackson, Henry
141 Fulton St.
New York City, N.Y.
. . . 1938 . . .

Jadco, Inc.
297 Dexter St.
Providence, R.I.
. . . 1980-1985 . . .

Japan, Sherman Specialty Co.
Merrick, N.Y.

Jay Shop, Inc.
197 Oakland Ave.
Pontiac, Mich.

Jennings & Graham
Cincinnati, Chicago,
Kansas City & San Francisco

Jens, F.E., Co.
Milwaukee, Wis.
. . . 1930's OE . . .

Jewel Emblem Mfg. Co.
1500 W. 59th
Chicago, Ill.
. . . 1928-1933 . . .

Joel, J.A., and Co.
147 Fulton St.
N.Y., N.Y.
. . . 1938 . . .

Johns, Robert
442-452 Wabash Ave.
Chicago, Illinois
. . . 1930's OE . . .

Johnston and Merhoff Co.
20 Brattle Sq.
Boston
. . . 1930's OE . . .

Jolle Jewelers International, Inc.
28-30 W. 36th
New York City, N.Y.
. . . 1961 . . .

Jonvan Mfr. Co.
Baltimore, Md.
. . . 1930's OE . . .

Jordan Ptg. Co.
411 Tenth St.
Oakland, Cal.
. . . 1909 . . .

Joy Products
24 W. 45th St.
N.Y., N.Y. 10036
. . . 1976-1984 . . .

Judson Press, (The)
Phila., Pa.; Boston, Mass.; Chicago, Il.;
Kansas City, Mo.; Los Angeles, Calif.;
Seattle, Wash.

Julian Art Studio
 Chicago

Kalamazoo Schools Work
Experience Program
1411 Oakland Dr.
Kalamazoo, Mich.

Keeshen Adv. Co.
Oklahoma City, Okla.
. . . 1933 . . .

Keil, A.J., Co., (The)
Betz Bldg.
Philadelphia
. . . 1920-1922 . . .

Keil & Styer Co., (The)
S.W. Cor. 17th & Tioga Sts.
Philadelphia, Pa.

Kelley-Strong Co.
220 Broadway
New York City, N.Y.
. . . 1925-1926 . . .

Kellow & Brown
428 Boyd St.
L.A., CA.
. . . 1916 . . .

Kennedy
Kansas City, Kansas
. . . 1930's OE . . .

Keyes-Davis Co., (The)
P.O. Drawer 1557
Battle Creek, Mi.
. . . 1968-1985 . . .

Keystone Badge Co.
806 Franklin St.
Reading, Pa.
. . . 1902-1985 . . .

Kinney Concepts
123 Stewart St.
Providence, R.I.
. . . 1985 . . .

Kinney Co.
. . . 1968-1981 . . .

Klcer Co.
2 Broadway
Paterson, N.J. 07505
(See: Merit Co.)
. . . 1980-1982 . . .

Klimpl Medal Co.
303 Fourth Ave.
New York City
. . . 1935 . . .

Knobby Krafters, Inc.
198 N. Main St.
Attleboro, Ma. 02703
. . . 1980-1985 . . .

Koza's Inc.
2910 S. Main
Pearland, Tx.
. . . 1985 . . .

Kratz Co. (The)
1130 Clark St.
Covington, Ky.
. . . 1942 . . .

Kraus & Sons, Inc.
245 7th Ave.
New York, N.Y.
. . . 1930's-1985 . . .

Kriebel & Bales
. . . 1941 . . .

L.A. Badge and Mfg. Co.
342 S. Broadway
Los Angeles, Cal.
. . . 1913 . . .

Lake, Fred L., and Co.
Dallas, Texas
. . . 1911-1924 . . .

Lane Stamp Co.
San Diego, Cal.
. . . 1938 . . .

Lauterer, Geo., Corp.
310 W. Washington St.
Chicago, Il. 60606
. . . 1906-1985 . . .

Lavenson Bureau For Advertisers
308-10 Walnut St.
Philadelphia, Pa.
. . . 1900 . . .

Leathertone, Inc.
153 Hamlet Ave.
Woonsocket, R.I.
. . . 1961-1985 . . .

Lehmberg, Wm.
Phila.
. . . 1912 . . .

Lenox Awards, Inc.
110 S. 11th Ave.
St. Charles, Ill.
. . . 1980-1985 . . .

Liberia de Quiroga
712 Dolorosa St.
San Antonio, Texas

Lilley-Ames Co., (The)
Columbus, Ohio
. . . 1922-1938 . . .

Ames Sword Co.
(Successor to: The Ames Manufacturing
Co.-Chicopee, Mass.)
F. 1834
(Purchased by Lilley Co. 1922-1923)

Lilley, M.C., and Co.
Columbus, Ohio
c.1860-1976 . . .

Lincoln Stamp & Seal Co.
1124 O St.
Lincoln, Nebraska
. . . 1938-1985 . . .

Linger, Claude R.
Burnsville, W.Va.
. . . 1939 . . .

Litchfield Corp.
25 Dey Street
New York City, N.Y.
. . . 1924-1925 . . .

Little Cross Crown System
UNCAS
Made in U.S.A.

Logo Co., (The)
California
. . . 1977 . . .

Lopez, A.R., & Bro.
Boston, Mass.
. . . 1912-1917 . . .

Lopez Badge and Novelties
Boston
. . . 1910 . . .

Los Angeles Badge & Novelty Co.
149 S. Main St.
Los Angeles, Calif.
. . . 1909 . . .

Lucke Badge & Button Co.
17-20 14th Rd.
College Point, N.Y.
. . . 1913-1973 . . .

Lynch, J.L.
325 W. Madison St.
Chicago, Ill.
. . . 1917-1925 . . .

Maclupe & Langley
301 Niagara St.
Buffalo,
and
156 Pearl St.
Toronto
. . . 1910 . . .

Madison Avenue Associates
Nashville, Tennessee

Magnum Advertising
P.O. Box 17376
Tampa, Florida
. . . 1985 . . .

Manee Novelty & Metal Co.
Malden, Mass.
. . . 1918 . . .

Manee Co.

Manitoba Stencil and Stampworks
Winnipeg
. . . 1930's OE . . .

Marburger, Alex
17 Ann Street
New York
. . . 1909 . . .

Marco Polos
320 Main St.
Southbridge, Ma. 01550
. . . 1985 . . .

Mart Line
4060 Pontoon Road
Granite City, Il. 62040
. . . 1984 . . .

Mason Costume and
Theatrical Supply Co.
Lancaster, Pa.
. . . 1930's OE . . .

Matthews International Corp.
6520 Penn Ave.
Pittsburgh, Pa. 15206
. . . 1980 . . .

Matthews, Jas. H., & Co.
. . . 1909-1968 . . .

Maxant Corporation, (The)
117 S. Morgan St.
Chicago, Il. 60607
. . . 1980-1983 . . .

Maxant Button & Supply Co.
. . . 1913-1952 . . .

Mayer, Geo. J., Co.
552 E. Market
Indianapolis, Ind.
. . . 1968 . . .

McCarthy, J.F.
Lynn, Mass.
. . . 1930's OE . . .

McGrath, James A.
Boston, Mass.
. . . 1930's OE . . .

Medallic Art Co.
Old Ridgebury Rd.
Danbury, Conn. 06810
. . . 1923-1985 . . .

Meek Co.
Coshocton, Ohio
. . . c. 1900 . . .

Mercantile Novelty Co.
St. Louis, Mo.
. . . 1930's OE . . .

Merit Co.
2 Broadway
Paterson, N.J.
(See: Kleer Co.)
. . . 1968-1980 . . .

Metal Arts Co., Inc. (The)
742 Portland Ave.
Rochester, N.Y. 14621
. . . 1942-1982 . . .

Metropolitan Equipment Co.
142 East 14th St.
New York
. . . 1905 . . .

Meyers, J.A., and Co.
Los Angeles
. . . 1930's OE . . .

Meyers Military Shop
Washington, D.C.
. . . 1930's OE . . .

Michigan Association of
Rehabilitation Facilities
938 Michigan National Tower
Lansing, Mich. 48933
. . . 1980-1981 . . .

Midwest Badge & Novelty Co., Inc.
4416 Excelsior Blvd.
Minneapolis, Mn. 55416
. . . 1930's-1985 . . .

Millenium Group
924 Cherry St.
Phila., Pa. 19107
. . . 1980 . . .

Miller and Co.
N.Y.
. . . 1930's OE . . .

Miller, Gordon B., & Co.
440 McMillan St.
Cincinnati, Ohio
. . . 1961-1985 . . .

Miller, W.F.
134 Park Row
New York
. . . 1898-1905 . . .

Minks Badge Co.
216 E. Baltimore S.
Baltimore, Md.
. . . 1907 . . .

Minks, Lewis, Jr.
Baltimore, Md.

Mitchell, C.G., Inc.
Cherry St.
Greene, N.Y.
. . . 1968 . . .

Montaco Graphics, Inc.
131 E. 10th Ave.
Conshohocken, Pa. 19428
. . . 1981-1985 . . .

Moore, T.F., Co.
Milwaukee, Wis.
. . . 1930's OE . . .

Moss Industries, Inc.
162 57th
Brooklyn, N.Y.
. . . 1950-1954 . . .

Moss, Henry, & Co., Inc.
. . . c. 1920's-1936 . . .
(See: Hall, Henry C.)

Moss, Samuel H., Inc.
36 E. 23rd St.
New York, N.Y.
F.1909-1985 . . .

Moss, Theo., Co., Inc.
2 Tillary St.
Brooklyn, N.Y.
. . . 1936 . . .

Mr. Button Products, Inc.
P.O. Box 68355
Indianapolis, In. 46268
. . . 1980-1985 . . .

Nadel and Shimmel
144 Park Row
N.Y.
. . . 1912 . . .

Napier-Browning Co.
105 W. 40th
New York, N.Y.
. . . 1915-1922 . . .
(See: Browning, George M.)

National Equipment Co.
12 E. 23d St.
New York
. . . 1898-1909 . . .

Newark Lithographing Co.
Newark, N.J.
. . . 1930's OE . . .

Newell Bros. Mfg. Co.
Springfield, Mass.
. . . C. 1898 . . .

Newell Bros. Button Co.
c.1840-1900

New England Flag and Regalia Co.
Stamford, Conn.
. . . 1930's OE . . .

New Haven Button Co.
New Haven, Conn.
. . . 1909-1918 . . .

Newman, L.
Indianapolis, Ind.
. . . 1930's OE . . .

Newman Manf'g. Co.
Cleveland, Ohio
. . . 1930-1934 . . .

Newton Mfg. Co.
Newton, Iowa
. . . 1980 . . .

Noble, F.H., & Co.
Chicago

Norsid Mfg. Co., Inc., (The)
43 Prospect
Yonkers, N.Y.
. . . 1950-1961 . . .

Northern Novelty Company
Fargo, N. Dak.
. . . 1959 . . .

Northwestern Stamp Works
43 East Third St.
St. Paul, Minn.
F.1882-1896 . . .

Norton Bros.
Chicago
. . . 1892 . . .

Novelty Supply Co.
208 Wood St.
Pittsburgh, Penn.
. . . 1927-1931 . . .

N.P.P. Inc.
(National Periodical Publications)
Creative Hse.
Chgo. 60641
. . . 1966 . . .

Offerman, F.J., Artworks, Inc.
299 Broadway
Buffalo, N.Y.
. . . 1938-1961 . . .

Offset Gravure Corp.
35-37 36th St.
Long Island City, N.Y.
. . . 1939-1943 . . .

O'Hara Dial Co.
Waltham, Mass.
F. 1833-1958

Ohio Badge Co., (The)
696 N. High St.
Columbus, Ohio
. . . 1904-1917 . . .

Okla. Nov. Ptg. Co.
Okla. City
. . . 1926 . . .

"Old Glory" Mfg. Co.
20 S. Wells
Chicago, Ill.
. . . 1938 . . .

Oleet and Co., Inc.
212 Astor St.
Newark, N.J.
. . . 1980-1985 . . .

Oleet, Harold K., & Bros.
60 Claremont Pl.
Mount Vernon, N.Y.
. . . 1968-1972 . . .

Oleet Bros.
Oleet

Olympic Button & Emblem
. . . 1950's . . .

Omaha Paraphernalia House
Omaha, Neb.
. . . 1906-1908 . . .

One World Advertising Specialties & Co.
11 Main St.
New Milford, Ct. 06776
. . . 1985 . . .

Orange Mfg. Co.
61 Hoyt
Newark, N.J.
. . . 1925-1945 . . .

Osborne Coinage Co.
1006 Bader
Cincinnati, Ohio
. . . 1961-1968 . . .

Oscarette Co.
211 W. 28th
New York City, N.Y.
. . . 1961-1968 . . .

Pacific Coast Stamp Works
400 S. River
Seattle, Wash.
. . . 1942-1985 . . .

Pacific Regalia Co.
Portland, Ore.
. . . 1902-1905 . . .

Pacific Stamp Works
1015 A St.
Tacoma
. . . 1909 . . .

P & F Sales
Regina, Saskatchewan
Canada
. . . 1937 . . .

Para Gift, Inc.
Chgo. 60610
. . . 1938 . . .

Paragon Co.
New Bedford, Ma.
. . . 1938 . . .

Parisian Novelty Co.
3510 S. Western Ave.
Chicago, Il. 60609
. . . 1905-1985

Pasquale Co., B.
2550 Marin
San Francisco, Ca. 94124
. . . 1952-1980 . . .

Paulich Spec. Co., Inc.
Cleveland, Ohio 44110
. . . 1976 . . .

P.C. Stampworks
Seattle
. . . 1942 . . .

Peacock Co., (The)
109 Wash'gT'n St.
Providence, R.I.
. . . 1920 . . .

Pearce & Feraille
10 S. 18th
Philadelphia, PA.
. . . 1905-1910 . . .

Penn Arts Mfg. Co.
3302 Franford Ave.
Philadelphia, PA.
. . . 1950-1968 . . .

Penn Rivet Corp., Plastics Div.
254 Huntingdon St.
Philadelphia, Pa.
. . . 1945 . . .

Personal Service Co.
Springfield, Il. 62702
. . . 1980 . . .

Pettibone Bros. Mfg. Co.
23 E. 77th St.
Cincinnati, Oh. 45216
. . . 1905-1985 . . .

Pettibone Manufacturing Co.
C.1880-1890 . . .

Pettibone
. . . 1900-1942 . . .

Phelps & Sons Mfg. Co.
110 Pennington
Newark, N.J.
. . . 1909-1923 . . .

Phelps
. . . 1899-1905 . . .

Philadelphia Badge Co., Inc.
1005 Filbert St.
Philadelphia, Pa. 19107
F.1900-1977 . . .

Philip German Badges & Buttons
25 N. 4th St.
Harrisburg, Pa.
. . . 1926-1931 . . .

Phillips, Albert
Baltimore, Md.
. . . 1930's OE . . .

Photo Button Co.
Indianapolis
. . . 1930's OE . . .

Photo Button Mfg. Co.
J.D. Basserman
556 North High St.
Columbus, O.
. . . c.1900 . . .

Photo Jewelry Mfg. Co.
269 Dearborn St.
Chicago, U.S.A.
. . . 1897-1901 . . .

Photopin Co.
Chicago
. . . 1930's . . .

Photovolt Corp.
90 Madison Av.
New York City, N.Y.
. . . 1968 . . .

Pictorial Productions, Inc.
Tuckahoe, New York
(VARI-VUE: flasher buttons)
. . . 1930's-1968 . . .

Pilgrim Badge
Boston 02215

Pilgrim Badge & Specialty Co.
216 Vassar
Cambridge, Mass.
. . . 1920-1968 . . .

Pilgrim Plastic Products Co., Div. of
Pilgrim Badge & Label Co.
268 Babcock St.
Boston, Ma. 02215
. . . 1961-1985 . . .

Pin-Lock Button Co.
174 S. Clinton St.
Chicago
. . . 1900 . . .

Pioneer Man'f'g Co.
252 Bowery
New York

Pioneer Novelty Mfg. Co.
329 E. 29th
New York City, N.Y.
. . . 1921-1924 . . .

Pitt Products Co., Inc.
197-201 Sussex Ave.
Newark, N.J.
. . . 1950 . . .

Plastic World, Inc.
Maspeth, N.Y.

Palxy Color, Inc.
11-01 40th Ave.
Long Island City, N.Y.
. . . 1980-1985 . . .

Porter, J.C.
Paterson, N.J.
. . . 1914 . . .

Pricing Press
105 Lafayette St.
New York City, N.Y.
. . . 1950 . . .

Printloid, Inc.
10-02 44th Ave.
Long Island City, N.Y. 11101
. . . 1945-1985 . . .

Promotion People, Inc. (The)
Chicago

Pudlin, M., Co.
286 5th Ave.
New York City, N.Y.
. . . 1924-1950 . . .

Pulver, F.F., Co.
Rochester, N.Y.
. . . 1902-1904 . . .

Pustet, Fr.
Cincinnati;New York
. . . 1919 . . .

Quimby Mfg. Co.
Minneapolis
. . . 1930's OE . . .

Rabinowitz, Jacob & Co., Inc.
338 W. 37th St.
New York, N.Y.
. . . 1950-1968 . . .

Raditz, I.H., & Co.
. . . 1954 . . .

Reading Badge and Button Co.
Reading, Pa.
. . . 1920's OE . . .

Reading Ribbon Badge Co.
11th Spruce Sts.
Reading, PA.
. . . 1904 . . .

Red Jacket Pencil Co.
Sanders Block
Nashville, Tn. 37201
(See: Sanders Mfg. Co.)
. . . 1942-1981 . . .

Reindl, Hugh M.
Milwaukee, Wisc.
. . . 1930's OE . . .

Reskrem Silver Mfg. Co.
76 Forsyth St.
New York City, N.Y.
. . . 1938-1950 . . .

Riley-Klotz Mfg. Co.
Newark, N.J.
. . . 1896-1900 . . .

Robbins Co., (The)
Attleboro, Mass.
F.1892-1938 . . .

Robbi Promotional Advertising
45 Academy St.
Newark, N.J.
. . . 1985 . . .

Rochester Celluloid Co.
Rochester, N.Y.
. . . 1903 . . .

Roehm, Edward R.
15 E. Grand River
Detroit, Mich.
. . . 1922-1938 . . .

Rogers, J. Earl
307 Ex. Place
New Orleans, La.
. . . 1915-1916 . . .

Ronemus & Co.
Signs & Novelties
Baltimore, Md.
. . . 1900 . . .

Rosenblatt, Geo. H.
180 B'way
New York City, N.Y.
. . . 1905-1920 . . .

Royal Button Works
505 Market
Philadelphia, Pa.
. . . 1915-1926 . . .

Royal Incentives
43 John St.
New York City, N.Y.
. . . 1945 . . .

Rudolph Bros. Mfg.
Philadelphia, Pa.
. . . c.1905 . . .

Russell Badge Mfg. Co., Inc.
417 Water St.
Wakefield, Mass.
. . . 1961-1985 . . .

Russell Mfg. Co.
. . . 1940-1950 . . .

Russell-Hampton Co., Inc.
2550 Wisconsin Ave.
Chicago, Il. 60515
. . . 1952-1985 . . .

Safford Industries Group
2425 W. Hubbard St.
Chicago, Il. 60612
. . . 1980-1985 . . .

Salt Lake Stamp Co.
384 W. 2nd S.
Salt Lake City, Utah 84101
. . . 1938-1985 . . .

Sanders Mfg. Co.
Sanders Block
Nashville, Tn. 37201
(See: Red Jackett Pencil Co.)
F.1918-1985 . . .

Sanger, H.H., Inc.
499-501 Fifth Av.
New York City, N.Y.
. . . 1968 . . .

Schiller Favor Corp.
348 E. Jefferson
Detroit, Mich.
. . . 1950 . . .

Schlechter, Ed H.
540 Hamilton St.
Allentown, Pa.
. . . 1909-1935 . . .

Schlechter, G.A., Co.
Reading, Pa.
. . . 1916 . . .

Schwaab, Inc.
11415 W. Burleigh Ave.
Milwaukee, Wisc.
. . . 1980-1985 . . .

Schwaab Stamp & Seal Co.
. . . 1938-1968 . . .

Schwartz, H.& S., Button Co., Inc.
240 W. 37th St.
New York City, N.Y.
. . . 1942-1961 . . .

Schwartz, Henry
15 Ann St.
New York City
. . . 1916 . . .

Schwerdtle Stamp Co.
168 Elm St.
Bridgeport, Conn. 06603
. . . 1930-1985 . . .

Scovill Mfg. Co.
Waterbury, Conn.
1850-1985 . . .

Abel Porter & Co.
F.1802-1820

Leavenworth, Hayden & Scovill
1821-1826

J.M.L. & W.H. Scovill
1827-1839

Scovills & Co.
1840-1849

Selby, J.T., Photo Buttons, Badges and
Novelties
50 N. Eutaw St.
Baltimore, Md.
. . . 1900-1930's OE . . .

Sentis Stencil Works, Inc.
480 Canal St.
New York, N.Y. 10013
. . . 1980-1985 . . .

Shapiro and Karr
Philadelphia, Pa.
. . . 1930's OE . . .

Sharkey Novelty Co.
Toronto, Canada
. . . 1930's OE . . .

Shaw, J.H.
Philadelphia, Pa.
. . . 1920's . . .

Shear, Charles
New York

Sheperd and Wilson
St. Paul, Minn.
. . . 1930's OE . . .

Shepherd Photo Co.
St. Paul, Minn.
. . . 1930's OE . . .

Short & Roehm Co. (The)
370 Orange St.
Newark, N.J.
[See: Sillcocks-Miller Co., (The)]
. . . 1927-1929 . . .

Shryock-Todd Notion Co.
St. Louis
. . . 1930's OE . . .

Shuler, G.A., Co.
Boston, Mass.
. . . 1930's OE . . .

Sillcocks-Miller Co., (The)
(Short & Roehm Co., Associates)
310 Snyder Ave.
Berkeley Heights, N.J. 07922
c. 1908-1982 . . .

Simon, E&H., Inc.
375 4th Ave.
New York City, N.Y.
. . . 1950-1968 . . .

Simon Co., (The)
. . . 1942 . . .

Sioux Calendar & Adv. Co.
Sioux City, Iowa
. . . 1920 . . .

Skemo Ltd.
Toronto, Canada

Slater, N.G., Corp.
230 W. 19th St.
N.Y., N.Y. 1011
. . . 1941-1985 . . .

Sleeper Stamp Co.
Sacramento, California
. . . 1930's OE . . .

Smith & Lamar
Nashville, Tn; Dallas, Tx.;
Richmond, Va.

Sommer Badge Mfg. Co., (The)
186 Emmet St.
Newark, N.J. 07102
F.1880-1985 . . .

Southard Co., Inc., (The)
555 E. Long St.
Columbus, Ohio 43215
. . . 1968-1985 . . .

Spencer & Co.
. . . c. 1930's . . .

Spencer, James, & Co.
Philadelphia, Pa.
. . . 1927-1934 . . .

Spencer, S.M., Mfg. Co.
131 Summer St.
Boston, Mass.
. . . 1938-1985 . . .

Spiegel Nov. Co.
17 Ann St.
N.Y.C.
. . . 1930's-1942 . . .

Spies Bros.
6 E. Monroe
Chicago, Ill.
. . . 1961-1968 . . .

Spokane Stamp Works
West 401 First St.
Spokane, Wash.
. . . 1961-1985 . . .

Stafford, N., Co.
New York City; Brooklyn, N.Y.
. . . 1931-1950 . . .

Stafford Mfg. Co., Inc.
143-145 58th
Brooklyn, N.Y.
. . . 1961-1968 . . .

Standard Badge Engraving Co.
Philadelphia, Pa.
. . . 1930's OE . . .

Standard Emblem Co., Inc.
7 Beverly
Providence, R.I.
. . . 1920-1968 . . .

Standard Printing & Publishing Co.
Huntington, W. Va.
. . . 1935 . . .

Standard Publishing Co.
Cincinnati, Ohio
. . . 1930's OE . . .

Standwood-Hillson Corp.
Brookline, Mass.
. . . 1928-1931 . . .

Star Engraving Co.
177 Minna St.
San Francisco, Ca.
. . . 1930's-1964 . . .

Steiner Engraving & Badge Co.
804 Pine St.
St. Louis, Missouri
. . . 1904-1937 . . .

Stephenson Mfg. Co.
230 E. Tutt
South Bend, Ind.
. . . 1926-1946 . . .

Stephenson Works Co.
. . . 1915 . . .

Stilz, Louis, & Bro. Co.
155 N. 4th
Philadelphia, Pa.
. . . 1968 . . .

Stimpson Edwin B., Co.
70 Franklin Ave.
Brooklyn, N.Y.
. . . 1916-1921 . . .

St. Louis Button Co., Inc.
Hernando, Miss.
. . . 1966-1976 . . .

St. Louis Button Co.
St. Louis, Mo.
F. 1893-1915 . . .

St. Louis Button & Mfg. Co.
. . . 1918-1965 . . .

Stoffel Seals Corporation
115 Main St.
Tuckahoe, N.Y. 10707
. . . 1961-1985 . . .

Stovall, H.S.
Weatherley, Mo.
. . . 1930's OE . . .

Strickrott, John F.
Topeka, Kansas
. . . 1930's OE . . .

Sullivan, James H.
Springfield, Mass.
. . . 1930's OE . . .

Sunset
Newark, N.J.
. . . 1930's OE . . .

Swift, Louis, & Co.
St. Paul
. . . 1930's OE . . .

Texas State Advertising Co.
6333 Gulf Frwy.
Houston, Tx.
. . . 1985 . . .

Think Ideas, Inc.
38 W. 32nd St.
New York, N.Y.
. . . 1970-1985 . . .

Thumb Things
680 S. Freeway Rd.
St. Paul, Mn. 55118
. . . 1980-1985 . . .

Tilton, H.W., Co.
Pembroke Arcade
Indianapolis
. . . 1899 . . .

Torsch & Franz Badge Co.
3 No. Liberty St.
Baltimore, Md.
. . . 1909-1959 . . .

Torsch & Lee
Baltimore, Md.
(See: Baltimore Badge & Novelty
Company)
. . . 1896 . . .

Torsch and Minks Badge co.
Baltimore, Md.
. . . 1930's OE . . .

Towle, E.J.
408 Dexter Ave. N.
Seattle, Wash.
(See: West Earth, Inc.)
. . . pre-1981 . . .

Trapp Print Shop
Topeka, Kansas
Chas. H. Trapp
. . . 1908 . . .

Trenton Advt. Nov. and Badge Co.
Trenton, N.J.
. . . 1930's OE . . .

Trimble A.G., Co.
3008 Jenkins Arcade
Pittsburgh, Pa. 15222
F.1913-1985 . . .

Tunnel City Regalia Co., (The)
Det., Mich.
Port Huron, Mich.
. . . 1930's OE . . .

Twelfth St. Badge & Novelty House
Phila., Pa.
. . . 1930's OE . . .

Uhl Bros.
Toledo, Ohio
. . . 1930's OE . . .

Union Litho-Metal Corp.
2608 N. Cicero
Chicago, Ill.
. . . 1961-1968 . . .

United Trophy Mfg. Inc.
610 N. Orange Ave.
Orlando, Fl. 32801
. . . 1985 . . .

Universal Badge Co.
3 School St.
Boston, Mass.
. . . 1931-1940 . . .

Universal Emblem Button Co.
103 State Street
Chicago, Ill., U.S.A.
. . . c.1900 . . .

U.U.U.
21st St., Marks Pl.
N.Y.C. 10002
. . . 1970's . . .

Van's Advertising Specialties and
Election Items Mfrs.
Box 217
Flanders, N.J. 07836
. . . 1980-1982 . . .

Votes Unlimited
Ferndale, N.Y.

Wade Button Co.
Boston, Mass.
. . . c.1880-1907 . . .

Wager, Wm. T.
2752 3rd Ave.
Bronx, N.Y.
. . . 1933 . . .

Ward, Bill, Inc.
Delaware

Walt Co., Inc.
New York City, N.Y.
. . . 1950-1968 . . .

Walter, N.C., & Sons
301 Degraw
Brooklyn, N.Y.
. . . 1922-1968 . . .

Waterbury Companies, Inc.
64 Ave. of Industry
Waterbury, Conn. 06720
. . . 1944-1985 . . .

Aaron Benedict
F.1812-1822

A. Benedict & Co.
1823-1828

Benedict & Coe
1829-1833

Benedict & Burnham Co.
1834-1848

Waterbury Button Co.
1849-1943

Waterbury Mfg. Co.
237 Grand
Waterbury, Conn.
. . . 1905-1928 . . .

Webb, F.M., & Co.
Seattle, USA
. . . 1930's OE . . .

Weber Badge & Novelty Co., (The)
Reading, Pa.
. . . 1906-1915 . . .

Weil Novelty Co.
New Haven, Conn.
. . . 1901 . . .

Weil, P.H.
New Haven
. . . 1916-1917 . . .

Weissler, I. Irving, Co.
381-383 Pearl St.
Brooklyn, N.Y.
. . . 1976-1980 . . .

Wendell-Greenwood Co., (The)
Minneapolis, Minn.
. . . 1916-1919 . . .

Wendell-Northwestern, Inc.
2430 E. Franklin Ave.
Minneapolis, Minn.
(See: Wendell's, Inc.)
. . . 1930's-1961 . . .

Wendell's, Inc.
2430 E. Franklin Ave.
Minneapolis, Minn.
(See: Wendell-Northwestern, Inc.)
. . . 1936-1938 . . .
. . . 1968-1985 . . .

West Earth, Inc.
4087 Dexter Ave. N.
Seattle, Wash.
(Successor to: Towle, E.J.)
. . . 1981-1985 . . .

Western Badge & Button Co.
1109 W. 7th St.
Los Angeles, Cal.
(See: Western Badge & Trophy Co.)
. . . 1915-1961 . . .

Western Badge & Novelty Co.
255 University
St. Paul, Minn.
. . . 1931-1977 . . .

Western Badge & Trophy Co.
1716 W. Washington Blvd.
Los Angeles, Cal.
. . . 1959-1983 . . .
1109 W. 7th St., L.A.
(See: Western Badge & Button Co.)

Western Badge Co.
Los Angeles
. . . 1930's OE . . .

Western Bargain House
Streetmens Novelties
272 E. Madison St.
Chicago, IL
. . . 1920 OE . . .

Western Specialty Mfg. Corp.
Cheyenne, Wyo.
. . . 1965-1985 . . .

Westminister Press (The)
Philadelphia, New York, Chicago,
San Francisco, St. Louis, Pittsburg,
Cincinnati, Nashville
. . . 1930's OE . . .

Westrich, T.C.
Chicago
. . . 1928 . . .

Weyhing Bros. Mfg. Co.
3040 Gratiot Ave.
Detroit, Mich.
. . . 1937-1985 . . .

Whitehead & Hoag Co.
272 Sussex Ave.
Newark, N.J.
. . . 1894*-1958 . . .

(*1894-1st patent obtained;
1896- production began.)
(Purchased by Bastian Bros. Co.)

White, Luther C., (L.C.), Co.
A sub. of the Ball & Socket Mfg. Co.
. . . 1901-1985 . . .
25 Willow St.
Cheshire, Ct. 06410
F.1851-1980 . . .

(Ball & Socket Mfg. Co. successor to:
Cheshire Mfg. Co. 1850-1901)

Whiteson, I.
. . . 1930's OE . . .

Wibbey, Thos.
Toronto
. . . 1913 . . .

Williams & Anderson Co.
812 Branch Ave.
Providence, R.I.
. . . 1961-1985 . . .

Williamson Stamp Co.
16 N. 3rd
Minneapolis, Minn.
. . . 1929-1945 . . .

Williamson Stamp Makers
Minneapolis
. . . 1930's OE . . .

Williamson, C.T., Wire Novelty Co.
Newark, N.J.
. . . 1905-1923 . . .

Wiltzies, M.H.
Milwaukee, Wisc.
Barclay St., N.Y.

Wojetcki, Michael
1037 Milwaukee Ave.
Chicago, Ill.
. . . 1912-1914 . . .

Wolff, Harold
Camden, N.J.
. . . 1939 . . .

Woodburn, W.J., & Son
Montreal, Canada

Wulff, Henry
195 Gensesee St.
Buffalo, N.Y.
. . . 1912 . . .

Sources:

Buttons, Badges, and Ribbons.

Thomas Register (1905-1985).

MacRae's Blue Book (1931-1982).

"Button History," *The Button Book,* Ted Hake.

Buttons in Sets, 1896-1972, Marshall N. Levin and Theodore L. Hake.

The Complete Checklist of American Button Makers, Manufacturers and Outfitters, 1710-1976. The New England Publishing Co.

"How Buttons are Made," Seminar conducted by Robert Levine and Kenneth Buck, Eleventh APIC National Convention, Chicago, Illinois, August 12, 1983.

The Collector's Encyclopedia of Buttons, Sally C. Luscomb, Bonanza Books, N.Y., 1967.

Smithsonian Institution, National Museum of American History, Washington, D.C., Trade catalogue collection.

Issues of the APIC *Newsletter* and *The Keynoter;* also, *The Political Bandwagon,* and *Political Collector.*

Leading mail auction catalogues.

A special thanks to Ted Hake for sharing his "list" and giving invaluable assistance.

DATING CELLULOID BUTTONS
by
Ted Hake

The original concept of dating celluloid buttons by studying changes in the back paper designs of a given manufacturer was developed by Stewart and Emily Barr, who specialize in buttons issued for governors, senators and other "local" candidates. Since exact election dates for these candidates are known, the Barrs were able to determine which years various back paper designs were in use. Their original research was published in *Collectibles Monthly* (November, 1978). The study concentrated primarily on ⅞" buttons from the 1894-1924 period and three manufacturers: Whitehead & Hoag, Bastian Brothers, and St. Louis Button Co.

To expand on the original research, hundreds of buttons carrying a specific date as part of the obverse inscription were assembled from the inventory of Hake's Americana & Collectibles. To make the study as broad as possible, buttons of every size, from all time periods and all manufacturers were included. The buttons were arranged by the year appearing on the obverse and then the back papers were examined.

Some obvious limitations to this dating method became apparent very quickly. Some companies did not use back papers at all, other companies used papers but never altered the design, and, as broad as the sample of dated buttons was, some companies were not represented by enough dated buttons to draw valid conclusions.

The sample of dated buttons was broad enough to draw conclusions about six button manufacturers. For a small company like C.J. Bainbridge, Syracuse, N.Y., about fifty dated buttons were studied while the sample for Whitehead & Hoag consisted of hundreds of buttons. Unfortunately, the companies did not consider the back papers important enough to cease using an "old" design immediately upon the adoption of a "new" design. Often a new design was introduced but the supply of papers with the old design was used until it ran out. This creates an overlapping time period when more than one back paper design was in use. For some companies, such as Western Badge and Novelty Co., the sample was large but did not cover every year. Thus, it is certain the Type II paper was used in 1910-1911 and the Type III paper was used in 1915-1916, but which design or designs were used from 1912-1914 remains a mystery.

The larger companies, Whitehead & Hoag, Bastian, and St. Louis, made many back paper design changes which are most helpful in drawing valid conclusions regarding dates. Still, these conclusions are certainly open to revision and refinement. Hopefully, readers will investigate their own collections to confirm the information offered here. Information about discrepancies or information that fills in gaps is welcomed. If enough new information is accumulated, an update to this section will be published. If you would like to receive any updates, please send a note to that effect to the publisher.

THE WHITEHEAD & HOAG CO. - NEWARK, N.J.

The following guidelines apply to ⅞" or smaller lapel studs and buttons:

1894
TYPE I
LAPEL STUD

Usually ¾" with a white metal rim surrounding a thin layer of celluloid that covers the paper. The reverse has a stud back surrounded by four triangular prongs. The cap of the stud is inscribed "WHITEHEAD & HOAG CO/NEWARK N.J./PAT. APP'D FOR". (See Type II)

1895
TYPE II
LAPEL STUD

A major design change eliminated the need for the obverse metal rim. Now the celluloid and paper edges are tucked under the metal back. The design and inscription of the reverse remains the same as Type 1.

1896
TYPE III
LAPEL STUD

The reverse design is similar to Types I and II except the four pronged fasteners are replaced by three punched holes arranged in a triangle around the stud.

	1896 TYPE IV	The first pin-back buttons were produced in 1896. The first back papers are covered with a thin layer of celluloid. Enclosed in a black circle is a circular inscription "THE WHITEHEAD & HOAG CO. NEWARK, N.J." and within that is a single patent incription also in a circular design "PATENTED JULY 11th 1894."
	1896 TYPE V	The celluloid covered Type IV paper was used very briefly and was replaced by a totally re-designed paper. The paper has a varnished finish rather than a celluloid covering and lists two patent dates as "JULY 17, 1894." and "APRIL 14, 1896."
	1896-1898 TYPE VI	Similar to Type V except a third patent date of "JULY 21, 1896" is included. Some papers have a varnished finish while others do not.
	1898 TYPE VII	A briefly used, but very attractive, design featuring a light blue border surrounding a shield outlined in gold. The patent dates are the same as Types V and VI.
	1898-1899 TYPE VIII	A thin black line separates the company name, city and state information at the top from the three patent dates listed below.
	1900-1901 TYPE IX	Similar to Type VIII except at the center printed in red is a union label reading "TYPOGRAPHICAL/UNION LABEL/ NEWARK NO 103".
	1901 TYPE X	Similar to Types VIII and IX except the union label is in black and the patent dates are listed on two lines instead of three.
	1901-1912 TYPE XI	In 1901 the union label was totally re-designed and reads "ALLIED PRINTING/TRADES COUNCIL/UNION LABEL/ NEWARK, N.J.". A number "3" appears to the right.
	1912-1940's TYPE XII	The back paper was re-designed for the last time in 1912. The long-term use of this design ends the usefulness of this method for dating buttons.

The following guidelines apply to 1¼″ and larger buttons:

1896
TYPE I

The obverse has a brass rim while the reverse has a tin cover with a pin soldered in a horizontal groove. Stamped in the metal in a circular design is "WHITEHEAD & HOAG C°/ NEWARK, N.J." with "BADGES" at the center. Below is "PAT. JUNE 12.94".

1896
TYPE II

Apparently the first open back button paper for the 1¼″ size. The paper is beige with a lightly varnished surface. The inscription reads "PIN BACK/PAT. APRIL 14, 1896/THE WHITEHEAD & HOAG CO./BADGES/FLAGS/BANNERS/ NEWARK, N.J.".

1896-1897
TYPE III

This paper is in a calendar button for January, 1897. A red rose with green leaves and stem is surrounded by a circle of red type "COMPLIMENTS OF THE WHITEHEAD & HOAG CO. NEWARK, N.J. U.S.A./BADGES, BUTTONS, ADVERTISING NOVELTIES ETC.".

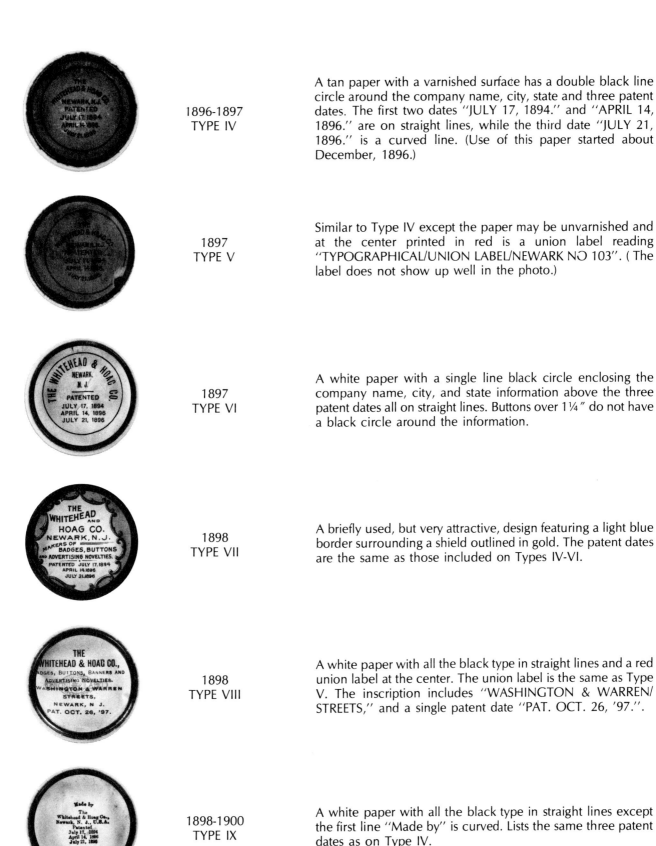

1896-1897
TYPE IV

A tan paper with a varnished surface has a double black line circle around the company name, city, state and three patent dates. The first two dates "JULY 17, 1894." and "APRIL 14, 1896." are on straight lines, while the third date "JULY 21, 1896." is a curved line. (Use of this paper started about December, 1896.)

1897
TYPE V

Similar to Type IV except the paper may be unvarnished and at the center printed in red is a union label reading "TYPOGRAPHICAL/UNION LABEL/NEWARK NO 103". (The label does not show up well in the photo.)

1897
TYPE VI

A white paper with a single line black circle enclosing the company name, city, and state information above the three patent dates all on straight lines. Buttons over 1¼" do not have a black circle around the information.

1898
TYPE VII

A briefly used, but very attractive, design featuring a light blue border surrounding a shield outlined in gold. The patent dates are the same as those included on Types IV-VI.

1898
TYPE VIII

A white paper with all the black type in straight lines and a red union label at the center. The union label is the same as Type V. The inscription includes "WASHINGTON & WARREN/ STREETS," and a single patent date "PAT. OCT. 26, '97.".

1898-1900
TYPE IX

A white paper with all the black type in straight lines except the first line "Made by" is curved. Lists the same three patent dates as on Type IV.

1900
TYPE X

Identical to Type IX except printed at the top is a light grey union label with an inscription identical to Type V.

**1900
TYPE XI**

The company name and a single patent date "PAT. OCT. 26, '97." form curved lines at the top and bottom enclosing the other information. Included is a union label reading "ALLIED PRINTING/TRADES COUNCIL/UNION LABEL/NEWARK" with a "3" to the right.

**1900-1901
TYPE XII**

A union label at the top is inscribed "•L•I•P•&•B•A•" and reads "AMERICAN/MANUFACTURE/UNION/LABEL". There are two patent dates reading "PAT. APRIL 14, 1896/JULY 21, 1896.".

**1900-1912
TYPE XIII**

The union label at the top reads "ALLIED PRINTING/TRADES COUNCIL/UNION LABEL/NEWARK" with a "3" to the right. The type is on straight lines and includes "Pat: April 14, 1896,/July 21, 1896.".

**1912-1948
TYPE XIV**

The back paper was totally re-designed in 1912 and then used without further changes, with two exceptions: (1) see Type XV, and (2) sometime after 1948 the union label was eliminated while the rest of the design remained unchanged. One known example of this paper (Type XVI, not illustrated) is in a button dated 1951. Possibly this design was used a few years before and/or after 1951.

**1933-1936
TYPE XV**

Circular type with the company name, city, and state surrounds the other information. The tiny union label on Type XIV is replaced with the slogan "MEMBER NRA".

ST. LOUIS BUTTON CO. — ST. LOUIS, MO.

The following guidelines apply to buttons of all sizes, with variations as noted:

**1899-1907
TYPE I**

Metal covered back with a long pin protruding from a punched hole near the top of the metal cover. Stamped inscription reads "ST LOUIS BUTTON CO ST LOUIS".

**1899-1907
TYPE II**

Same as Type 1, but stamped inscription reads "ST LOUIS BUTTON CO/620 N. BR.D.W.Y. ST LOUIS".

1900
TYPE III

The first open back St. Louis button seen is from 1900. The paper lists the company, name, city, and state between two black dots and two thin black lines at the top and bottom. (The four other dark spots on the lower third of the the photo are holes and stains.)

1905-1919
TYPE IV

1¼″ and larger sizes have the number "105" to the right of the union label. The words "Manufactured By" are in upper and lower case. Carries the patent inscription "Pat. Aug. 8, '99".

1908-1925
TYPE V

1″ and smaller sizes do not have any number to the right of the union label, but may have a number "15" below the union label. The words "MANUFACTURED BY" are in upper case. Carries the patent inscription "Pat. Aug. 8 (no comma as in Type IV) '99". (Note: A variation of this design without the patent date was also used circa 1924-1928.)

1923-1928
TYPE VI

1¼″ and larger sizes have a "10" to the right of the union label. The words "Manufactured by" are in upper and lower case. Carries the patent inscription "Pat. Aug. 8, '99".

1912-1929
TYPE VII

The company imprint is enclosed in a stylized shield design. A number "28" appears below the union label. Carries the patent inscription "PAT. AUG. 8, '99".

1924-1939
TYPE VIII

⅞″ and smaller sizes have "MFRS." above a union label inscribed at the center "AMALGAMATED LITHOGRAPHERS OF AMERICA".

1928-1949
TYPE IX

1¼″ and larger sizes have "MANUFACTURERS" spelled out in upper case. Otherwise, the design is identical to Type VIII.

1944-1957
TYPE X

The inscription "ST. LOUIS BUTTON CO. MFRS., ST. LOUIS, MO. is repeated over the entire paper with no other design or inscription.

BASTIAN BROTHERS — ROCHESTER, N.Y.

The following guidelines apply to buttons of every size:

1905
TYPE I

At the center is a ½" circular company imprint with a tiny union label.

1906-1907
TYPE II

Imprint includes the inscription "SEND FOR CATALOGUE GET A COLLECTION OF BUTTONS".

1907-1920
TYPE III

"•L•I•P•&•B•A•" is inscribed across the center of the union label.

1908
TYPE
IV

1915
TYPE
V

The above two papers saw limited use, apparently only in 1908 and 1915. Both include a union label with a number "19" to the right.

1921-1946
TYPE VI

"AMALGAMATED LITHOGRAPHERS OF AMERICA" appears at the center of the union label.

1916-1940's
NO PAPER
TYPE VII

Beginning in 1916, Bastian eliminated the button paper from the ⅞" size buttons and replaced it with a design stamped directly into the metal back. The design features crossed tongs and a tin snip. The words "UNION LABEL" are across the center with "B.B.CO." above and "ROCH.N.Y." below.

1939-1941
Lithographed
Tin
TYPE VIII

Very few lithographed tin buttons carry the Bastian Bros. name. The only examples found are from 1939-1941 and feature a repeating design printed in red on the reverse. There are three union imprints. One pictures crossed tongs and a pair of tin snips, the second is inscribed "TRADES COUNCIL", and the third is inscribed at the center "AMALGAMATED LITHOGRAPHERS OF AMERICA". The words "BASTIAN BROS. CO./ROCHESTER, N.Y./MADE IN U.S.A." also appear.

KEYSTONE BADGE CO. — READING, PA.

The following guidelines apply to buttons of every size:

1902-1914
TYPE I

The union label imprint is prominent and says "UNION LABEL" on a horizontal line.

1915-1936
TYPE II

A keystone trademark is prominent and the union label is very small. The label says "TRADES COUNCIL" on a horizontal line.

WESTERN BADGE AND NOVELTY CO. — ST. PAUL, MINN.

The following guidelines apply to buttons of every size:

1903-1911
TYPE I

A number "27" is to the right of the union label.

1910-1911
TYPE II

A number "54" is to the right of the union label.

1915-1916
TYPE III

"•L•I•P•&•B•A•" is inscribed across the center of the union label.

1921-1935
TYPE IV

A large letter "B" and large letter "S" begin and end the slogan "BADGES/BANNERS/BUTTONS". A union label and number "27" also appear which are similar to the imprint used on the earliest papers, but on those papers there is no large letter "S".

1924-1957
TYPE V

Black bars are above and below the company name, city, state, and union label.

C.J. BAINBRIDGE BADGES AND BUTTONS — SYRACUSE, N.Y.

The following guidelines apply to buttons of every size:

1907-1910
TYPE I

The initials "C.J." are used.

1910-1941
TYPE II

The name "BAINBRIDGE" is used without initials.

COLLECTIBLES REFERENCE BOOKS
BY TED HAKE

1. *ENCYCLOPEDIA OF POLITICAL BUTTONS 1896-1972 (BOOK I)*. A price guide picturing 4,000 presidential campaign buttons and novelty items. Includes election histories and statistics for each campaign. Each item has its own code number used by collectors to identify their items and communicate with other collectors. Recognized as an indispensible reference since its publication in 1974.

   8½"x11", 256 pages   Softbound $32.00
   Includes most recent price supplement for Book I   Hardbound $42.00

2. *POLITICAL BUTTONS BOOK II 1920-1976*. This book prices and pictures 4,000 additional buttons and related presidential campaign items not included in Book I. Campaigns from 1952 through 1976 are covered more thoroughly in this book than in Book I. Complete election statistics are included and each item has a code number to facilitate communication among collectors. Recognized in the hobby as an essential reference work.

   8½"x11", 256 pages   Softbound $32.00
   Includes most recent price supplement for Book II   Hardbound $42.00

3. *POLITICAL BUTTONS BOOK III 1789-1916*. The finest collections throughout the country were photographed to assemble this remarkable record of American political history since George Washington's era. The book prices and pictures 4,000 presidential campaign items such as portrait badges, ribbons, textiles, tokens, posters, china, canes, mechanical novelties, flags, ferrotype and cardboard badges, celluloid badges and many other unusual campaign collectibles. Complete election statistics are included and each item has a code number. This is the first and only comprehensive reference work on presidential campaign artifacts of the 19th century.

   8½"x11", 256 pages   Softbound $32.00
   Includes most recent supplement for Book III   Hardbound $42.00

PLEASE NOTE: The above three books are companion volumes covering all presidential elections from 1789 through 1976. There is no duplication. Together they illustrate and evaluate 12,000 presidential campaign collectibles.

---

4. *BUTTONS IN SETS* by Marshall N. Levin & Theodore L. Hake. Listings of individual buttons comprising over 100 sets issued between 1896 and 1972. One example is pictured for each set with other information. Major sections include Comics, Movies, Baseball, TV/Radio, Western, and others. Includes revised prices for *The Button Book*, published in 1972, but now out of print.

   6"x9", 88 pages   Softbound $12.00

5. *NON-PAPER SPORTS COLLECTIBLES: AN ILLUSTRATED PRICE GUIDE* by Ted Hake & Roger Steckler. Over 5,000 listings of buttons, charms, coins, discs, pencil clips, pen/pencil bats, press pins, records, statues and tabs relating to baseball, football, boxing, bowling, basketball and hockey. Includes every All-Star press pin in color, photos of all undated World Series press pins, photos of all undated World Series phantoms, photos of all Super Bowl press pins and photos of hundreds of other items issued as sets or singles. The book covers items issued since 1896 and every item is evaluated.

   6"x9", 200 pages   Softbound $20.00

6. *SIX GUN HEROES: A PRICE GUIDE TO MOVIE COWBOY COLLECTIBLES* by Ted Hake & Robert D. Cauler. Another standard reference for the field. Over 500 examples of western character collectibles are pictured plus biographies and filmographies for Hopalong Cassidy, Roy Rogers, The Lone Ranger, Tom Mix, Gene Autry, and other Western heroes.

   8½"x11", 140 pages   Softbound $11.50
   Includes most recent price supplement.

All prices include U.P.S. postage. Please provide a street address. Pennsylvania residents add 6% sales tax.

Dealers write for quantity discount schedule.

MAIL/PHONE BID AUCTIONS
&
PRICED SALE CATALOGUES

Each year we publish six auction or sales catalogues. Each catalogue illustrates 3,000 items in more than one hundred collecting specialties. Both pin-back buttons and larger items are offered. Categories include comic characters, Disneyana, toys, movies, western and space heroes, radio premiums, political items, advertising collectibles, transportation, aviation, space flight, expositions, sports, Boy Scouts, Santa, famous people, wars and many others. A sample copy of our next catalogue is available for $5.00 from:

Hake's Americana & Collectibles
P.O. Box 1444 York, PA 17405

INDEX